Also by William Nester

Haunted Victory: The American Crusade to
Destroy Saddam and Impose Democracy on Iraq

The Revolutionary Years, 1775–1789:
The Art of American Power During the Early Republic

The Hamiltonian Vision, 1789–1800:
The Art of American Power During the Early Republic

The Jeffersonian Vision, 1801–1815:
The Art of American Power During the Early Republic

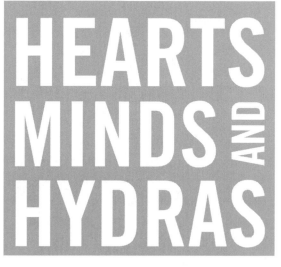

HEARTS MINDS AND HYDRAS

FIGHTING TERRORISM IN
AFGHANISTAN, PAKISTAN,
AMERICA, AND BEYOND—
DILEMMAS AND LESSONS

WILLIAM NESTER

Potomac Books
Washington, D.C.

Library of Congress Cataloging-in-Publication Data
Nester, William R., 1956–
  Hearts, minds, and hydras : fighting terrorism in Afghanistan, Pakistan, America, and beyond : dilemmas and lessons / William Nester.—First edition.
      pages ; cm
  Includes bibliographical references and index.
  ISBN 978-1-59797-950-4 (hardcover : alkaline paper)—ISBN 978-1-59797-951-1 (electronic) 1. Terrorism—United States—Prevention. 2. War on Terrorism, 2001–2009. 3. United States—Foreign relations—21st century. 4. Terrorism—Government policy—United States. I. Title.
  HV6432.N428 2012
  363.325'160973—dc23
                                                                      2012023475

Printed in the United States of America on acid-free paper that meets the American National Standards Institute Z39-48 Standard.

Potomac Books
22841 Quicksilver Drive
Dulles, Virginia 20166

First Edition

10 9 8 7 6 5 4 3 2 1

CONTENTS

ACKNOWLEDGMENTS

I cannot express enough my deep gratitude to Elizabeth Demers, the senior editor at Potomac Books, first for wanting to publish my Art of American Power series and then for carefully editing each book. She made numerous corrections and wonderful suggestions that greatly strengthened my books. She is an outstanding professional in her field.

I also owe a great deal to Elizabeth Norris and Aryana Hendrawan, the respective copyeditor and production editor, for their own excellent editing of this book. It is such a great pleasure to work with such wonderful people as Elizabeth Demers, Elizabeth Norris, and Aryana Hendrawan.

INTRODUCTION

We had to destroy the village in order to save it.
　　—American Vietnam War saying

We thank God for appeasing us with the dilemmas in Iraq and
Afghanistan. The Americans are facing a delicate situation in
both countries. If they withdraw they will lose everything.
If they stay they will continue to bleed to death.
　　—Ayman al-Zawahiri

My martyrdom would lead to the birth of thousands of Osamas
　　—Osama bin Laden

Bring 'em on!
　　—George W. Bush

A story recently surfaced about the novel way a CIA officer nurtured an intelligence source in Afghanistan. His target was a tribal leader in his sixties who
could potentially reveal a gold mine of information about the insurgency in his region. The chief claimed to be against the Taliban but revealed little more for fear
of retaliation. He had more on his hands than the war. He was the husband to four
wives who were all much younger than he, and he ruefully admitted that keeping
them happy was ever-more challenging. The officer said he had just the thing

to perk up the chief's love life, handed him four hits of Viagra, and promised to return within the week to see how he was doing. The chief was ecstatic when the officer reappeared and thereafter eagerly shared information for a steady supply of the love pills. And thus were at least five hearts and minds swayed in that war.[1]

Humor aside, that story reveals some of the counterinsurgency dilemmas faced by the United States in Afghanistan and elsewhere. The officer was well aware that any arms or money he gave the chief could be passed on to the insurgents while he received disinformation in return. Viagra, however, was a new and very personal source of power, one the chief was likely to keep to himself; whether it made him any more truthful was more problematic. But even if the chief's information was solid, how long could that Viagra edge last? Sooner or later the Taliban would learn how effective that inducement proved to be, and they would begin handing out their own love potions to fence-sitters like the chief. And then the CIA officer and his colleagues elsewhere would be back at square one in that "whack-a-mole" struggle.

Terrorism, or the threat or use of violence against innocent people for political goals, is not a part of every insurgency or armed rebellion against an established authority.[2] Terrorism is, however, an integral part of the insurgencies and civil wars in Afghanistan and Pakistan. Although terrorism and insurgency differ, the strategies to fight them overlap when an insurgency uses terrorism as one of its tactics.

Virtually all insurgencies are provoked by exploitive, repressive, corrupt, brutal, and inept governments that worsen vicious cycles of mass poverty, exploitation, violence, hatred, and despair. Yet those horrific conditions alone are not enough to spark an insurgency. That takes brilliant, ruthless leaders with an organization that mobilizes people to fight against their exploiters, and an ideology to fight for, along with a radical agenda for change. In insurgencies most people are the rope in a tug-of-war between the rebels and the authorities and just wish that the war would end. The side that can win their support—their "hearts and minds" as the saying goes—has a good chance of winning the war. Fighting an insurgency involves a core dilemma that is perhaps best compared to Hercules's battle against the hydra. As if the beast's nine snarling heads were not formidable enough, two more would rapidly grow back for every one Hercules lopped off.

Although known much more for his brawn than his brain, Hercules finally solved that exasperating dilemma. Before resuming battle, he heated his sword red-hot, and with each mighty swing, the blade created and then instantly seared shut the gaping wound left by another severed head. And so Hercules eventually killed the hydra.

Every war poses an array of interrelated dilemmas to the participants, from the highest leaders to the lowest foot soldiers. No war is packed with more dilemmas than an insurgency that wields terrorism as one of its tactics. Insurgencies are often like hydras. Once an insurgency begins, the brutal measures a government takes to eliminate militants often provoke countless others to join the enemy ranks. The reason why is simple. Tactical victories often breed strategic defeats. Traditional "search, destroy, and withdraw" missions that rely on firepower to wipe out rebels often destroy the livelihoods and injure or kill the loved ones of innocent people caught in the crossfire. That can transform once-cowed people with something to lose into enraged revolutionaries devoted to destroying the government and supporters that ruined their lives. Thus do the hydra's heads multiply with the decapitations. Former United Nations secretary general Kofi Annan succinctly explained the hydra dilemma: governments "that resort to excessive use of force and indiscriminate repression when countering terrorism risk strengthening the base for terrorists among the general population."[3]

The Americans and their allies in Afghanistan and, increasingly, Pakistan undoubtedly wish they could find as easy a solution as that of Hercules to killing the hydra of insurgency and terrorism that they face. While that multiheaded hydra lurks in any insurgency, that core dilemma was exacerbated and many others unnecessarily conjured up in both Afghanistan and Iraq. The initially successful American offensives that toppled enemy regimes in Kabul and Baghdad were soon transformed into grueling, worsening guerrilla wars across those countries.

Many reasons account for that. The most crucial were self-defeating decisions made by the Bush administration, whose policies were shaped by neoconservatism and hubris rather than a careful analysis of the genuine threats, American interests, and reasonable options. Indeed, the more America's position deteriorated in both wars, the more dead set the neoconservatives became to stay the course. Although the Americans were eventually able to contain and diminish the insurgency in Iraq, that in Afghanistan not only steadily intensified but spread into neighboring Pakistan.

The near abandonment of the war in Afghanistan and the neoconservative crusade in Iraq were godsends for al Qaeda and all other enemies of the United States. Ayman al-Zawahiri, al Qaeda's second in command, expressed their elation: "We thank God for appeasing us with the dilemmas in both Iraq and Afghanistan. The Americans are facing a delicate situation in both countries. If they withdraw, they will lose everything, and if they stay, they will continue to bleed to death."[4]

The United States is warring against the hydra of insurgency in Afghanistan and Pakistan, as it did earlier in Iraq. Alas, there is no elegant solution like the one Hercules found. As President Barack Obama succinctly put it, "We've inherited a mess."

This book analyzes some of the more prominent dilemmas haunting American policymakers struggling to win those related wars. Specifically, it will explore which strategies and tactics worked, which failed, and why. In doing so, hopefully we can gain greater insights into the nature of that all-too-real beast of insurgency and terrorism, what feeds it, and what can starve it.

1

September 11, 2001

The pictures of airplanes flying into buildings . . . filled us with disbelief, terrible sadness, and a quiet unyielding anger. . . . Terrorist attacks can shake the foundations of our biggest buildings, but they cannot touch the foundation of American resolve.
—George W. Bush

The Attack

Who was the first to glance out and spot the airliner flying low and straight toward the 110-story North Tower of the World Trade Center? How many seconds elapsed before puzzled curiosity surged into gut-wrenching dread and sharp calls for others to look? How fast did it take for dozens, then scores, and finally hundreds of people on ever-more floors to crane their necks or dash to the windows to see?

The airliner hit the North Tower at 8:48 on a sunny morning with a slight breeze from the northeast. As the airliner crashed through the glass windows and steel girders, its jet fuel exploded into a fireball that incinerated hundreds of office workers in seconds and engulfed several stories. Thousands of people above and below the inferno rushed for the exits and down the seemingly endless flight of stairs.

The first news bulletins reported that an airliner had accidentally struck one of the World Trade Center towers. As stunned viewers grappled with that horror, the second airliner slammed into the South Tower at 9:03 a.m. There was no doubt now that terrorism was the cause. Word of the disaster raced through the country and around the world. Americans switched on their televisions and sat transfixed by the unfolding nightmare. Then came the report that a third airliner had nosedived into the Pentagon at 9:39 a.m. Soon television sets were split between shots of the World Trade Center towers and the Pentagon belching flames and smoke. Minutes later at 9:59 a.m., a floor on the South Tower collapsed, pancaking those below and dragging the building down in an avalanche of shattered concrete, steel, and glass. A fourth hijacked airliner crashed in rural western Pennsylvania at 10:10 a.m. The north tower pancaked at 10:28 a.m. Quarter-mile-high twin pillars of dust and smoke swirled like ghosts above the towers and lingered for days before finally dispersing. Although the exact figure may never be known, eventually 2,987 people were either confirmed dead or missing and presumed dead, with 2,752 at the World Trade Center, 184 at the Pentagon, and 40 on the plane that crashed in Pennsylvania.[1]

The Reaction

When these horrors erupted, President George W. Bush was arriving at an elementary school in Sarasota, Florida, before an audience of reporters, teachers, and parents.[2] His political advisor Karl Rove informed the president of the first attack shortly after it occurred, before he entered the classroom. Then Andrew Card, the chief of staff, whispered news of the second attack to the president as he was seated in the classroom. For another five to seven minutes Bush continued listening to the children read aloud as the adults' cell phones began to ring and they began to quietly discuss the news before Rove whispered that they should go. Bush excused himself and left the room with his entourage. He reappeared at 9:30 a.m. to announce to the startled audience "an apparent terrorist attack on the country."

Meanwhile Vice President Dick Cheney swiftly took charge at the White House. As Cheney, along with National Security Adviser Condoleezza Rice and essential officials, hurried to the secure underground bunker known as the Presidential Emergency Operations Center, he ordered the evacuation of the White House, Congress, and all three hundred thousand federal workers. He urged Bush to fly to a secure military base far from the capital until the immediate threat could be assessed. His most important advice was for the president to order that any more hijacked passenger jets be shot down by F-16s that were currently circling Washington. Bush agreed and as a further precaution had all flights within the United States grounded and incoming flights turned back. There was not much else for Cheney and Rice to do but sit tight, evaluate the stream of reports, and discuss with Bush, key aides, and speechwriters how best to respond.

The other principal power-holders were elsewhere. Defense Secretary Donald Rumsfeld had been in his Pentagon office when the airliner hit but was safe. Secretary of State Colin Powell was breakfasting with Peruvian president Alejandro Toledo in Lima before attending a meeting of the Organization of American States; he was taken immediately to his airliner for the long flight back to Washington. CIA chief George Tenet was at his headquarters in Langley, Virginia. Attorney General John Ashcroft was at the Justice Department. Federal Reserve chair Alan Greenspan was just arriving from a banking conference in Switzerland.

Bush was whisked away at 9:55 a.m. on Air Force One for a zigzagging flight toward Barksdale Air Force Base near Shreveport, Louisiana. The plane touched down around noon. At 12:16 p.m. news organizations received a taped statement by Bush, who vowed "to hunt down and punish those responsible for these cowardly acts." Air Force One took off at 1:37 p.m. and at 2:50 p.m. touched down at Offutt Air Force Base, the nuclear command center near Omaha, Nebraska.

The president began a teleconference with the National Security Council (NSC) at 3:30 p.m.. George Tenet was certain that Osama bin Laden was behind the attacks; passenger lists revealed al Qaeda agents on the flights that nosedived into the Pentagon. But the CIA director cautioned those eager for vengeance that any decision had to await a full assessment of who had committed the atrocities and how they could best be found and destroyed. For now all Bush could do was wait impatiently until Washington was secured from further attacks. His return flight took off at 4:26. Just before 7:00 he strode into the White House.

A tense George W. Bush addressed the horrified nation that night at 8:30. His most memorable lines declared that "the pictures of airplanes flying into buildings . . . filled us with disbelief, terrible sadness, and a quiet unyielding anger. . . . Terrorist attacks can shake the foundations of our biggest buildings, but they cannot touch the foundation of American resolve. America was targeted for attack because we're the brightest beacon for freedom and opportunity in the world. . . . Today our nation saw evil, the very worst of human nature. And we responded with the best of America." So how then would his administration respond to the attacks? He asserted his commitment to "find those responsible and . . . bring them to justice. We will make no distinction between the terrorists who committed these acts and those who harbored them."[3]

2

Know Your Enemy
Al Qaeda versus Its Enemies

Then fight and slay the pagans wherever ye find them, and seize
them, beleaguer them, and lie in wait for them in every stratagem.
—Koran, 9:4–7

Know your enemy, know yourself.
—Sun Tzu

Among the more poignant figures of Greek mythology was Cassandra of Troy, who was able to foresee disasters but was unable to convince anyone of what was coming, let alone what could prevent it. If there were a patron saint of experts, it would be Cassandra. Experts often find their in-depth analyses of threats ignored by those in power, especially by ideologues with simplistic good-versus-evil views of the world, in which they personify all that is good and anyone who opposes them all that is evil.

That willful ignorance violates the most fundamental principle of power articulated by Sun Tzu over 2,300 years ago in his book, *The Art of War*. Sun Tzu insisted that the first vital step to take in any struggle was to "know your enemy, know yourself," for he "who knows neither the enemy nor himself will invariably be defeated."[1] Only after carefully analyzing the ends, means, strengths, and weaknesses of oneself and one's enemy can one begin to devise the strategies and tactics with the best chance of victory.

And the key maxim in guiding that analysis comes from yet another ancient thinker, this one Greek. When Hippocrates warned to "do no harm," he was speaking of the doctor's duty to his patient. But that advice can be just as wisely applied to war. If the enemy is a terrorist group or insurgency, then the "do no harm" principle would mean avoiding acts that proliferate the heads of the hydra.

Why Do They Hate Us?

What then are the motives, ends, means, strengths, and weaknesses of the group that attacked the United States on September 11, 2001?[2] President George W. Bush offered an interpretation during a televised address nine days later. After posing the rhetorical question, "Why do they hate us?" he asserted a popular view of al Qaeda: "They hate our freedoms: our freedom of religion, our freedom of speech, our freedom to vote and assemble and disagree with each other. . . . These terrorists kill not merely to end lives, but to disrupt and end a way of life. With every atrocity they hope that America grows fearful, retreating from the world and forsaking our friends. They stand against us because we stand in their way."[3]

The president was only partly right. Al Qaeda and all other Islamists hate America not so much for what it is but for what it does. Al Qaeda is primarily warring against America for its policies, not its culture, although it does note the relationship between them. A fatwa, or binding Muslim legal opinion, issued by al Qaeda on February 23, 1998, condemned the United States for "occupying the lands of Islam, the holiest of places, the Arabian Peninsula, plundering its riches, dictating to its rulers, humiliating its people, terrorizing its neighbors, and turning its bases in the Peninsula into a spearhead through which to fight the neighboring Muslim peoples." To eliminate those abominations, al Qaeda calls on "every Muslim who believes in God and wishes to be rewarded to comply with God's order to kill the Americans and plunder their possessions wherever he finds them." That command includes killing all "Americans and their allies—civilians and military" and is an "individual duty for every Muslim who can do it in any country in which it is possible to do it."

That war declaration listed al Qaeda among several other groups, including the World Islamic Front for Jihad against Jews and Crusaders, the Islamic Army, the

Islamic Army for the Liberation of Holy Places, the Group for the Preservation of Holy Sites, and the Islamic Salvation Foundation. Al Qaeda and its allies have a clear set of goals beyond merely killing Americans. For the relative short term, there are four: (1) drive the United States and other Western powers from the Middle East and greater Muslim world; (2) destroy Israel; (3) replace all apostate regimes ruling Muslim peoples with Islamist rule guided by sharia; and (4) re-establish the caliphate, or the unity of all Islamist states under one Islamist ruler, which is believed to have previously existed from the death of Mohammad in 632 until the Turkish republic abolished it in 1923. Over the long term, Islamists seek to convert everyone on earth to the true faith.

It is essential to distinguish between al Qaeda the organization and al Qaeda the movement. As counterterrorism expert Daniel Byman succinctly put it, "al Qaeda is not a single terrorist group but a global insurgency."[4] Osama bin Laden, his organization, and his movement committed themselves to a truly revolution-ary vision. Their holy war, or jihad, can be understood as a global insurgency to destroy an American-, Western-, and infidel-dominated world, the collapse of which will unite all humanity in peace, prosperity, justice, and eternal salvation realized by submission to Allah, the Koran, and Sharia or Islamic law. To that end, any means is justified. Osama bin Laden described the September 11 attacks as a blow against "the values of this Western civilization under the leadership of America. . . . Those awesome symbolic towers that speak of liberty, human rights, and humanity have been destroyed."[5]

Theological Justifications

Theology empowers al Qaeda with legitimacy in the hearts and minds of count-less Muslims. Jihad, or holy war, is the God-sanctioned means to al Qaeda's ends. While "jihad" literally means "striving," its intrinsic meaning is war in the name of Allah. There are two ways of jihad: one a holy war to purify the world of infi-dels and the other a holy war to purify oneself of sin. Ideally the two complement each other. Yet theologically, one form of jihad far surpasses the other in impor-tance. Of the 199 references to jihad in the Hadith, or sayings of Mohammad, all refer to war against the unfaithful. The notion of a lesser jihad did not clearly emerge until the Sufi mystical movement of the eleventh century.[6]

That certainly has been the practice of jihad.[7] Muslims distinguish the "House of Islam" (Dar al-Islam) from the "House of War" (Dar al-Harb). There are two types of enemies in the House of War: polytheists and monotheists like Christians and Jews, who are people of the Book. Polytheists must be given the choice to convert or die. The faith of People of the Book must be respected, although they occupy a secondary, restricted, and penalized status once they are conquered. Jihad is the only just war. All other wars are condemned, especially wars between Muslims.

Thus, armed with the doctrine of jihad, Osama bin Laden and all his fellow Islamists insist that they are merely the latest spearpoints of a God-given mission that is nearly fourteen hundred years old.

Historically and theologically, Islam and imperialism were synonymous from the religion's founding until relatively recent times. Mohammad himself was a warrior as well as a prophet, and he led his followers in numerous battles against his enemies. In just one century after Mohammad's death in 632 CE, Muslim armies expanded westward across North Africa and crossed the Gibraltar straits to conquer most of the Iberian peninsula; in its deepest penetration of western Europe, a Muslim army was defeated near Tours, France, in 732. Other Arab armies overran the Middle East and Central Asia and reached the Indus and Oxus rivers. Eventually this sustained burst of Arab imperialism lost its impetus, and the vast caliphate, or unified Muslim world, broke up into separate realms. The Turks (first the Seljuks and then the Ottomans) picked up that fallen banner when they overran the Middle East, captured Constantinople in 1453, and drove deep into the Balkans; Turkish armies twice besieged Vienna, in 1529 and 1683.

By the eighteenth century, however, the Ottoman Empire begun to crumble as had previous Arab empires. Many of the faithful blamed this decline on the presumed impiety of those in power. Reform movements arose to purge Islam of decadence, corruption, and heresy, and return the faith to the purity of its earliest years, when Mohammad strode the earth. Muslim puritans became known as Salafists, and the movement, Salafism. The most puritanical and persistent of those Salafist movements emerged in the Arabian Peninsula.

Muhammad ibn Abd al-Wahhab was born in 1703 into a family of Islamic clerics and was educated at madrassas, or religious schools, in Medina and Basra.

He became a fervent follower of the puritanical teachings of Taqi ad-Din Ahmad ibn Taymiyyah, a thirteenth-century theologian. Wahhab's teachings were so extreme that he was expelled from city after city across the Middle East until he returned to his homeland. There he was embraced by Muhammad ibn Saud, a tribal chief. Together they wielded the sword and the crescent to carve out a small empire in the western and central Saudi peninsula. Saudi Arabia is the legacy of this jihad.

The most important recent theological expression of this revolutionary creed of puritanism and jihad was expounded by the Egyptian Sayyid Qutb in his book *Signposts*. In his early life, Qutb journeyed to Europe and America but was repulsed by the decadence and faithlessness (*jahiliyya*) that he observed. He returned to Egypt, developed his theology, worked with the puritanical Muslim Brotherhood, was imprisoned on charges of sedition by Gamal Abdel Nasser's regime, and was executed in 1965. He has been celebrated ever since as an Islamist martyr, and his thoughts have guided Islamist militants.

After the teachings and conquests of Mohammed himself, Osama bin Laden was most influenced by Wahhabism and Sayyid Qutb. That combined theology has been an enormous source of power for al Qaeda by legitimizing for believers anything it does in religious terms. In August 1999, he called on "young Muslims to devote their life to . . . jihad [because] there is only one way to earn the life thereafter. Follow that way and the world will fall in your lap."[8]

Osama bin Laden was crystal clear about the type of war that he waged until virtually the moment he was killed: "This war is fundamentally religious. Under no circumstances should we forget this enmity between us and the infidels. For us the enmity is based on creed."[9]

The Origins and Rise of Osama bin Laden and al Qaeda

If al Qaeda's ends and means are clear enough, the continuities and changes in its power, organization, and relationship to other militant Islamist groups is much more ambiguous. Al Qaeda is perhaps best understood as the core of a network of Islamist groups that share the same ends and means.

Al Qaeda and its affiliates are linked not only by a common ideology but by either a native or acquired language of Arabic (God's voice in the Koran) and by financial, operational, and propaganda links, as well as, for many, blood or marriage ties. The network has a horizontal, or global, link that in turn reaches down into national or subnational jihads. The global web can either give or take money, operatives, safe havens, and even meaning to or from more local struggles. The result is "a global insurgency" in which "al Qaeda and similar groups feed on local grievances, integrate them into broader ideologies, and link disparate conflicts through globalized communications, finances, and technology." Before September 11, al Qaeda had operational links with other transnational Islamist groups, as well as most national or subnational groups; since then the links have become more virtual and inspirational than operational. But at no time did al Qaeda act as the headquarters for the global Islamist insurgency. Operations by other groups were encouraged and assisted rather than commanded.[10]

David Kilcullen, an expert counterterrorist practitioner and theorist, explains that the traditional Middle Eastern patron-client relationship best explains the al Qaeda movement. He defines this relationship as "an intricate, ramified web of dependency . . . and patterns of patronage . . . [bolstered by] marriage relationships, money flows, alumni relationships, and sponsorship links." As such "the military activity is actually subordinate, being merely one of the shared activities that the network engages in, while the core is the patronage network. . . . Jihad is simply one activity that the network does; it is not the network itself." He explains that "each local insurgency is driven partly by local issues, partly by factors in the broader jihad. Regional and global players prey upon and exploit local factors in order to further their objectives."[11]

Osama bin Laden, al Qaeda's founder and leader and the contemporary world's most notorious Islamist, had an unlikely upbringing for that status. He was born in Riyadh on March 10, 1957, the seventeenth son and one of fifty-seven children of Mohammed bin Awad bin Laden, who had made billions of dollars overseeing construction projects for Saudi Arabia. Given the demands of his father's business, his father's early death in a plane crash in 1968, and his plethora of siblings, Osama spent very little time with him. That isolation was reinforced by a falling out between his father and his mother, a Syrian. Osama filled that emotional void by attaching himself to authoritative father figures who personified the ideals of Islamism and Arab manhood.[12]

He tried to follow in his father's footsteps by enrolling as a student in engineering and public administration at King Abdulaziz University in 1978. There he supplemented his technical schooling with an ever-deeper study of Islamism in classes and in mosques. During those years his most influential Islamist teacher was Mohammed Qutb, Sayyid's brother. Four events in 1979 radicalized that scion of wealth and privilege—the Camp David peace treaty between Egypt and Israel, Iran's Islamist revolution, the brief takeover of Mecca by Islamists, and the Soviet invasion of Afghanistan. That stunning succession transformed what had been Osama's growing interest in Islamism and jihad into an unquenchable obsession.

The Soviet invasion of Afghanistan in December 1979 gave Osama bin Laden a practical outlet for his ideals. He was only twenty-three years old when he first briefly visited Peshawar, Pakistan, on the Afghanistan frontier in 1980. He hurried back the following year after receiving his university degree in public administration. In Peshawar he fell under the influence of Abdullah Yusuf Azzam, a Palestinian, Islamic scholar, and member of the Muslim Brotherhood. In 1984, Azzam and bin Laden founded the Maktab al-Khidmat (Bureau of Services) to recruit, equip, train, and dispatch Arab and other foreign jihadists to the war in Afghanistan. They split the duties, with Azzam managing the operation in Peshawar while bin Laden traveled frequently to Saudi Arabia and Muslim communities elsewhere to raise funds and recruits. From then through 1992, an estimated thirty-five thousand foreign fighters, mostly Arabs but including Muslims from around the world, may have been mobilized for the Afghanistan war, although probably only a fraction of them ever reached a battle front.

Among the Arabs who did get to fight was Osama bin Laden. His first battle was at Khost near Jalalabad in 1986. It was Azzam's mishandling of that battle—which resulted in the unnecessary deaths of hundreds of their men—that first distanced bin Laden from his partner. Bin Laden's status swelled in April 1987, when he and his men finally defeated a week-long Soviet siege of their compound at Jaji near Khost. Azzam was jealous that his former pupil and now partner appeared to have surpassed him in adulation among their so-called Afghan Arabs.

Technology rather than faith was the most decisive source of power in that war. The Soviets were eventually defeated by Afghans armed with American

Stinger antiaircraft missiles and billions of dollars worth of other weapons and equipment. With Stingers, the mujahideen destroyed the Soviet control of the air and then encircled and attacked the Soviets and their allies holed up in cities, towns, and bases. As the cost in blood and treasure soared, Moscow eventually realized that victory was nothing more than a mirage and began extracting itself from the quagmire. The last Soviet troops withdrew from Afghanistan in February 1989. The debilitating costs of that war were a major reason why the Soviet empire and communism collapsed soon thereafter.[13]

Meanwhile, having accomplished its mission, Washington quite understandably turned its back on Afghanistan, not imagining that another threat, Islamism, would arise from the ruins of that devastated country. Shamshad Ahmad, Pakistan's former foreign secretary, explained that the United States "left us in the lurch with all the problems stemming from that war—an influx of refugees, the drug and gun running, and a Kalashnikov culture."[14]

As the Soviets retreated from Afghanistan, Azzam and bin Laden sought a new target and new organization for the foreign fighters. Bin Laden agreed with Azzam's declaration that their "duty will not end with victory in Afghanistan; jihad will remain an individual obligation until all other lands that were Muslim will return to us so that Islam will reign again."[15] But they became estranged over just what the next target for jihad should be. Azzam called for joining the war against Israel, while bin Laden increasingly leaned toward attacking the United States. Those differences broke the relationship between them. Azzam was killed by a car bomb in Peshawar on November 24, 1989. Whether Osama bin Laden was behind that murder was known only to him and perhaps a few select others who survive from that time. One thing is certain: from then until he was killed in May 2011, Osama bin Laden was the most prominent Arab jihadist leader.

Bin Laden and his closest followers founded al Qaeda on August 11, 1988. Al Qaeda means "The Base," a reference to both a guest house in Peshawar where recruits stayed and the advanced camps in Afghanistan where they were sent. The name seemed appropriate for the new group. Bin Laden became al Qaeda's emir, or prince, to whom al Qaeda members had to swear a personal oath. That institutional authority was reinforced by his powerful, quiet charisma. His calm, soft-spoken yet authoritative statements and decisions inspired not just confidence but a zealous devotion among his followers, countless among whom were willing to die for him. He was for the militant Muslim world what Che Guevara has been for western Marxists, a near God-like figure who exemplifies the movement's highest ideals and its most extreme sacrifices.

Yet bin Laden was no dictator. As the senior operations chief, he chaired the Advisory Council (Shura) that manages five committees. The Political Committee discussed and issued fatwas. The Military Committee planned and implemented terrorist attacks and supervised training. The Finance Committee raised and dispersed funds. The Foreign Purchase Committee bought all needed goods and services. The Security Committee gathered, analyzed, and disseminated intelligence, as well as protecting the group itself. Decisions were made by consensus, usually after prolonged and animated debate.

From al Qaeda's inception, Ayman al-Zawahiri was bin Laden's deputy, until he took over following the latter's death. Zawahiri joined Egypt's Muslim Brotherhood when he was fourteen. Although he eventually went to medical school and became a doctor, leading an Islamist revolution inspired by the teachings of Sayyid Qutb was his true vocation. He rose up through the ranks of the Egyptian Islamic Jihad and eventually became its emir. He was arrested, imprisoned, and tortured for suspicion of being part of the plot to assassinate President Anwar Sadat in 1981. Upon being released, he journeyed to Peshawar in 1986 and soon met with bin Laden. Zawahiri replaced Azzam as bin Laden's esteemed confidant and partner.

Bin Laden soon found ample justification for turning against the United States. Saddam Hussein ordered the brutal conquest of Kuwait on August 2, 1990, and implicitly threatened Saudi Arabia with invasion. Bin Laden offered Riyadh his al Qaeda forces to join the Saudi military in defending that kingdom and eventually expelling the Iraqi army from Kuwait. The Saudi government rejected bin Laden's offer and instead let American and other foreign troops mass in the kingdom first for Operation Desert Shield to protect Saudi Arabia, and then for Operation Desert Storm to rout the Iraqis from Kuwait. Saudi Arabia's Council of Senior Ulema, the highest clerical body, issued a fatwa allowing the stationing of those foreign troops. Despite the fatwa, bin Laden and countless others across the Muslim world were outraged by the presence of infidel troops in the country with Islam's holiest shrines at Mecca and Medina.

Several motivations prompted bin Laden to move al Qaeda to Khartoum, Sudan, in 1992. That year the mujahideen, or holy warriors, finally captured Kabul and expelled the pro-Soviet Afghans from the rest of the country. Now there was no apparent reason for al Qaeda to remain in Afghanistan. In December 1992, the United States led an UN peacekeeping and humanitarian mission to Somalia, an act bin Laden interpreted as the latest invasion of a Muslim country. He began planning to send his men to resist that foreign force. Those operations would be much easier to conduct if he could establish a base in northeast Africa.

Sudan offered just such a possibility. A 1989 military coup transformed Sudan into an Islamist government led by the brilliant theologian Hassan al-Turabi. To bolster the new regime, Turabi invited bin Laden to bring his money and men to Khartoum. In return for a $5 million fee, bin Laden and his followers joined Turabi's National Islamic Front. Bin Laden soon launched a number of development projects, including roads, warehouses, food-processing plants, chemical factories, and other businesses. He became a major shareholder in Sudan's Military Industrial Corporation, which was trying to develop weapons.

Yet jihad remained his primary focus. In 1993 he blessed a plan by freelance terrorist Ramzi Yousef to attack the United States itself. Yousef formed a small cell from a mosque in Jersey City led by the radical Islamist Sheik Omar Abdel Rahman. On February 26, Yousef left a rental truck packed with 1,500 pounds of explosives in the garage underneath one of the World Trade Center towers. The explosion killed 6 people, injured 1,042, and was the first Islamist terrorist attack on American soil.

Al Qaeda meanwhile tried to drive the American-led UN peacekeeping force from Somalia. An al Qaeda bomb exploded in Aden, Yemen, at a hotel where Americans sometimes stayed, although none were among the victims. Bin Laden sent scores of operatives into Somalia, where they fought alongside the Vanguard of the Somali Islamic Salvation. Minor skirmishes between UN troops and local warlords and their foreign allies flared through the summer and into the autumn of 1993. The climax was a battle on October 3, when American rangers tried to capture Mohammed Farah Aidid, the most aggressive Somali warlord. The

Americans lost eighteen dead and seventy-eight wounded, while they killed or wounded over a thousand fighters and civilians. The battle was a tactical win and strategic defeat for the United States. The Clinton White House recognized that destroying Aidid and other warlords was not worth the price. The last American troops pulled out of Somalia on March 1, 1994. Bin Laden and his followers rejoiced in what they saw as a victory over the United States and plunged into planning other operations elsewhere.

During the mid-1990s, bin Laden dispatched operatives to join Muslims fighting the Russians in Chechnya and the Serbs in Bosnia and Herzegovina. Fortunately bin Laden's efforts to get weapons of mass destruction (WMD) failed. Scam artists bilked al Qaeda out of $1.5 million for enriched uranium that was never delivered. Bin Laden's apparent goal was a radiological bomb. Al Qaeda agents exploded a truck bomb at the Military Cooperation Program in Riyadh on November 13, 1995, killing six and wounding more than sixty. That was the first al Qaeda attack inside Saudi Arabia itself. The Saudis found and defused two other bombs that month. This attack convinced King Saud to actively ally with the Clinton administration in fighting al Qaeda.

When Sudan's government expelled al Qaeda in May 1996, practical concerns about wealth and power trumped Islamist principles. The Clinton White House shut down its embassy in February 1996, after receiving threats of a pending terrorist attack. Washington, Brussels, and Riyadh put more pressure on Khartoum to kick out al Qaeda. Foreign investors and aid donors began to pull out of Sudan. The Sudanese government itself feared al Qaeda's growing power. The development of Sudan's oil fields made the country less dependent on bin Laden's investments. Bin Laden himself wore out his welcome by criticizing Sudan's government for diverting Islamist forces to the civil war in the south rather than against western targets. In early 1996, he threatened to invest his money elsewhere. That was the last straw for President Omar al-Bashir, who sent bin Laden an eviction notice.

The timing for al Qaeda's latest move could not have been more fortuitous. They packed up and headed back to Afghanistan, where they were welcomed by the Islamist movement called the Taliban, which was in the process of taking power.[16]

The Taliban's Origins and Rise

Mullah Mohammad Omar, the Taliban's founder and leader, was as zealous a warrior as he was a Muslim. Indeed for him the duty of jihad made the two identities synonymous. He fought against the Soviets from their 1979 invasion until the mujahideen took power in 1992, when he finally returned to his home in a village near Kandahar. He founded the Taliban (meaning "students") movement in 1994. With his austere piety, powerful charisma, and indomitable will, he attracted more and more followers.

Omar soon found a new enemy to war against. The mujahideen proved to be just as brutal, corrupt, and inept as the Soviet puppet regime under Mohammad Najibullah, whom they had overthrown. Omar led his Taliban followers against a vicious local warlord, who had kidnapped and raped two girls. They killed and hanged him from a tank barrel as a warning to others and as inspiration for the oppressed to fight back against their oppressors. The Taliban began expelling or killing other warlords in the region and converting the population. Although the Taliban spread mostly among Afghanistan's Pashtun people, who comprise about 40 percent of the population, it soon attracted the attention of a powerful foreign patron.

The interest of Pakistan's Inter-Services Intelligence (ISI) agency in the Taliban was both ideological and practical. Islamists composed most of the ISI's ranks from top to bottom. The ISI had been the funnel through which most American and other foreign arms and money had reached the mujahideen fighting the Soviets. But, like the Taliban, the ISI soured on the mujahideen after they took power because of their blatant violations of Islamist ideals. There was also a practical interest. The ISI could enlist the Taliban as fighters to vanquish the warlords who used their control of the road network to shake down Pakistani truck drivers. So the ISI backed the Taliban with crucial supplies of money, arms, equipment, and recruits from madrassas in Pakistan.

The Taliban captured Kandahar in 1994 and over the next two years steadily expanded their control over most of Afghanistan. The Taliban chief's ambitions grew with his power. On April 4, 1996, he unsealed a shrine in Kandahar, cloaked himself in a robe said to have been worn by Mohammed, and declared himself the caliph, or leader of all Muslims. That claim inspired a final Taliban push that captured Kabul in September 1996. The Taliban swiftly consolidated control over most of Afghanistan. The only region that the Taliban failed to overrun was the northeast, defended by the Northern Alliance under the command of Ahmad Shah Massoud.

The Taliban imposed a harsh puritanical regime based on select Koran verses. All men had to grow beards at least as long as a fist from their chins. Women were forbidden to work or go to school, had to wear a burqa (a head-to-toe covering with a screen for seeing), and had to be accompanied by a male relative whenever they left their homes. Kite flying, chess playing, dancing, music, computers, pictures, dolls, stuffed animals, television, movies, gambling, and pigeon raising were all forbidden.

The Taliban are not just killjoys. They take over and rule people through the most vicious forms of terror. Anyone who resists is tortured, beheaded, and left to rot as a warning to others. Adulterers are stoned to death, with their own children throwing the first rocks. Theft is punishable by the amputation of the offending hand. Women without burqas or unaccompanied by a male relative are publicly whipped. Through mosque pulpits and village cadres, the Taliban unleashes an unrelenting stream of sermons, warnings, and announcements of the latest apostates to be executed.

There was at least one area where the Taliban turned a blind eye to sharia. Islamic law forbids addictive drugs. The Taliban not only never banned opium growing, but they skimmed huge profits from its production, from its refinement into heroin, and from smuggling it across the borders. The country's limited poppy eradication program in 2000 was designed to prop up sagging prices from overproduction rather than fulfill an Islamic principle.

The Taliban compounded the suffering of the Afghan people when they forced all private relief organizations to leave Afghanistan in July 1998. The United Nations organizations shut down their operations the following month. In March 2001 the Taliban defied most of the international community's sensitivities by destroying two ancient giant statues of Buddha at Bamiyan.

Given the Taliban's viciousness, nearly all countries avoided establishing diplomatic relations with the regime. Only three governments eventually did recognize the Taliban as Afghanistan's legitimate government. Having nurtured the

Taliban, Pakistan was the first to recognize them, in May 1997, followed by Saudi Arabia and the United Arab Emirates. And then there was al Qaeda.

Al Qaeda's War against America

Osama bin Laden and his followers certainly felt ideologically at home sheltered within such a puritanical Islamist regime. The Taliban allowed al Qaeda to carve out its own autonomous realm within Afghanistan made up of compounds, munitions depots, and training camps, all with revenues raised from the heroin trade, truck transportation, a variety of businesses, and protection fees paid by businesses and families. In return al Qaeda directly paid the Taliban up to $20 million a year and encouraged charities to channel some of their donations to Kabul, while al Qaeda experts trained Taliban fighters. Swiftly the Taliban and al Qaeda became ever-more entwined and interdependent. As one analyst put it, "under the Taliban, Afghanistan is not so much a state sponsor of terrorism as a state sponsored by terrorism."[17]

From that safe haven bin Laden and his inner circle began planning a series of attacks against American and other targets that culminated spectacularly and horrifically with September 11. Those attacks did not come out of the blue. On September 2, 1996, bin Laden issued a *bayan*, or doctrinal manifesto, that served as his first declaration of war against the United States. To justify killing American soldiers, the forty-page document cited Washington's backing of Israel's exploitation of Palestinians and its alleged mistreatment of Muslims in Bosnia, Chechnya, Somalia, Kashmir, the Philippines, Eritrea, Tajikistan, and elsewhere. Much more chilling was the fatwa issued on February 23, 1998, by al Qaeda and an umbrella organization of other groups called the World Islamic Front for Jihad Against the Jews and Crusaders. That war declaration called for killing any Americans—soldiers or civilians—anywhere and anytime.

Al Qaeda operatives eventually began acting on that command. Although to date al Qaeda has launched only a few direct attacks against American assets, they have been notorious for their effectiveness and destructiveness. The twin embassy bombings on August 7, 1998, killed 213 in Nairobi and 11 in Dar es Salaam, and wounded about 5,000 between the two capitals, although only 12 Americans were among the dead. The suicide boat attack on the USS *Cole* on October 12,

2000, killed 17 sailors, wounded a score more, and crippled the billion-dollar ship. To date, no attack has been more devastating than that of September 11, 2001, which killed nearly 3,000 people and blew a hundred-billion-dollar hole, literally and figuratively, in America's economy.

The horrors of terrorist acts and the difficulty in uncovering definitive evidence over who commits them has given al Qaeda an undeserved reputation for omnipotence. Some attacks attributed to al Qaeda were actually committed by unrelated groups, such as Hezbollah's bombing of the Khobar Towers in June 1996. Others came with al Qaeda's blessing but were essentially the freelance operations of affiliates, like the bombings of the World Trade Tower in 1993, the Bali nightclub in 2002, the Madrid train station in 2004, and the London transit system in 2005.

This destruction was wrought on a financial shoestring. Although the 9/11 attacks may have cost as much as $500,000, the other attacks were much cheaper. By one estimate, the bombings of the American embassies cost only about $50,000, the USS *Cole* less than $10,000, the Bali nightclub about $20,000, the Madrid train station about $10,000, and the London transit system about $2,000.[18]

Al Qaeda's annual operating costs were about $30 million before September 11. Much of that was rent—al Qaeda paid the Taliban up to $20 million a year to stay in Afghanistan from 1996 to 2001. Al Qaeda gets money from an array of sources, the most important of which are donations from mosques, charities, and other sponsors. It earns money from smuggling gold, guns, drugs, and other illegal products. It once earned a good income from various legitimate businesses, like construction, but most of those have been shut down. Reports that Osama bin Laden funded al Qaeda out of his own fortune, estimated to be as much as $300 million, were false. He actually received only a million dollars a year from 1970 until 1994, when his family succumbed to international pressure and cut off his allowance.[19]

With each strand of income so tenuous, al Qaeda tries to squeeze its dollars for all their worth. The 9/11 hijackers actually returned $36,000 to the group's coffers on the eve of the operation. Not all the operatives were so honest. Jamal al-Fadl was an agent in Sudan who became embittered when al Qaeda rejected his request for $500 to pay for his wife's caesarian section. Out of vengeance and greed, he siphoned off over $100,000. He got caught, but rather than being executed, he was simply told to repay what he stole. He eventually defected in 1996 and became a critical source of information on al Qaeda.[20]

Al Qaeda is unique. No other terrorist group has ever mobilized as many resources and operated in as many countries. As Michael Scheuer explained, al Qaeda "is larger, more ethnically diverse, more geographically dispersed, younger, richer, better educated, better led, and more military trained and combat experienced" than any other terrorist group in history.[21] Most terrorist groups have a very short lifespan. Bruce Hoffman estimates that nine of ten organizations die within the first year, and only half of the survivors last another decade.[22] Al Qaeda celebrated its twenty-first birthday the same year the George W. Bush administration finally left office.

Several key factors explain al Qaeda's resilience. Patience and methodical planning have been essential. The attacks on the American embassies, USS *Cole*, World Trade Center, and Pentagon took years to realize from conception to execution. An obsession with security has been equally vital, although scores of top-ranking al Qaeda leaders have been killed or captured, topped by Osama bin Laden's death in May 2011. Others have escaped justice or filled the empty positions. Then there is al Qaeda's ability to adapt to new challenges and opportunities. Following 9/11, the United States led a concerted assault on al Qaeda cells around the world, focusing on its headquarters in Afghanistan. Al Qaeda responded by reinventing itself—it flattened its organization, minimized its links with its affiliates, and concentrated on inspiring Islamists around the world to organize and strike independently as part of a broader movement. Finally, the Bush administration's blunders in its "war on terror" swelled the ranks of al Qaeda and other militant Islamist groups with countless zealots.

Al Qaeda is also unique in its priorities. Previous Middle East terrorist groups concentrated their efforts on attacking Israel and pro-Western Arab governments. For Al Qaeda, the United States is the primary enemy whose defeat would lead to the collapse of those Western allies. Bin Laden explained that "if we cut off the head of America, the kingdoms in the Arab world will cease to exist."[23]

Much of al Qaeda's history involves training and dispatching terrorists back to their homelands. It nurtured Islamist groups in such far-flung countries as Thailand, the Philippines, Indonesia, Chechnya, Georgia, Algeria, Bosnia and

Herzegovina, Kosovo, Somalia, and Yemen. Al Qaeda may have trained as many as twenty thousand men from 1996 through 2001 in Afghanistan.[24] It then tapped the best of those fighters to join its own organization, with possibly as many as three thousand jihadists heeding the call. While Muslims from around the world filled al Qaeda's ranks, Khalid Sheikh Mohammed, 9/11's mastermind, estimated that 70 percent were Saudis and 20 percent were Yemenis, with the rest from elsewhere.[25]

Al Qaeda magnifies its numbers by weaving a network of alliances with dozens of other Islamist organizations. To those groups it offers not merely trained fighters but also funds and access to the global network of safe houses, mosques, and charities. The al Qaeda network of operatives and affiliates continues to span scores of countries and continents around the world.

Most worrisome has been al Qaeda's repeated attempts, from its inception, to get its hands on nuclear, biological, chemical, and radiological WMD as bombs, a mission that bin Laden declared "a religious duty" for Muslims.[26] That effort was deemed so vital that bin Laden put his deputy, Ayman al-Zawahiri, in charge. To date, these efforts appear to have failed. Even if al Qaeda does have such deadly materials, getting them to a prime target and detonating them may be beyond its capability. Then again, perhaps it does have that power and is just biding its time. Only al Qaeda's leaders know for sure.

3

Know Your War
Terrorism versus Counterterrorism

*You cannot kill your way out of an insurgency. You're not
going to defeat everyone out there. You have to turn them.*
—General David Petraeus

*In recent years, the lines separating war, peace, diplomacy,
and development have become increasingly blurred.*
—Robert Gates

*Do not try to do too much. . . . It is their war and you are
there to help them, not to win it for them.*
—T. E. Lawrence

Warfare is the way of deception.
—Sun Tzu

Having assessed the nature of one's enemy and oneself, the next step in winning
a war is to fulfill a maxim by that great theorist and practitioner of warfare, Carl
von Clausewitz: "The statesman and the commander have to . . . establish the
kind of war on which they are embarking, neither mistaking it for, not trying to
turn it into, something that is alien to its true nature. This is the first of all strategic
questions and the most comprehensive."[1] Sun Tzu put it more succinctly: "Know
your war."

Terrorism and Revolution

Terrorism is a kind of war. On that most people seem to agree. The trouble is that, like God, just what constitutes terrorism is in the eyes, mind, and heart of the beholder. Few concepts evoke more impassioned debates over its meaning. Walter Laqueur counted over a hundred definitions. Yet the most exasperating problem is not so much in defining as in applying the term. President Ronald Reagan captured that conundrum when he admitted that "one man's terrorist is another man's freedom fighter."[2]

Nonetheless, experts can extract a working meaning of terrorism from the labyrinth of popular images or politicized uses. Most definitions boil down to terrorism as the unlawful threat or use of destruction against the lives or property of innocent people for political ends. That conception is pliable enough to embrace terrorism committed by states as well as subnational or transnational groups. Yet it would still provoke debate over the meaning of "unlawful," "innocent," and "political." One thing, however, is certain. As Vladimir Lenin asserted, terrorism is about evoking terror.

There is a reason for the seeming madness. As Gary Sick put it, "Terrorism is the continuation of politics by other means." Most terrorist groups do more than target innocent people with indiscriminate destruction. They are driven not just by murderous hatred but also by ideals and visions of a better future that they believe terrorism can bring. They are fighting for as well as against certain people and ideals. Terrorism is said to be most often the tactic of the weak, exploited, and enraged against the strong, rapacious, and unjust. Bruce Hoffman explains that "terrorists perceive themselves as reluctant warriors, driven by desperation—and lacking any viable alternative—to violence against a repressive state, a predatory rival ethnic or nationalist group, or an unresponsive international order."[3]

Thus most terrorists are would-be Robin Hoods, righting wrongs, punishing villains, and liberating oppressed people. Although terrorism is clearly a crime, it is motivated by political rather than monetary or pathological ends. People choose to become terrorists ultimately because they have made a rational choice that they have no other means of satisfying their drive for justice and vengeance. So any one person or group of people who follow that path would be terrorists, as the term is commonly understood.

Terrorism and insurgency have distinct meanings, but more often than not, terrorism is a tactic of a revolutionary movement. There are far more would-be than genuine revolutionary movements that use terrorism. Historically, political revolutions (the rapid, systematic change of one political, economic, social, and cultural system into another) are as rare as terrorist groups spouting revolutionary slogans are numerous.

So-called revolutionary conditions do not necessarily breed revolutions. Scores of countries around the world suffer mass poverty, corruption, brutality, and exploitation in which the rich are getting richer and fewer while the poor are getting poorer and more numerous and desperate. Relatively few of those countries have revolutionary movements trying to destroy the government and create something radically new atop its ruins. To be viable, that movement must include a leadership, organization, and ideology dedicated to revolution.

Revolutions do not have to be violent but usually are. Those with power want to keep it and will do all that they can to crush any challengers. Revolutionaries thus must use violence as one of many means to erode and eventually topple those at the top. Mao Tse-tung, one of history's greatest practitioners and theorists of revolution, explained that the path to destroying a hated government and taking power unfolds in three stages: hit and run, take and hold, and circle and destroy.[4]

Terrorism is usually wielded in that opening hit-and-run stage of a revolutionary group's struggle to transform itself into the spearhead of a mass evolving movement. According to Bruce Hoffman, at that time the terrorists "do not function in the open as armed units, generally do not attempt to seize or hold territory, deliberately avoid engaging enemy military forces in combat, and rarely exercise any direct control or sovereignty over either territory or population."[5]

A reputation for being powerful enhances one's power. People tend to obey, fear, emulate, or want to join those with power, and are either indifferent to or exploitive of those without power. Terrorist groups try to make up for their relative paucity in operatives and operations by promoting the image that they are far more powerful than they really are. Much like the Wizard of Oz, they play a smoke and mirrors game by manipulating images.

During that initial stage, paradoxically, the revolutionaries at times terrorize the very hearts and minds of the people they are trying to champion and enlist.

In their minds, they do so for a very good reason. They try to make up for their few numbers with the "rope-a-dope" strategy of provoking the government into overreacting to their attacks with indiscriminate violence and repression that in turn drives more and more fence-sitters to join the terrorists.

But the hit and run stage involves more than terrorism. The movement is organizing an alternative underground political, economic, and social system that will supposedly better the lives of most people. Thus ever-more people join the revolution both because of the beguiling pull of the movement's good works and ideals and the violent push of blind government retaliation atop chronic exploitation, injustice, and repression.

At some point, the revolutionary leaders judge that they have won over enough hearts and minds that they can begin to take and hold territory. The violence escalates to ever-larger groups of armed forces fighting one another as the government launches campaigns to crush the insurgents and retake that territory. If the insurgents can not only fend off those attacks but expand their control over more land and people, then the struggle for power reaches the third stage. The insurgents now field armies that they use to circle the government forces in their strongholds and cities and, slowly, systematically destroy them.

Having taken power, the revolutionaries now must hold it against those who would, in Winston Churchill's chilling words, "strangle the monster in its cradle." The rebels systematically destroy all vestiges of the old order and plant in its ruins the political, economic, and social institutions and values of their revolutionary vision. That is easier said than done. Historically, non-liberal revolutions have simply replaced one system of dictatorship, exploitation, corruption, and brutality for one far more efficient and rapacious.

In the twentieth century, a handful of communist and non-communist groups successfully used terrorism as a critical tactic in an array of means to take and hold power. The communist revolutions in China, Vietnam, Cuba, and Cambodia most clearly followed Mao's three-stage strategy followed by the systematic transformation of those countries. Noncommunist movements like the Irish Republican Army (IRA), the Palestinian Liberation Organization (PLO), the African National Congress (ANC), and Hezbollah in Lebanon never got beyond the first stage of terrorist hit-and-run tactics. Bloody stalemates were followed by deals cut with the governments they were fighting. Those groups agreed to give up terrorism and revolution in return for sharing power within existing or reformed democratic systems. The Taliban in Afghanistan did follow Mao's three-stage strategy for taking power by 1996 but failed to consolidate that power and were deposed by the United States in late 2001; recently they have made a startling comeback in Afghanistan and Pakistan.

"Old" versus "New" Terrorism

While terrorism may be as old as humanity, globalization has transformed both its means and ends. Increasing numbers of experts distinguish "old" from "new" terrorism.[6] A key distinction is the cause for which a group commits terror. Old terrorist groups tended to espouse varying mixes of Marxism and nationalism and were defiantly secularist. Religious extremism characterizes new terrorism. That change has been abrupt and sweeping

Another difference is the scale of violence. Old terrorism tried to minimize the number of innocent victims and maximize publicity for the cause. As expert Brian Jenkins famously put it, "Terrorists want a lot of people watching and a lot of people listening and not a lot of people dead." The reason why was simple. While all politics is a form of theater, this is most important to terrorist groups whose success depends on winning understanding, sympathy, and support for their causes; too much death and destruction will alienate most of the audience.[7]

New terrorism seeks to destroy as many lives and as much property as possible for two reasons. One is that most groups are fired by apocalyptic visions of good versus evil, the rapidly approaching end of time, and their God-given mandate to devastate God's enemies. Another motivation is that as groups proliferate, they compete ever-more fiercely for the mass media's attention; the worse the body count, the bigger the media coverage.

Although neither variety wants to get caught, the old terrorists tried to get away while the new are willing to commit suicide for his or, increasingly, her cause. Suicide bombing is a serious terrorist threat. From 1980 to 2003, suicide bombings accounted for only 3 percent of all terrorist attacks but nearly half of all fatalities. That figure is an underestimate because it does not include victims from 9/11 or Iraq. Nine out of ten of those suicide bombings were motivated by the drive to eliminate foreigners from their land. The number of suicide bombings and proportion of suicide bombings to all terrorist attacks are steadily increasing.[8]

Yet another distinction is the scope of operations. Old terrorist groups generally confined their efforts to destroying one state and operated in that country and a few others. New terrorists seek to defeat or destroy entire classes of countries and operate in dozens or even scores of countries around the world.

The sources of support are becoming just as diverse. Old terrorist groups usually benefited from the shelter, money, arms, and training of a sympathetic state. Globalization allows new groups to be far more self-reliant. Today's terrorists have a source of tremendous power unavailable to previous generations of terrorists—the Internet. With laptop computers and a cybercafé, terrorist groups can raise consciousness, publicity, recruits, and money while plaguing their enemies with viruses and worms. The array of technologies available to terrorists is constantly expanding. The terrorists that attacked hotels and restaurants in Mumbai, India, in November 2008 used such technologies as global positioning system handsets, satellite phones, satellite-generated street and building maps, and voice-activated Internet systems.

Failed Psyches versus Failed Societies

Regardless of whether someone is an old or new terrorist, how could anyone murder innocent people? Some mix of nature and nurture may offer an explanation. So are terrorists more likely to rise from failed psyches or failed states? The answer may appear clear enough. There are literally billions of people around the world mired in poverty, repression, and despair. Only a tiny sliver of that population would ever join a terrorist group, let alone commit vicious atrocities in its name.

Yet if failed psyches offer more likely explanations, the attempts to identify a definitive terrorist profile have been a chimera.[9] Terrorists come from virtually all professions, income levels, and backgrounds. Most studies, however, belie the notion that a society's most desperate are the most inclined to become terrorists. A study of Hezbollah members found that they were on average better off and more educated than most of the population. The 9/11 hijackers were mostly well educated and middle class. Osama bin Laden himself came from one of the world's wealthiest families. Indeed terrorist groups have at times bedeviled affluent societies like those of America, Europe, and Japan. Revolutionary leaders in any country tend to emerge from privileged backgrounds, with their drive and vision to change the world animated by a profound sense of injustice combined with enough wealth and education to understand and act on radical alternatives.

Terrorists are no different from nearly everyone else on the planet in at least one respect—they are sane, and their acts are rational. That is a fundamental requirement for membership in virtually any terrorist groups. People with psychological problems are hard to control and easy to spot and thus could disrupt and expose the group whose survival depends on strict secrecy and discipline.

Yet, regardless of the personal backgrounds of terrorists, most do indeed come from countries with appalling poverty, repression, exploitation, and corruption; these nations also have an ever-widening gap between the haves and have nots. These conditions push alienated, enraged, and vengeful people along the path to terrorism. How far that person goes depends on the pull of a leader, organization, and ideology that can explain and provide the means of destroying the people and system that is responsible for those abysmal conditions. One final key is whether a government can repress those who would rebel against it. A tottering or outright failed state will breed more terrorists than a government that is as efficient at crushing dissent as it is at exploiting the population.[10]

Clinton Watts established a profile for foreign fighters in both Iraq and Afghanistan. That fighter is most likely from a country in the Middle East or North Africa with "a high infant mortality rate, a high unemployment rate, and few civil liberties." He was more likely to be recruited by a returning fighter or a local religious leader than from the Internet. "He is not necessarily impoverished but has time on his hands and a lack of purpose, making him more susceptible to radicalization. . . . If he has experienced fighting, he will elect to fight; if not he will elect to be a suicide bomber." The countries that supplied the most fighters in proportion to their populations were Libya, Saudi Arabia, and Yemen. Watts argues that, armed with that knowledge, American and allied counterterrorist strategies can and should work with the governments of countries most likely to produce such fighters and work to alleviate the socioeconomic conditions that breed them.[11]

Terrorism-as-Crime versus Terrorism-as-War

So just how is any terrorist group, especially the more virulent, newer versions, best fought, let alone defeated? There is certainly no dearth of advice.[12]

The National Strategy for Combating Terrorism, issued by the Bush administration in February 2003, was more a pep talk than a coherent plan and was summarized by the four Ds—defeat, denial, diminish, and defend:

> We will defeat terrorist organizations of global reach through relentless action. We will deny terrorists the sponsorship, support, and sanctuary they need to survive. We will win the war of ideas and diminish the underlying conditions that promote the despair and the destructive visions of political change that lead people to embrace, rather than shun, terrorism. And throughout, we will use all the means at our disposal to defend against terrorist attacks on the United States, our citizens, and our interests around the world."[13]

UN secretary general Kofi Annan one-upped the Bush administration with a 2005 program that highlighted "five Ds," which included "dissuading disaffected groups from choosing terrorism, denying terrorists the means to carry out attacks, deterring states from supporting terrorists, developing state capacity to prevent terrorism, and defending human rights in the struggle against terrorism."[14]

However sensible those two approaches may be, both the president and secretary general may have jumped the gun, so to speak. Which brings us back to Sun Tzu and his admonition to "know the enemy, know yourself."[15] Any strategy for winning or avoiding defeat must begin with understanding and comparing the interests and powers of one's enemy and oneself. Every terrorist group is unique, no matter how similar many may appear. Each differs in its organization, operations, finance, popular support, goals, and threat. Thus, any one-size-fits-all strategy is doomed to failure. What works in one struggle may be self-defeating in the next. Any successful strategy will be tailored to blunt that terrorist group's unique strengths and exploit its weaknesses. And to do that one must understand one's own unique strengths and weaknesses.

Even if terrorism is a kind of war, a core question for policymakers is whether to treat it as acts of war or crime. Neoconservatives insist that the best way to fight terrorism is to wage a full-scale war against all who practice it. Lawrence Freedman powerfully critiques that approach:

> First, defining obnoxious criminal acts as warlike dignifies them and gives the perpetrators an unnecessarily heroic status. Second, instead of being framed in terms of law enforcement and the successful prosecution of the perpetrators, they are framed in terms of military victory. Third, in a gloves off war, governments can do things that they cannot do when the problems are described in more civilian terms. . . . Fourth, and finally, power within governments shifts to the military and the Pentagon civilians, leading to a harsh policy with scant hope for diplomatic initiatives, let alone attention to the conditions which breed terrorism.[16]

From a realist perspective, that war or crime decision depends on the strength, operations, and motivations of the group that commits terrorism. The smaller the group's numbers, the more restricted its operations, and the more motivated it is by hatred and vengeance rather than by a coherent ideology, the more sensible it would be to wield a terrorism-as-crime strategy that emphasized police investigations and criminal court trials to apprehend and prosecute suspects. But if terrorism is a tactic of a mass revolution that is trying to destroy an established authority and replace it with a completely different political, economic, and social system, then a counterinsurgency strategy that protects the population and addresses underlying socioeconomic problems would certainly be more appropriate.[17]

Any successful campaign against al Qaeda and its affiliates clearly demands a hybrid of both strategies. Islamist operatives in states where the rule of law prevails can be investigated, apprehended, and prosecuted. A legal approach, however, will not work in failed or failing states where an Islamist movement threatens to take power or has taken power. Just what mix of methods might best counter the terrorists will vary from one country to the next. The bottom line of any strategy is whether it works.

Hearts and Minds

Winning hearts and minds is crucial for a successful counterinsurgency strategy, a reality expressed by the 1940 Marine Corps Small Wars Manual: "In major warfare, hatred of the enemy is developed among troops to arouse courage. In small wars, tolerance, sympathy, and kindness should be the keynote of our relationship with the mass of the population."[18]

The key to winning that battle for hearts and minds is to match the enemy's network with one's own so that one can oppose him at every level and in every way. So if al Qaeda has morphed from a hierarchy into a flatter, more defused network of networks, the American and allied counterterrorist efforts must somehow try to get appropriate government and private organizations to become more flexible, decentralized, responsive, and, above all, interactive with one another.

Those who commit and those who fight terrorism are engaged in a multidimensional war in which the battle of images, ideas, and ideologies is among the most crucial. It is not enough to discredit the enemy's ideology; a successful counterterrorist strategy must promote a positive vision that can appeal to the hearts and minds of the population at stake.

Thus public relations is an essential tactic in any war against a terrorist group. Terrorists and counterterrorists exploit the mass print and electronic media to sell their respective cause and denigrate that of their enemy. If terrorism is a tactic of a revolutionary movement, then the ultimate goal is to capture the hearts and minds, or allegiance, of more and more people. To do so, the insurgents try to create an image or mystique about themselves, usually as Robin Hood–type saviors of the people against a brutal, corrupt, and inept government. At times that image is actually true. Regardless, counterinsurgents must do everything possible to demystify and debunk the enemy. They must pull the curtain aside and reveal the Wizard of Oz to be a tiny man at the controls of a machine rather than the all-powerful demigod that he tried to appear as. The terrorists must be exposed as the true enemy of the people due to their harming the very people they claim to represent through murder, exploitation, and extortion. President Barack Obama and his administration tried to do that by releasing unflattering images of Osama bin Laden seized during the SEAL operation that killed him.

Hearts and Wallets

Regardless of what strategy prevails, at least one vital factor will be constant. Much is rightfully made of the battle for hearts and minds, but the struggle for hearts and wallets may be just as crucial. Terrorism is expensive, and the bigger the group and the more wide-ranging its operations, the greater the expense. There is more to terrorism than simply destroying things and people. Terrorists need not only weapons but food, shelter, clothing, medical care, and incomes for themselves and often their dependents. People must be organized and trained in various skills in secure locations. The cause must be promoted to as many potentially sympathetic or outright supportive hearts and minds as possible. In many cases corrupt people with public or private power must be paid off. And, of course, it takes money to make money.

Terrorists can raise money from a variety of sources, including running legitimate businesses, soliciting donations, or engaging in criminal activities. For most Islamist groups, charities are the most vital source of money. Billions of dollars have been raised by passing the hat at thousands of mosques around the world. Proving that a charity is a front for a terrorist group is hard; shutting it down is harder. Governments in Muslim and non-Muslim countries alike can be reluctant to interfere in religious matters. Faced with overwhelming evidence, a government may prohibit a charity. This action usually only briefly disrupts the operation, as the charity is reopened under a new name with a new headquarters.

Narcoterrorism, or the nexus between drug smuggling and terrorism, is an increasingly important source of money. The global illegal drug trade in 2008 was estimated to be worth at least $322 billion. While the share of that skimmed by narcoterrorism is difficult to estimate, all analysts agree that it is growing steadily. Annually skimming hundreds of millions of dollars from the heroin trade is ever-more vital for the Taliban and al Qaeda.[19]

Making money is not enough. The money must be moved from where it is made to where it is needed. All along it must be stored or transferred safely and secretly. There is as diverse an array of ways to move money as to make money. It can be transferred via the Internet or cell phones, carried by couriers, or passed through an informal remittance system known as *hawala*, a kind of third world version of Western Union. Thus a key counterterrorist strategy involves trying to disrupt and ideally eliminate the ability of terrorists to make and move money. "Following the money" is the best way to reveal not just the sources and destinations of that essential source of terrorist power but the agents and refugees who accompany it.

Each step along the way demands a different strategy. The most challenging is trying to drain the financial swamp that terrorists tap for their livelihood. The more diverse the sources of money, the tougher they are to cut off. Donors can be exposed and, as appropriate, shamed, intimidated, or incarcerated so that they are deterred from giving more. Legal means can be found to shut down legitimate businesses. The most difficult, of course, is eroding criminal sources of money like smuggling, protection, prostitution, and so on.

Terrorist groups once could fairly safely invest their money in banks, stocks, and other legitimate financial havens under the phony names of front companies or people. That option is increasingly risky, given the ever-more sophisticated means that authorities wield to find and freeze such investments. Increasingly, terrorists rely on their own informal banking system. But that too has its costs. To prevent theft as well as detection, the money must be spread in smaller amounts to more diverse locations, which can make for an accounting nightmare. Operating costs climb and movement slows when the funds must be transferred by networks of couriers and hawala transactions.

Yet despite sophisticated means of doing so, trying to find terrorist money is the counterterrorist equivalent of searching for the proverbial needle in a haystack. In 2011 over $2 trillion dollars a day was transferred across international borders; a week's worth of such transactions equaled what America's economy generated that entire year! Remittances by foreign workers to their homes surpassed $350 billion. Somewhere in all that were hundreds of millions of dollars of money transferred by terrorist groups.[20]

Conquest versus Containment

States can and at times do become sanctuaries for international terrorism and crime. Iran, Pakistan, Yemen, Lebanon, Somalia, and Colombia are only the most prominent examples of countries whose governments either actively support or are incapable of eliminating terrorist groups in their midsts.

What can be done about that? In the United States neoconservatives and realists champion rival strategies. Neoconservatives assert that Washington has no choice but to conquer and convert such a country into a democracy. Citing the historic tendency for such crusades to be disastrous for American interests, realists reject that knee-jerk response and instead insist that any policy must be tailored to the specific nature of that regime's threat to the United States. On rare occasions the conquest and conversion strategy may be the best option; usually, it simply plays into the rope-a-dope strategy of America's enemies.

As an alternative to conquest and conversion, containment has historically been a far less costly and far more successful strategy. The reason is simple—it is a lot easier to change behaviors than regimes. The larger the territory and the more diverse, numerous, anti-Western, and radical the population of a belligerent state, the more absurd the conquest and conversion strategy and the more sensible the containment strategy become.

It is falsely believed that containment is a purely defensive strategy that leaves the initiative to the enemy. A better name for containment is "constriction," with the image of an anaconda methodically crushing its prey. The means would include all appropriate diplomatic, economic, covert, and even military actions that erode both the specific threats that regime poses and that regime's legitimacy in the hearts and minds of the population. Like any other successful assertion of power, containment depends on the capacity and will of those who wield it.

Deterrence is an essential part of containment. Deterrence works only if the enemy does not attack because it believes that the retaliation would be certain and devastating. Yet deterrence is hardly a foolproof strategy. Leaders and their advisers frequently miscalculate the capacity and determination of their enemies. The result is often an unwanted war and an even more unwanted defeat.

And then there are states, groups, and individuals for whom deterrence might not work under any circumstances. Islamist groups that champion holy war, martyrdom, and suicide attacks are often put in that category. Can Islamist terrorists be deterred?

These groups face a dilemma—they at once enhance and diminish their power when they take over a state. The monopoly they enjoy over the country's sources of power can be at once a blessing and a curse. Those resources are vulnerable to international economic sanctions and attack by American missiles, bombs, and Special Forces. It can be as difficult to hold as to take power. The new revolutionary regime faces the same hearts and minds dilemma as the regime it overthrew.

Thus theoretically even the most radical regime can be deterred and thus contained. The key is for the White House to communicate to that regime just what behavior is unacceptable, as well as the devastating consequences if it chooses to behave that way. At the same time the United States must have not just the capacity but the will to act on its threat should deterrence fail.

If the government of a nation-state can be deterred, what about a terrorist group without a mailing address? In a commencement address at West Point on May 27, 2006, President George W. Bush declared that the "terrorists have no borders to protect or capital to defend. They cannot be deterred—but they will be defeated."[21] Actually terrorism can be deterred, even the suicide version. The key to deterring terrorists is to feed their fear that they will get caught before they reach their target. This entails three vital components: "We must be able to identify the adversary; the adversary must know that we have the capability to cause them great harm as well as the willingness to use that capability; and the adversary must wish to avoid the harm we can cause."[22]

Ideally that fear begins in their lairs. Terrorists must be made to exist in constant dread that their safe houses are death traps, that at any second black-clad Special Forces will burst in tossing stun grenades, or that a Hellfire or cruise missile will obliterate the building. The measures the terrorists take to avoid detection and thus destruction in their hideouts will divert crucial resources from preparing and executing attacks. That line of deterrence is only nurtured by successful attempts to find and capture or kill terrorists. The brilliant SEAL operation that killed bin Laden has had such effects on al Qaeda and its affiliates.

It is far better to capture than kill the terrorist leaders who are gold mines of information that can be used to devastate the group. If that is not possible, then killing them is the next best option, although that usually has relatively little impact on the terrorist group. Leaders can be replaced, while charismatic leaders killed in action become martyrs. Yet killing a key leader in a group with ambitious lieutenants and no clear line of succession can ignite a self-destructive power struggle. After bin Laden's death, weeks passed before al Qaeda announced that Ayman al-Zawahiri was able to suppress his rivals and declare himself the leader.

The next line of deterrence is promoting the fear that they will get caught en route to their target. The enhanced security measures since September 11 for obtaining visas, catching planes, and crossing international borders most likely have had a powerful deterrent effect on would-be terrorists.

The final line of deterrence is at the target itself. That involves determining which targets would be the most likely and hardening them. Just what that hardening entails will vary. Obviously there are classes of targets like airports, planes, ports, or shipping containers that can benefit from the same or similar measures.

Overwhelming retaliation can be an appropriate strategy of containment. Here again it works only if the enemy believes that the threat is credible and the results would be worse than giving in. The Taliban apparently believed that the Bush administration would not invade Afghanistan if it did not give up bin Laden and other al Qaeda leaders after September 11. That belief was understandable. After all, President Bush and his fellow neoconservatives had ignored the advice of experts that al Qaeda was "a clear and present danger" and chose not to retaliate even after it was revealed in January 2001 that al Qaeda was behind the suicide bombing of the USS *Cole* the previous October. Likewise, Saddam Hussein believed that the Bush administration's threat to attack Iraq was a bluff. Those miscalculations resulted in the initial rout of the Taliban and al Qaeda from Afghanistan and the destruction of Saddam Hussein's regime.

Some threats can only be confronted with appropriate military force after all other measures have failed. For instance, should Tehran break its promise not to develop nuclear weapons, or an Islamist revolution take over Pakistan with its hundred or more nuclear weapons, then a military strike that eliminates that nuclear threat might be the best option. That would involve not a suicidal "conquer and convert" invasion but instead a "smash, grab, and run" operation that secures those nuclear weapons and materials. The political fallout of such an operation would be the equivalent of kicking a hornet's nest. But if the array of other containment measures are in place, then any attempts to retaliate decisively would be blunted.

Powell versus Petraeus

The outright conquest and conversion of a country could only be legally, morally, and, most important, strategically justified if its government were responsible for a massive attack on the United States. By that criteria the Bush administration was as justified in going to war in Afghanistan as it was unjustified in warring against Iraq.

That aside, the initial campaigns in both Afghanistan and Iraq were models of what is called the Revolution in Military Affairs (RMA), which includes wielding an array of cutting-edge technologies in communications, targeting, and precision firing that allows forces to be fewer, faster, and deadlier. Standard equipment includes laptop computers, smartphones, global positioning systems, unmanned aerial vehicles (UAVs), and "smart" bombs and missiles. The RMA is not just about hardware. Soldiers too must be smarter. All those high-tech marvels give unprecedented information and destructive power to soldiers down through the ranks to the lowest private. To maximize that potential power, each soldier's powers of reason and intuition must be developed to make critical and creative decisions of life and death, and victory and defeat. That "Netcentric warfare" lets commanders fine-tune the destruction so that it cripples a government's ability to wage war but does not cripple a country's ability to recover.

While an RMA is most effective at destroying a nation-state's conventional military forces, it can also be asserted in unconventional wars. When terrorism is among the tactics a popular revolutionary movement wields to take over a country or countries vital to America's defense, then the United States military will have to play a prominent role. In that situation, counterterrorism and counterinsurgency are essentially synonymous. But that raises a question: just what is the most effective method of fighting terrorists when they morph into insurgents?

Andrew Bacevich, a West Point graduate, Vietnam War veteran, and military theorist, identifies two broad schools of contemporary American warfare, the Powell Doctrine and the Petraeus Doctrine.[23] Two different ground commanders in Iraq—Gen. Ricardo Sanchez, who served from June 2003 to June 2004, and Gen. David Petraeus, from January 2007 to September 2008—exemplified those perspectives. That debate was resolved among reasonable observers when Sanchez's strategy exacerbated, and Petraeus's strategy quelled, the Iraqi insurgency.

The Powell Doctrine emphasizes the launching of overwhelming force against an enemy so that wars are "brief, decisive, and infrequent." The strategic and tactical key to this philosophy is "search, destroy, and withdraw." When the war is conventional, the Americans can actually field fewer troops than the enemy as long as those troops and bombs are concentrated in devastating numbers against the enemy's military, economic, and political infrastructure and ultimately obliterate its ability to fight. After systematically eliminating the enemy threat and imposing terms, the American military can be swiftly withdrawn.[24]

This doctrine also recognizes that an insurgency takes much longer to defeat than a conventional enemy. In such a war, the tipping point is the ratio of ten soldiers to each insurgent. The greater the ratio, the greater the chance of smothering the insurgency; the lesser the ratio, the more likely the insurgents will not only survive but prosper and ultimately prevail.[25]

Under the Petraeus Doctrine, the strategic and tactical emphasis is to "clear, hold, and build" in order to win the hearts and minds of the population and thus win the war. That in turn depends on developing the economic, social, and political infrastructure that gives people security with which to develop their living standards and quality of life.

The U.S. Army and Marine 2006 Counterinsurgency Manual, edited by Petraeus, explores that strategy in depth. An insurgency is defined as "an organized movement aimed at the overthrow of a constituted government through the use of subversion and armed conflict. . . . Counterinsurgency is military, paramilitary, political, economic, psychological, and civic actions taken" to defeat an insurgency.[26] The emphasis is on "securing the population" rather than "destroying the enemy" since the enemy diminishes as the population becomes more secure: "The civilian population is the center of gravity—the deciding factor in the struggle. Therefore civilians must be separated from insurgents to insulate them from insurgent pressure and to deny the insurgent 'fish' the cover of the civilian 'sea.' By doing so the counterinsurgents can militarily isolate, weaken, and defeat the insurgents."[27]

Expert Jessica Stern offers a succinct explanation of terrorism's sources and the best counterstrategy: "While there is no single root cause of terrorism . . . alienation, perceived humiliation, and lack of political and economic opportunities make young men susceptible to extremism. It can evolve easily into violence when government institutions are weak. . . . Thus the best way to fight them is to ensure that they are rejected by the broader population. Terrorists and guerrillas rely on getting at least some popular support."[28]

Successfully fighting an insurgency involves first understanding its unique, complex nature and then committing the most appropriate forces to eventually overwhelm each of its dimensions. That takes time, although how much depends on the nature of the insurgency and what resources can be mustered to counter it. Patience is essential, but being a quick study is even more important. No counterinsurgency motto is more important than "learn and adapt" since "the side that learns faster and adapts more rapidly . . . usually wins."[29]

The Petraeus Doctrine seeks to revolutionize the way Americans and their allies understand and conduct counterinsurgency. To that end the manual identifies eight Zen-like paradoxes for practitioners to constantly meditate and then act upon: (1) Sometimes the more force is used, the less effective it is; (2) The more successful the counterinsurgency is, the less force can be used and the more risk must be accepted; (3) Sometimes doing nothing is the best reaction; (4) Some of the best weapons for counterinsurgency do not shoot; (5) The host nation doing something tolerably well is normally better than us doing it well; (6) If a tactic works this week, it might not work the next week, and if it works in this province, it might not work in the next; (7) Tactical success guarantees nothing; and (8) Many important decisions are not made by generals.[30]

A counterinsurgency strategy that focuses on defending the population rather than searching out and destroying guerrillas demands vast numbers of troops. The general tipping point is one soldier for every fifty inhabitants. The greater the ratio of soldiers to inhabitants, the more secure the population, the more likely they can work and live in relative peace, and the more likely they will be loyal to the government. Ideally that ratio is met not by deploying foreign boots on the ground but by raising and deploying native forces. The reason is simple: even in the best of causes, the transition from liberator to occupier to imperialist oppressor can be swift in the eyes of a population.

According to a Rand Corporation study, "by far the most effective strategy against religious [terrorist] groups has been the use of local police and intelligence services, which were responsible for the end of 73 percent of [terrorist] groups since 1968."[31] The key element behind that success is the ability to understand, penetrate, and rally the people away from the insurgents and behind the government. Local police are the best able and foreign troops the least able to do that.

However, in failed or destroyed states like Afghanistan or Iraq, foreign troops are essential to securing the country and then rebuilding that country's security forces. But a dilemma is embedded in that necessity. The presence of foreign troops often feeds rather than starves a counterinsurgency. Even the best-trained troops can literally and figuratively trample local sensitivities, customs, and people. Search and destroy missions—especially the midnight raids of shouting soldiers, kicked-in doors, screaming women and children, and suspects shot or dragged away—are hardly the most convincing way to win hearts and minds. So ideally foreign troops should remain in the background, training the native troops, evaluating intelligence sources, and backing rather than leading operations.

Thus steadily training, equipping, and deploying national security forces is a key part of any counterinsurgency strategy. To that end, Arthur Keller, a former CIA operative with extensive experience in the Middle East, offered these lessons:

> Keep your footprint small. Don't use trainers who don't know the language or culture. Don't let the locals become dependent on American air power. Train them in tactics suited to their circumstances. Don't ever let the locals think mighty America will fight their battles or solve all their problems for them; focus on getting them ready to fix their own problems. Keep the folks in Washington out of the way of the people doing the work in the field.[32]

While that process is unfolding, what should the foreign troops do about the rebels? Smearing any insurgents and their supporters as "terrorists" and trying to wipe them all out only strengthens the insurgency. "You cannot kill your way out of insurgency," General Petraeus explained. "You're not going to defeat everybody out there. You have to turn them."[33]

Self-destructive behavior is not confined to Washington. The American-backed governments of Iraq, Afghanistan, and Pakistan are ever-more critical of the United States for an array of exaggerated or all too real sins. The worst charge is that American forces are killing too many civilians in their operations against the militants. That may be true, although the Americans are doing all they can to minimize such "collateral damage." But most American operations are deft surgical strikes compared to the often blind hammer blows inflicted by Iraqi, Afghan, and Pakistani troops when they do stir from the security of their bases. Biting the hand that feeds oneself is ultimately self-defeating. By making the United States the scapegoat for their own failures, those governments only erode their already fragile grip on their respective countries, and a key element of the counterinsurgency strategies in those countries is gently but firmly convincing the native leaders of that folly.

In Iraq and Afghanistan virtually all men are armed, dangerous, and members of local militias. Each of those hundreds of militias are political wild cards, ropes in the tug-of-war between insurgents and counterinsurgents. The militias know their turf, the people, places, and resources of their territory, whether it's a neighborhood, a village, or an entire valley. Their primary loyalty is to the clan, village, or tribe that they are organized to defend. They will fight with or against anyone that defends or enhances their particular interests. It is easy to alienate and tough to entice such militias.

As the saying goes, the loyalty of a militia member cannot be bought, but it can be rented. Part of Washington's belated "clear, hold, and build" strategies in both Afghanistan and Iraq involve buying the cooperation of the militias. Here is yet another dilemma. This strategy might actually conflict with attempts to build a viable national government, army, and police. American co-opting of local militias in Iraq and Afghanistan means arming, training, and funding groups that are at best autonomous and at worst opposed to the states that Washington is trying to develop in those countries.

There is another way to enlist a militia's arms, if not its hearts and minds. A militia group can be terrorized into a temporary loyalty, as the Taliban has proven. A Taliban threat to behead the militia chief and his sons will most likely cause them to submit. They might only resist if American, allied, or government forces are present and strong enough to defend them. Tragically, that is rarely the case.

The conservative nostrum to never negotiate with terrorists is another self-defeating strategy. In reality, the insurgent coalitions in Afghanistan and Iraq are composed of numerous groups and individuals with often vastly differing motivations and commitments to the cause and the fighting. That gives counterinsurgents the opportunity to play off the groups against one another, best achieved by trying to co-opt rather than kill. Daniel Markey, a former State Department South Asia expert, explains: "You fight, you talk, you fight, you talk. By talking you can divide your enemies. But if by talking, you're just giving your enemies a breathing space, then don't talk."[34]

Building Nations and Draining Swamps

Perhaps the central dilemma in counterinsurgency is the chicken and egg relationship between security and development. A country cannot develop unless it is secure, and it cannot be secure unless it develops.

Legitimacy is the bottom line of development and thus security. Seymour Martin Lipset defines legitimacy as "the capacity of a political system to engender and maintain the belief that existing political institutions are the most appropriate and proper ones for the society."[35] Nearly two and a half millennia ago, Sun Tzu offered this timeless advice on how a state bolsters its legitimacy: "If orders are consistently implemented to instruct the people, then the people will submit. If orders are not consistently implemented to instruct the people, then the people will not submit. One whose orders are consistently carried out has established a mutual relationship with the people."[36]

The more people who question or outright resist a political system's legitimacy, the greater the chance that that state will be overthrown and replaced. Insurgencies break out and persist for good reasons. People rebel because a government has failed not just to satisfy their fundamental needs, wants, and rights, but has wielded its power to repress and exploit them.

A government establishes legitimacy by alleviating rather than worsening problems. Thus the most logical and effective counterinsurgency strategy is to resolve the grievances that first sparked the rebellion. That in turn robs the insurgency of its appeal. The result is to lock the insurgents into a vicious cycle of fewer recruits, funds, operations, and legitimacy. But to do that, there must be a willing and able government, which brings us back to this chicken and egg dilemma.

The central goal for a counterinsurgency strategy is to build up faster than the insurgents tear down. Dell Dailey, the State Department's counterterrorist coordinator, explains that "our most important task in the war on terrorism is not the 'destructive' task of eradicating enemy networks, but the 'constructive' task of building legitimacy, good governance, trust, rule of law, and tolerance. Systems that are characterized by an absence of political choice, honest governance, economic opportunity, and personal freedoms can create incubators for extremism. Ignoring the human-development problem is not an option." He estimates that "addressing the conditions that terrorists exploit" is two-thirds of the counterterrorist effort.[37]

Larry Diamond, who was a senior adviser to the Coalition Provisional Authority in Baghdad and is a development expert, offers a succinct analysis of the four key components necessary in "any effort to rebuild a shattered, war-torn country: political reconstruction of a legitimate and capable state; economic reconstruction, including the rebuilding of the country's physical infrastructure and the creation of rules and institutions that enable a market economy; social reconstruction, including the renewal (or in some cases, creation) of a civil society and political culture that foster voluntary cooperation and the limitation of state power; and the provision of general security, to establish a safe and orderly environment."[38] He goes on to explain how the four are interrelated and when one fails it erodes the others. But of the four, security comes first. Without order and stability there will be little or no political, economic, and social development. The result is "nothing but disorder, distrust, and desperation—an utterly Hobbesian situation in which fear pervades and raw force dominates."

State building and nation building are inseparable but distinct. State building involves creating the institutions of government that are essential for nation building, or developing the economy, forging national unity, suppressing crime and rebellion, and resolving popular grievances. The nation building—or "drain the swamp" strategy—tries to eliminate the festering socioeconomic conditions that may breed terrorism and terrorists. As President Bush put it, "We fight against poverty because hope is an answer to terrorism."[39]

Education is a key to development and thus is a key counterinsurgency strategy. The more deficient a country's school system, the greater the appeal of Islamist madrassas. Thus educating girls and boys alike is crucial; historically, Islamism's appeal has fallen as female literacy has risen.[40]

A state's legitimacy depends on rooting its institutions in that country's political culture. Erecting lasting liberal democratic institutions in an authoritarian political culture may be a fool's mission. There is an inherent contradiction in imposing democracy from above upon people whose culture and history are shaped only by authoritarianism. The result at best is an illiberal democracy characterized by mass corruption, favoritism, ineptness, brutality, and injustice—the ingredients for the eruption of a rebellion. The countries of Latin America offer as many examples. For nearly two centuries since they threw off Spanish rule and drafted American-style liberal constitutions, the Latin American countries have seesawed between dismal versions of military and civilian rule. Liberalism has yet to supplant authoritarianism in Latin America's political and cultural gardens.

At the very least, any teacher of democracy should be a model to the student. The failure to practice what is preached can tragically skew the results. The Bush White House essentially sacrificed nation building in Afghanistan and Iraq on the altar of political payback and ideological correctness. Eventually tens of billions of taxpayer dollars were handed over in no bid or insider contracts to huge Republican Party campaign contributors like Halliburton and Bechtel. Overhead and often blatant theft devoured up to half of those payments, leaving very little left for the actual projects. Hundreds of projects never got beyond the blueprints or were started but never completed. Regardless, American taxpayers paid the bills. The result was to grossly undermine the counterinsurgency campaigns in both countries. The American occupation's corruption, ineptness, and brutality alienated literally millions of people, turned thousands into insurgents and terrorists, and squandered tens of billions of dollars, tens of thousands of local lives, and thousands of American lives.

If state building is a Herculean challenge, nation building may well be a Sisyphean condemnation. Imperialism, rather than nationalism, formed the frontiers of most of the world's nearly two hundred countries. Political frontiers were imposed by foreign generals or diplomats who split peoples sharing linguis-tic, tribal, or religious identities and grouped them with their traditional enemies. It is hard enough to forge a nation among people sharing the same language and culture, and nearly impossible in a land of Babel. Separatism has at time afflicted even wealthy multinational states like Belgium or Canada. These tensions worsen with poverty. The world's poorest countries tend to rely on a mineral or crop or two for export, and sometimes they do not even have that. Often a group within the state holds a monopoly over what little wealth that country produces and uses in part to put down and exploit everyone else. These conditions are ripe for rebellion.

Intelligence and Counterintelligence

A successful counterterrorist strategy has many crucial, interrelated elements. None is more vital than intelligence, or the collection, analysis, and sharing of the right information with the right people at the right time. There is just as much an art of spying as there is of war. Here, too, Sun Tzu offers eternal advice. Being a spymaster demands nothing less than the "wisdom of a sage." The reason why is that spying is ubiquitous not just to war but to life—"there are no areas where one does not employ spies." So to master the art of spying is to master the art of life itself. That in turn demands being "benevolent and righteous" and "subtle and perspicacious."[41] CIA director Michael Hayden elaborated just what counterter-rorist intelligence entails. The

> core mission . . . remains what it is always has been: to provide a first line of defense for the American people against foreign adversaries. We collect intelligence and run operations to counter threats before they do us harm; we provide our leaders with sophisticated analysis of the chal-lenges that they face; and we apply world class scientific prowess to give our operations an edge our adversaries cannot match. In this effort we work closely with our partners in other intelligence agencies, the diplo-matic community, law enforcement, and the military.[42]

Each step of the intelligence cycle is fraught with its own dilemmas and dangers. There is an operational race between terrorists and counterterrorists in which each tries to keep as far ahead of the other as possible. When terrorists come up with a new method (say, hijacking jetliners and slamming them into skyscrapers), counterterrorists try to come up with better methods of preventing that from happening. The most dynamic race is over surveillance, with counterterrorists using ever more sophisticated means of trying to spy on terrorists, and terrorists using every possible means, from the most traditional to the most cutting edge, to avoid detection.

Ideally the information is taken directly from the source through the recruitment of agents, eavesdropping, theft, or some other means. That, of course, is not always possible, and attempts to do so when it is possible can be counterproductive. The central CIA National Clandestine Service (NCS) mission of "recruiting agents and stealing secrets" is always a calculated gamble. Getting caught can be an embarrassment in friendly countries and fatal in unfriendly countries.

Then there is the problem of assessment. Discerning information gold from scree, or noise from signals, is the essential analytical challenge. In her classic study of the Pearl Harbor intelligence failure, Roberta Wohlstetter explained how the "relevant signals, so clearly audible after the event, [were] partially obscured before the event by the surrounding noise." She offered insights into the dilemmas of anticipating threats: "There is a tendency in our planning to confuse the unfamiliar with the improbable. The contingency we have not considered seriously looks strange; what looks strange is therefore improbable; what is improbable need not be considered seriously."[13]

Obviously pooling intelligence among appropriate institutions within a government and with foreign allies is essential to counterterrorism. Indeed Daniel Byman calls "foreign liaison . . . the single greatest element of successful counterterrorism."[44] Yet there are dilemmas here as well. Intelligence services jealously guard their sources and methods both to keep them secure and for the power they hold. Even within a government, intelligence tends to be overclassified and undershared. Ideally all counterterrorist organizations should enjoy access to the same crucial databases, whether it be watch lists, telephone logs, flight lists, credit histories, and so on, along with data-mining capabilities. That remains an elusive goal.

American military leaders on the ground in Afghanistan face a constant intelligence dilemma. They need the cooperation and information of local police, officials, tribal leaders, and the general population. Yet they must withhold plans of operations for fear of them being passed on to the insurgents. As a result, mid-night raids can terrorize and outrage a community. And that is if the operations successfully nabs or kills the enemy. If the innocent are incarcerated or killed, the result often is to push the local population into the hands of the enemy.

"Warfare is the way of deception," said Sun Tzu. "Thus although you are ca-pable, display incapability. . . . When committed to employing your forces, feign activity. When [your objective] is nearby, make it appear as if it is distant; when far away, create the illusion of being nearby."[45] Just as one tries to deceive others, one avoids being deceived. Modern practitioners distinguish between

> denial, in which information is used in a "defensive" way by keeping it both secret and hidden . . . and deception, in which information is used in an "offensive" way to mislead or confuse an adversary and which can include the use of both truthful and overt as well as false information in such a way as to influence a rival nation's perceptions. The discovery and uncovering of the first, and protection against the second, are "the two great purposes of intelligence."[46]

Information is gathered with the fear that it may be disinformation delib-erately planted by one's opponent. False information is an especially egregious problem in Afghanistan and Iraq, where warlords and chiefs feel no compunction in ridding themselves of ancient enemies by labeling them al Qaeda or Taliban. It is especially problematic when the American military calls in an air strike to attack an "al Qaeda" or "Taliban" leader, only to later learn that a chief simply found an effective way to kill off a rival.

Yet at times the fear of being deceived may be worse than or part of the threat. Michelle Van Cleave, former national counterintelligence executive, iden-tifies the paradox whereby "the more alert we are to deception, the more likely we are to be deceived." There is the natural fear that critical information can leak or be stolen. Fortunately, the chance of that happening is not as great as in the past. The odds of an Islamist group somehow penetrating intelligence net-works and siphoning off critical information is far lower than when Soviet bloc agents played the same game during the Cold War. However, those worse odds do not stop the Islamists from trying. Van Cleave revealed that "some 40 terrorists had been caught trying to infiltrate U.S. intelligence agencies as of 2005," while at least 35 terrorist groups along with most governments are trying to steal American secrets.[47]

If intelligence is all about getting the secrets of others, counterintelligence tries to prevent others from getting one's own secrets. At a certain point these different operations overlap. Counterintelligence involves the four key steps of identifying a foreign intelligence threat; assessing its danger, strengths, and vulnerabilities; neutralizing that threat; and, finally, exploiting that threat to provide intelligence on the other side's capabilities and intentions.[48]

Ideally, that fourth step leads to the penetration of "the opposition's own secret operations apparatus: to become, without the opposition's knowledge, an integral and functioning part of their calculations and operations…Most importantly, you are in a position to control his actions . . . by tailoring intelligence for him to your purposes, by influencing his evaluation, mislead him as to his decisions and consequent actions."[49]

Winners and Losers

Determining just who is winning a war against a terrorist group appears to be simple enough. If the number of terrorist attacks and victims goes down, then it would seem that the government is winning. Victory is measured by what does not happen. If the opposite is occurring, then the terrorists are ahead. The key question for Defense Secretary Donald Rumsfeld was, "Are we capturing, killing, or deterring and dissuading more terrorists every day than the madrassas and the radical clerics are recruiting, training, and deploying against us?" But of course it is more complicated than that, as the State Department's 2007 report on global terrorism explained: "Incarcerating or killing terrorists will not achieve an end to terrorism."[50]

The key element of terrorism—terror—cannot be easily measured. And while the number of attacks and victims is evident enough, it is far more difficult to get accurate figures on the number and morale of terrorists and their supporters, along with their short- and long-term plans. Paul Pillar, a former CIA analyst, warns that a "central lesson of counterterrorism is that terrorism cannot be 'defeated'—only reduced, attenuated, and to some degree controlled. Individual terrorists or terrorist groups sometimes are defeated; terrorism as a whole never will be. Expectations must be kept realistic"[51]

Thus a lull in the war should not be mistaken for victory. A group can lie in wait for years before launching another strike. And even when a terrorist group is effectively destroyed, the collateral destruction can create breeding grounds for new terrorist groups. Reversals of fortune can be swift. In January 2006, Afghanistan was touted as a counterterrorist success, and Iraq was condemned as a failure. Yet a mere two years later when George W. Bush relinquished power to Barack Obama, these situations had completely flipped.

4

Clinton and Bush versus al Qaeda before September 11

We knew and we warned that al Qaeda was planning a major strike.
—Jim Pavitt, CIA Deputy Director for Operations

That's a no brainer. Of course it's a violation of international law, that's why it's a covert action. The guy is a terrorist. Go grab his ass.
—Al Gore

The system was blinking red.
—George Tenet

Clinton Team Policies

Terrorism was off the political radar map when Bill Clinton took the oath of office on January 20, 1993. It briefly hogged center stage with the attack on the World Trade Center on February 26, 1993, before being elbowed aside by an array of other, more pressing domestic and international issues, each with its own array of powerful, competing interest groups. Despite the horror of that attack, most Americans preferred to believe that their country was relatively immune from international terrorism.

That belief was understandable. Even at the CIA, the terrorist threat took decades to creep up the priority agenda. Terrorism became a serious international problem in the late 1960s and into the 1970s with the proliferation of Palestinian and Red Army groups that conducted ever-more outrageous hijackings, kidnappings, and murders. Yet vicious as those groups were, they appeared to pose little direct threat to the United States.

That perception changed with Hezbollah's terrorist campaign against America's diplomatic, military, and intelligence presence in Lebanon from 1983 to 1984. The onslaught included bombings of the Marine barracks and American embassy that killed or wounded several hundred Americans; the kidnapping of several Americans for ransom; and the abduction, prolonged torture, and murder of Beirut CIA station chief William Buckley in 1984. The result was a humiliating defeat as the Reagan administration not only withdrew the American peacekeeping mission from Lebanon but actually tried to appease Hezbollah by ransoming hostages. Reagan and his inner circle did not stop there. They committed a series of felonies known as Iran-Contra that further empowered not just Hezbollah but also its sponsor, Iran.

Meanwhile, Langley pressured the White House for permission to create a Counterterrorism Center (CTC). Permission was finally granted in 1986. From the beginning the CTC focused mostly on Middle East terrorist groups that were at that time nearly all secularist and Marxist, except for Hezbollah. The 1993 attack on the World Trade Center prompted the CTC to explore more deeply the relationship between Islamism and terrorism. Osama bin Laden and al Qaeda, however, were not yet on the target, let alone the bull's-eye. As late as January 23, 1995, an executive order signed by President Clinton did not include al Qaeda on a list of twelve Middle East terrorist groups deemed so dangerous that they and their state supporters would suffer economic and travel sanctions.

The bin Laden file at Langley was at that time not just thin but mostly positive. The CIA was aware of bin Laden and his role with the Bureau of Services during the 1980s. Milt Bearden, the Islamabad station chief from 1986 to 1989, explained that bin Laden "actually did some very good things" by putting "a lot of money in a lot of the right places in Afghanistan" and was not regarded as "someone who was anti-American." A CIA report in April 1993 described bin Laden as an "independent actor who sometimes works with other individuals and governments" to promote "militant Islamic causes."[1]

It was not until January 1996 that the CIA concluded that al Qaeda was a powerful terrorist organization that posed an imminent threat to Americans. That month the CIA set up a special "virtual station" devoted to bin Laden and al

Qaeda. Analyst Michael Scheuer was asked to organize and lead that station, which he named after his son. Alec Station was unique. It was the only CIA station dedicated to a single terrorist organization and was initially set up at a secure site in northern Virginia, outside Langley, to encourage independent thinking. It began with a dozen analysts and a modest budget but expanded greatly in the years ahead.

When Alec Station was established, the United States had no significant assets in Afghanistan. The Americans had shut their embassy in Kabul in January 1989, and the nearest CIA station was in Islamabad. The U.S. Agency for International Development had ended its aid program there in 1994. But Alec Station got a windfall its first year when Jamal al-Fadl defected from al Qaeda in May 1996 and provided a gold mine of information, the most important of which was a range of ongoing plans for terrorist attacks. That reinforced intelligence gleaned from other sources. The result was to unravel more of al Qaeda's links with terrorist groups and attacks around the world.[2]

As 1996 opened, the threat appeared most imminent in Khartoum, where al Qaeda and an array of affiliates were headquartered. The word was that bin Laden was planning attacks on Americans and the American embassy in retaliation for his mistaken belief that the CIA was behind an assassination attempt on him.

President Clinton agreed to the CIA's advice to shut the Khartoum embassy and work with other American allies to pressure Khartoum to expel al Qaeda. That policy succeeded. Faced with crippling international economic sanctions and fearful that al Qaeda and terrorist groups threatened his rule, President Omar al-Bashir ordered bin Laden and his followers to leave Sudan. Bin Laden had no choice but to comply.

The terrorist attack (experts still debate whether it was committed by al Qaeda or Hezbollah) on the Khobar Towers on June 25, 1996, that killed 19 and wounded 372 Americans at their residence outside Riyadh, Saudi Arabia, was a watershed moment for the Clinton White House. Henceforth counterterrorism would be a core element of President Clinton's foreign policy. On June 21, 1996, he issued Presidential Decision Directorate 39 (PPD–39), which asserted that the United States would "deter, defeat, and respond vigorously to all terrorist attacks on our territory and against our citizens." It recognized that the "acquisition of weapons of mass destruction by a terrorist group . . . is unacceptable. There is no higher priority than preventing the acquisition of this capability or removing this capability from terrorist groups potentially opposed to the United States."

To these ends, President Clinton authorized the CIA to mount "an aggressive program of foreign intelligence collection, analysis, counterintelligence, and covert action." One of the powers Clinton gave the CIA became known as extraordinary rendition. This involved capturing and spiriting away terrorist subjects "by force . . . without the cooperation of the host government." When the White House legal counsel questioned the policy's legality, Vice President Al Gore replied with a laugh: "That's a no brainer. Of course it's a violation of international law, that's why it's a covert action. The guy is a terrorist. Go grab his ass."[3]

The CIA apprehended nearly a hundred terrorists during the last five years of the Clinton White House. President Clinton reviewed and approved every one of those snatches. Two were especially gratifying. Both took place in Pakistan with the aid of its security forces. Ramzi Yousef, who led the 1993 World Trade Center bombing, was captured in 1996; he is currently serving a 240-year sentence in a federal prison with no chance of parole. Mir Aimal Kansi, who shot and killed two CIA employees outside of the Langley headquarters in 1993, was captured in Pakistan in 1998, brought back to the United States, put on trial, found guilty of murder, and executed in 2002.

Clinton backed his get-tough counterterrorist policy with plenty of cash, doubling the counterterrorism budget from $5.7 billion in 1996 to $11.3 billion in 2001; the FBI's counterterrorist budget alone rose 280 percent during those years.[4]

Clinton understood that the United States could not go it alone, that any successful counterterrorist campaign had to be an international effort. To that end he began enlisting as many allies as possible. His first step was to get the Group of Seven to concentrate on counterterrorism during its July 1996 summit at Lyon, France, which occurred the month after the Khobar Towers bombing. They agreed to overhaul the Financial Action Task Force, which was originally set up in 1989 to fight money laundering, so that it would target terrorist financial accounts. By the time Clinton left office, over thirty countries had joined in that effort. But he was unable to get America's allies to do more. The White House "felt resistance to their request for better coordination" because the "Europeans were skeptical of claims about the size and dangerousness of al Qaeda."[5] Nonetheless the Clinton administration did successfully lead the effort to negotiate and sign the International Convention for the Suppression of the Financing of Terrorism in 1999.

Another essential element of Clinton's policy was to overhaul America's intelligence and counterterrorist institutions. The worst deficiency was in the CIA. During the 1990s, the CIA suffered an array of problems that hobbled its ability to collect and analyze information vital to American interests. Like the Pentagon, the CIA found its budget and personnel slashed as part of the post–Cold War peace dividend. The NCS, then called the Directorate of Operations, shriveled with massive retirements and few new recruits. Morale suffered sharp blows with the revelations in 1994 and 1996 that CIA officers Aldrich Ames and Harold Nicholson had spied for the Soviets. From 1991 to 1997, the CIA had four different directors, none of whom were able to revive the agency's sinking morale and effectiveness.

President Clinton finally resolved this chronic leadership problem by tapping George Tenet to head the agency on July 11, 1997. There had never been a director with Tenet's background. Armed with a bachelor's degree in international relations from Georgetown University, he got a job as a congressional staffer and eventually worked for intelligence committees. Impressed with the strength of Tenet's mind and character, a series of powerful mentors nurtured his political and analytical skills and placed him in increasingly important positions before he was named deputy CIA director in 1995.

Tenet got to work rebuilding the CIA's morale, budget, personnel, and missions, the most important of which became counterterrorism. Like President Clinton, he recognized the threat that terrorism posed to America. In May 1998, he warned Congress that the terrorist threat "is growing more diverse, complex, and dangerous. . . . It's easier and easier for smaller and smaller groups to do serious damage, with less visibility and warning. The potential for surprise has increased enormously."[6]

As that threat worsened, President Clinton recognized the need for an expert within the White House who could coordinate policy and think creatively. On May 22, 1998, he created the Counterterrorism Security Group (CSG) and appointed Richard Clarke to be its national coordinator, or "czar." Clarke was an excellent choice, renowned for his powerful mind, storehouse of knowledge, and hard-driving management style. He had spent more than two decades working on an array of intelligence issues for the Defense and State departments and knew Washington's political labyrinth inside out. Clarke would sit at the table with the president and other policy "principals."

Unfortunately, that new post complicated rather than eased counterterrorism policy. Clarke, along with Michael Scheuer, Alec Station's chief, tended to demand more aggressive measures than the CIA's Counterterrorist Center, which included both area experts and operatives with years of field experience, deemed prudent; having confined their careers to Washington, Clarke and Scheuer did not appreciate just how culturally, politically, and technically challenging paramilitary operations could become overseas, especially in remote and alien places like Afghanistan.

It was bin Laden's fatwa on February 23, 1998, calling on all good Muslims to kill any Americans anywhere, anytime, that prompted President Clinton to issue PDD-62 and PDD-63, which laid out a comprehensive counterterrorism strategy. Within that strategy were specific measures and authorizations for the CIA to take bin Laden, preferably alive, possibly dead.

Unfortunately, capturing bin Laden turned out to be an impossible mission. He and al Qaeda's other leaders knew they were being tracked and evaded detection. They rarely got together and rarely stayed long in any one place. They might enter a house at dusk and then leave after it got dark. A motorcade would suddenly break up, with vehicles peeling off in different directions. Further fouling this shell game was the reliability and timeliness of information sent back by Afghan spies on the ground. Surveillance satellites and, eventually, drones high above could not precisely identify bin Laden. And even if a consensus formed that the target was most likely bin Laden and should be attacked, hours would slowly pass for cruise missiles to be programmed, launched, and propelled to the target. By that time he could be far away. As if the intelligence and technical weaknesses were not troubling enough, there were other worries. A strike that missed him would only provoke al Qaeda to take added security measures to avoid similar strikes. Nearly any strike would most likely kill or wound innocent civilians and destroy their homes and livelihoods, which could push them and outraged others into the Islamist cause. Finally, a miss would make the United States look weak and flailing, rather than decisive and omnipotent. All this would make a future similar strike even more problematic.[7]

There was one consistency in the terror chief's movements that slightly upped the dismal odds of a successful hit. Periodically he returned to the compound at Tarnak Farm, outside Kandahar, where three of his wives, many of his children, and a community of followers lived. The CIA's only asset in the region was a friendly tribe whose chief deployed men to spy on the movements of bin Laden and his followers. The CIA developed a plan for thirty of that tribe's fighters to invade the compound, capture bin Laden, and take him to a remote location where he would be picked up by an American aircraft.

The CIA task force in charge of the operation split over whether the potential gain was worth the likely cost. The Afghan allies were fierce fighters but lacked the training and temperament to distinguish enemy fighters from noncombatants. Dozens of women and children might be killed in the crossfire. And bin Laden himself, along with his guards, would most likely fight to the death. Or he might not even be there during the attack. Each likely scenario posed different degrees of a public relations disaster. Eventually, the plan was shelved.

After the embassy bombings on August 7, 1998, President Clinton shifted the mission to the outright killing of bin Laden and his henchmen. On August 20, seventy-five cruise missiles slammed into al Qaeda's Zhawar Kili training camp near Khost, Afghanistan, where bin Laden and his inner circle were said to be meeting, and thirteen missiles hit the al Shifa chemical plant in Khartoum, which an intelligence report concluded produced both commercial products and weapons.

But killing bin Laden proved to be an only slightly less daunting mission. The attack on the camp missed decapitating al Qaeda's leadership by hours—they had already moved on to another location—but did kill twenty-six and wound thirty-five militants who stayed behind. It is quite possible that bin Laden and his inner circle hurried away after being tipped off by a high-ranking Pakistani official; the White House gave Islamabad forty-eight hours notice of the strike, since the missiles flew over Pakistan's territory. This was not the only trouble with the attack. Although missiles destroyed the al Shifa factory, to the White House's embarrassment, international inspectors found no traces of chemical weapons.[8]

Upon learning that bin Laden had escaped, President Clinton approved a plan to enlist the efforts of Pakistan, Saudi Arabia, the United Arab Emirates, and Yemen to deny the terrorists shelter and money. He also called on the CIA to work with Pakistan's ISI to create and launch a special commando unit to seek out and destroy bin Laden. But the ISI snookered the Americans, using its resources to beef up rather than undermine both al Qaeda and the Taliban. When it was clear that plan had failed, Clinton urged the Saudi government to pressure the Taliban into expelling al Qaeda. In September 1998, Prince Turki al-Faisal, Saudi Arabia's intelligence chief, met with Mullah Omar in Kandahar, but Omar rejected the demand.[9]

President Clinton then asked the Pentagon to plan a powerful strike that would devastate Taliban as well as al Qaeda targets. The Pentagon rejected that option, with Gen. Hugh Shelton, the chairman of the Joint Chiefs of Staff, and Gen. Anthony Zinni, who headed Central Command (which would be responsible for that campaign) leading the charge. They argued that such an attack would cause more harm than good by provoking sympathy for the regime and possibly destabilizing neighboring Pakistan. Given that resistance, the president was forced to shelve the idea.[10]

Daniel Benjamin and Steven Simon, who were then White House advisers, recalled an encounter that captured that gap between the White House and the Pentagon:

> At the end of one meeting in the Cabinet room, Clinton approached Joint Chiefs Hugh Shelton and said, "You know, it would scare the shit out of al Qaeda if suddenly a bunch of black ninjas rappelled out of helicopters into the middle of their camp. It would get us enormous deterrence and show those guys we're not afraid." Shelton, a huge, powerfully built man, blanched. The NSC followed up with a request for a new military plan, a small package that did not require using the entire 101st Airborne Division.[11]

Yet the Pentagon balked even at that modest request and never got around to writing up any contingency plans for attacking Afghanistan. The military brass remained paralyzed by the "Desert One syndrome" nearly two decades after the

Pentagon's inept and tragic failure to rescue the fifty-two American hostages in Iran in April 1980. The CIA, however, developed its own plans. After September 11, it would be Langley rather than the Pentagon that led the war against al Qaeda and the Taliban in Afghanistan, much to the fury of then defense secretary Donald Rumsfeld.

All along, the FBI was as uncooperative as the Pentagon. Louis Freeh, who had been appointed director in 1993, hated Bill Clinton and did what he could to thwart any White House initiatives while aiding the conservative efforts to destroy his presidency. That Freeh used his power in a vendetta against the president was troubling enough, but he proved to be an inept leader. On his watch came the debacles of Ruby Ridge, Waco, Oklahoma City, the Atlanta Olympics, and Robert Hanssen's treason.[12]

Attorney General Janet Reno was an unwitting ally of Freeh. She not only made no effort to either reform or fire her subordinate but passively went along with every investigation of the Clinton administration demanded by Special Counsel Kenneth Starr, no matter how obviously they were driven by ideology and politics rather than the law. As a result both the FBI and the White House were nearly paralyzed by political games rather than focused on dealing with their respective duties.

Reno also complicated the attempts to target bin Laden with reminders that assassinations were illegal. This was finessed when, in August 1998, Clinton signed a Memorandum of Notification authorizing the CIA to use deadly force if merited by self-defense. That loophole would certainly be needed if Special Forces tried to get bin Laden. He and his guards would die fighting rather than submit. But missiles rather than commandos remained the preferred method of killing him.

The next possible chance to kill bin Laden came in late 1998. Gary Schroen, the Islamabad station chief, had gathered credible evidence that on December 20, bin Laden would be staying at a residence in the governor's compound in Kandahar. There were potential bonuses. Mullah Omar, the Taliban's leader, and his entourage might also be staying there, and fifty-two Stinger missiles were possibly stored in a warehouse on the grounds. Schroen urged the president to "hit him tonight" because "we may not get another chance." But cautious heads once again prevailed when General Zinni pointed out that collateral damage among ci-vilians and their homes in the neighborhood could be heavy, and a nearby mosque might be hit. The evidence for bin Laden's presence was thin. The attack was called off. [13]

The Clinton White House recognized that Pakistan was the key to the back door of the al Qaeda and Taliban. It was well known that Pakistan's ISI aided both terrorist groups. President Nawaz Sharif was deaf to White House demands that his government sever these ties. Sharif's overthrow by mostly Western-leaning Gen. Pervez Musharraf in a military coup on October 12, 1999, appeared to of-fer a chance to get Pakistan to act against the Taliban and al Qaeda. Clinton met with Musharraf twice to discuss an array of vital issues, with the ISI's support for the Taliban and al Qaeda central. Sandy Berger, the national security adviser, recalled that Clinton "pressed Musharraf very hard and told him to use Pakistan's influence with the Taliban to get bin Laden. He was very tough on that." To that Musharraf could only offer the feeble reply: "I will do as much as I can."[14]

Another possible chance to kill bin Laden arose when he was reported to be falcon hunting with an entourage of United Arab Emirate princes in a remote area of Helmand Province in February 1999. There was an airfield nearby where guests and supplies were flown in. The counterterrorist team debated two op-tions, a cruise missile attack or a rendition by Special Forces. The commando raid was scrubbed because of the time it would take to organize and launch as well as the mission's danger. Michael Scheuer, the Alec Station head, presented a colorful counterargument: "Let's just blow the thing up. If we kill bin Laden and five sheikhs are killed, I'm sorry. What are they doing with bin Laden? He's a terrorist. You lie down with the dog, you get up with fleas."[15] But eventually the familiar arguments for prudence shot down that opportunity.

The friendly tribe reported in May 1999 that bin Laden was at a safe house in Kandahar. This sparked another debate over whether the intelligence was "action-able" and, if so, whether the chance of killing bin Laden was worth the collateral damage. Looming over this debate was the recent American bombing in Belgrade of the Chinese embassy, which was mistaken for a military supply warehouse. If American intelligence could bungle such fundamental intelligence in a European capital, what confidence was there in a tribal report beamed from Afghanistan? In the end, this possibility was also rejected.

Ahmad Shah Massoud, who led the Northern Alliance opposed to the Taliban, offered in December 1999 to launch a rocket attack on al Qaeda's Derunta training camp. In return, he wanted massive aid from the United States. The White House worried that it might get dragged into a war that Congress might not authorize and the American people might not support. In the end, Massoud was asked to stand down for the moment.[16]

Test flights of the Predator, a UAV that was not then armed with Hellfire missiles, began in September 2000. The hunt for bin Laden grew more intense after the terrorist suicide boat attack on the USS *Cole* on October 12. Twelve successful flights were made over Afghanistan before the next president was inaugurated. Three Predator flights appeared to spot bin Laden. Each time analysts and policy makers debated whether it was really him and, if so, whether cruise missiles could be targeted and launched in time to reach and kill him. The final decision was always no.

Meanwhile President Clinton tried to increase pressure on the Taliban to turn over bin Laden and other al Qaeda leaders. On July 4, 1999, he issued an executive order placing unilateral economic sanctions on Afghanistan that cut off trade and froze $220 million worth of gold that Afghanistan's government had deposited with the Federal Reserve for safekeeping. The sanctions were essentially a symbolic measure, since the United States had little trade with that country, and no other governments joined the sanctions. Nor was the impoundment of gold any more effective, since the Taliban had no trouble financing itself through the heroin trade.

The Taliban blatantly used Afghanistan's Ariana Airline to smuggle al Qaeda terrorists, arms, and heroin around the world. The Clinton White House was able to get the UN Security Council to impose sanctions against Ariana for international flights on November 11, 1999, and on November 14 to pass Resolution 1267, which declared both al Qaeda and the Taliban terrorist organizations, thus requiring all member states to sever ties with them.

The Clinton administration's most important coup was thwarting the Millennium Plot masterminded by Abu Zubaydah, one of al Qaeda's operations leaders. According to George Tenet, "In a frenzy of activity . . . CIA launched operations in fifty-five countries against thirty-eight separate targets."[17] This effort paid off. On New Year's Eve 1999, al Qaeda planned to bomb four sites in Jordan frequented by foreign tourists, including the Radisson Hotel in Amman, as well as Los Angeles International Airport and the USS *The Sullivans* anchored at Aden, Yemen. Jordanian intelligence intercepted messages among the plotters and eventually arrested twenty-eight suspects starting on December 12, 1999. Alert customs officers arrested Ahmed Ressam, who tried to drive into the United States from Canada with his car packed with explosives for bombing the Los Angeles airport. A fortuitous bungle saved the USS *The Sullivans*; the overloaded suicide boat sank with all the explosives. Jim Pavitt, then the CIA's deputy operations chief, recalled that "we told the president that there would be between five and fifteen serious attacks against . . . U.S. soil. But we did much . . . more than warn. With our allies and our partners around the world we launched immense efforts to counter those threats. Hundreds of terrorists were arrested, multiple cells of terrorism were destroyed."[18]

The last foreign policy success of the Clinton administration was UN Security Council Resolution 1333 of January 19, 2001, which called on the Taliban to expel bin Laden, prevented any foreign travel by Taliban officials, froze Taliban and al Qaeda assets, and imposed an arms ban on the Taliban but, pointedly, not on the Northern Alliance. The Taliban replied by rejecting the demand to expel bin Laden with the explanation that Afghan culture forbids surrendering a guest to his enemies.

In all, despite struggling against an array of political and ideological enemies, along with bureaucratic and intelligence handicaps, the Clinton White House was able to chalk up some successes in the struggle against al Qaeda. One thing is certain: CIA director George Tenet explained that "the Clinton administration understood fully the nature of the threat we were facing."[19]

Countering terrorism had been a key component of President Clinton's foreign policy following the June 1996 Khobar Towers bombing. Thereafter he made the international terrorist threat a major theme in all his foreign policy speeches. He expressed his most notable warnings at George Washington University in August 1996, at the Naval Academy in June 1998, and in his January 2000 State of the Union address. In the latter speech, he predicted that "the major security threat this country will face will come from the enemies of the nation-state: the narco-traffickers and the terrorists and the organized criminals who will be organized together, working together, with increasing access to more sophisticated chemical and biological weapons."

Nearly all Americans heeded those warnings. A 2000 Gallup poll revealed that 94 percent of Americans thought that international terrorism was a serious threat to the United States. Tragically the new administration did not understand the terrorist reality and would reject these warnings.

Bush Team Policies

The first crucial dilemma with which the Bush administration entangled itself was a failure to heed Sun Tzu's admonition, "Know your enemy, know yourself." Al Qaeda was not among the enemies and threats the president and his fellow neoconservatives pointed to during their first nine months in power. Yet al Qaeda proved to be the only genuine enemy and threat the United States then faced. Just what should the Bush White House have known about al Qaeda before September 11, 2001? [20]

Osama bin Laden and al Qaeda were household words when George W. Bush took the presidential oath on January 20, 2001, to protect the U.S. Constitution and defend the United States. The informed public knew that al Qaeda had declared war against America in 1996 and 1998 and attacked the United States with the embassy bombings in 1998 and the suicide boat bomb against the USS *Cole* in October 2000, just before the election.

Key Clinton administration officials briefed their incoming Bush counterparts on the nature of the al Qaeda threat. These briefings began the day after the contested election for both the Bush and Gore campaigns and then intensified after the five conservative members of the Supreme Court named Bush as president and he began appointing his key advisers. National Security Adviser Sandy Berger warned his replacement, Condoleezza Rice, that "you're going to spend more time during your four years on terrorism generally and al Qaeda specifically than any issue." When Clarke briefed Rice on al Qaeda, "her facial expression gave me the impression that she had never heard the term before."[21]

Then, from Bush's inauguration on January 20, 2001, until September 11, counterterrorist chief Richard Clarke and CIA director George Tenet repeatedly warned that al Qaeda was plotting more attacks, including in the United States. In the Presidential Daily Briefs (PDBs) alone, there were forty intelligence articles devoted to al Qaeda. The most notorious blared the headline, "Bin Laden Determined to Strike in U.S.," which Bush received on August 6, more than a month before the actual attack; the report carefully explained that al Qaeda was planning to hijack airliners and slam them into buildings. Pavitt recalled that the United States had "very good intelligence of the general structure and strategies of the al Qaeda terrorist organization. We knew and we warned that al Qaeda was planning a major strike." Tenet stated that the first nine months after the Bush team took power, "The system was blinking red." [22]

The Bush administration symbolically expressed their disinterest in terrorism and intelligence when the president took away Tenet's cabinet rank and demoted Clarke from a principal to a deputy; although Tenet would still meet with Bush, astonishingly Clarke was not allowed to brief the president until after September 11. That bureaucratic downgrade, however, could not stifle their warnings. Over the next eight months, Tenet and Clarke would issue numerous analyses of the al Qaeda threat and calls for a meeting of the principal policy makers to devise a strategy to counter that threat.

The first warning and accompanying plea came on January 25, from Clarke to the White House. Rice dismissed that warning and those that followed. Two months later in March, Tenet and Clarke submitted their Blue Sky memo, requesting authorization for the CIA to war systematically against al Qaeda around the world, including in the United States, and kill Osama bin Laden without first trying to capture him. The White House killed the plan. In his memoir, Tenet asks the haunting question: "If the new administration had embraced our Blue Sky concept wholeheartedly and granted us all the authorities we sought . . . would we have been able to prevent 9/11?" He admits that the question can never be answered. [23]

The CIA tried again in May to convince the Bush administration of the dire threat posed by al Qaeda. The CIA's Cofer Black, head of the CTCenter, explained that al Qaeda was planning a "spectacular" attack against the United States. Tenet hurried to the White House to warn Rice and Hadley. They acknowledged the warning but did nothing about it. From May through June, the National Security Agency (NSA) picked up thirty-three messages that indicated a pending attack within the United States, but the Bush White House dismissed those reports.

The warnings that Tenet and Clarke submitted included an al Qaeda plot to hijack airliners and slam them as flying bombs into prominent buildings. Indeed, using jetliners as weapons was already a well-known terrorist strategy. In recent years plots had been thwarted to hijack and crash aircraft into the Eiffel Tower, the CIA headquarters, and the Genoa summit of the G8 (which included Bush himself), or to explode jetliners simultaneously over the Pacific Ocean. In February the president learned that bin Laden had discussed with the son of Sheik Omar Abdel Rahman, who inspired the 1993 World Trade Center attack, the idea of hijacking an airliner to use as ransom for his father.[24]

President Bush not only refused to mobilize the government for a pending al Qaeda attack, but he even refused to retaliate against past al Qaeda attacks. Within days of taking power, the Bush administration received the first of a series of reports that revealed concrete evidence that al Qaeda had attacked the USS *Cole* on October 12, 2000. Tenet personally explained the situation to Bush on January 25. Yet Bush refused to retaliate, claiming that to do so would be merely "swatting flies."[25]

The Bush administration also received an intelligence report that in late January, some of the leaders of al Qaeda, Islamic Jihad, Hamas, Hezbollah, and other groups from Egypt, Pakistan, Algeria, Jordan, Qatar, and Yemen would meet in Beirut. This presented a golden opportunity to decapitate much of the top leadership of al Qaeda and an array of affiliated terrorist groups with a few cruise missiles. Again Bush chose not to act.[26]

The essence of the CIA's warnings to the Bush administration eventually became public knowledge. In February Tenet explained that "the threat from terrorism is real, it is immediate, and it is evolving. . . . Terrorists are seeking out 'softer' targets that provide opportunities for mass casualties. . . . Usama bin Laden and his global network . . . remain the most immediate and serious threat. . . . He is capable of planning multiple attacks with little or no warning." He returned to the Senate in March to declare: "For me the highest priority must invariably be on those things that threaten the lives of Americans or the physical security of the United States. With that in mind, let me turn to the challenges posed by international terrorism. . . . Osama bin Laden and his global network . . . remain the most immediate and serious threat."[27]

Bush rejected pleas that the counterterrorist budget be increased as it had under the Clinton administration. He not only froze the total budget but slashed the proposed FBI counterterrorist budget of $1.5 billion by two-thirds, to $500 million. In August when Carl Levin, the Senate Armed Service Committee chair, tried to transfer $600 million from missile defense to counterterrorism, Bush threatened to veto the entire defense budget. Bush also cut $200 million from the budget of the Federal Emergency Management Agency (FEMA), whose duties included being the first responder to any terrorist attack.

The president's measures to undermine his predecessor's counterterrorism policy did not stop there. He also canceled Clinton's policy of a standby alert for cruise missile crews on submarines and warships within range of al Qaeda targets in Afghanistan, along with Predator drones armed with Hellfire missiles to be flown and circled over terrorist sites. For nine months the CIA impatiently awaited word from Bush to approve the Clinton administration's plan to stalk and ideally kill bin Laden. Had Bush approved that plan, it would probably not have prevented September 11 but might have eliminated the terrorist chief when he was relatively more vulnerable. On April 30 the deputies' committee did recommend approval of a CIA plan to aid Ahmad Shah Massoud's Northern Alliance, but nothing would happen without the president's approval, and that would not come until after September 11.

Meanwhile, although frustrated after being thwarted at every turn, Tenet and Clarke did what they could to war against al Qaeda. On June 30, Tenet ordered all station chiefs in friendly countries to share all al Qaeda intelligence with their counterparts and work together to roll up any terrorists cells. On July 3, Tenet called the intelligence chiefs of twenty countries and asked them to arrest any al Qaeda suspects.[28]

Tenet and Clarke also sought to strike directly against bin Laden. They, along with Cofer Black, led the push to arm the Predator and get it in the skies above Afghanistan as soon as possible. On February 21, 2001, a Predator UAV successfully fired three Hellfire anti-armor missiles and destroyed a tank. Successful tests followed on May 22 and June 7. During the latter test, a missile destroyed a replica of Osama bin Laden's Tarnak compound. Now the Americans had the ability to kill bin Laden in real time rather than hope he stayed put while a cruise missile traveled several hours from a remote ocean site to his lair. Unfortunately, this effort was impeded by a turf battle between the CIA and the air force over who should have operational control; ironically, neither wanted this job and tried to pass it to the other.

None of the thirty-three meetings that Condoleezza Rice chaired for the NSC before September 11 focused on al Qaeda. It was not until September 4, nearly nine months after taking power, that Bush held his first cabinet meeting that addressed the broad subject of terrorism.

Rice was even reluctant to take up the deputies' time with the issue. It was not until July 10 that she grudgingly convened a deputies meeting to discuss al Qaeda. Tenet recalled that the CIA briefer pulled no punches in his presentation, starting with his opening line: "There will be a significant terrorist attack in the coming weeks or months." He went on to describe that pending attack as "spectacular." Rice then "turned to Clarke and said, 'Dick do you agree? Is that true?' Clarke put his elbows on his knees and his head fell into his hands and he gave an exasperated yes." When Rice asked what should be done, Black replied, "This country needs to go on a war footing now." But this did not fit into the Bush team's playbook. Deputy Defense Secretary Paul Wolfowitz rejected the warning and, along with Rice, pushed through a decision calling for further study of the issue.[29]

That counterterrorism policy review was completed by a designated team on August 13. The policy was nearly identical to President Clinton's, with only the semantic difference of goals switched from "rolling back" to "permanently eroding." The NSC's deputies finally approved that plan, but not until September 4.

Rice had this report rewritten as National Security Presidential Directive 9 (NSPD-9). Bush was supposed to sign off on it by September 10. The administration's persistent indifference to al Qaeda is revealed by the fact that NSPD-9 was preceded by eight other NSPDs that took priority; Bush was apparently too busy with other matters to read and approve the NSPD-9 while it was sitting on his desk. It would not have made any difference on September 11, but at least signing off on such a vital issue would have reassured many that the president was in charge and ready to act against the only genuine geopolitical threat then facing America. Yet in all of Bush's statements before September 11, he never once cited al Qaeda as a threat to the United States.

Eight months after counterterrorist chief Richard Clarke first began pressing for one, a principals meeting devoted to al Qaeda took place on September
4. Clarke explained to Rice that "the real question" they faced was if "we are
serious about dealing with the al Qaeda threat. . . . Decision makers should imag-
ine themselves on a future day when [the White House] has not succeeded in
stopping al Qaeda's attacks and hundreds of dead Americans lay dead in several
countries, including the U.S. What would those decision makers wish that they
had done earlier? That future day could happen at any time."[30] Indeed that day
was just a week away. The meeting adjourned with no consensus on what to do.

Much later, when all those briefings, reports, and warnings from November
2000 until September 2001 were revealed, the Bush White House's initial response was to deny they happened; then in the face of overwhelming evidence, to
dismiss their importance; and finally, to stonewall any request by congressional
intelligence committees for full reports. Rice claimed that Bush "doesn't recall
seeing anything. I don't recall seeing anything." If true, this means that neither
the president nor the national security adviser were paying attention to such vital
intelligence presented through repeated warnings by key advisers. Cheney later
tried to cover up that denial with the claim that there was "no special threat." But
his response was just as troubling.[31]

Utter incompetence and negligence was not confined to the Bush White
House. The FBI ignored several warnings in February, July, and August 2001
from field agents about suspicious activities by Arabs at flight schools. The most
explicit was a July 5 memo from Phoenix agent Kenneth Williams, who urged
the systematic investigation of Middle Eastern men at flight schools, noting that
they might be al Qaeda agents who could get jobs as pilots, security guards, or
maintenance workers at airports; at least one was connected to Abu Zubaydah,
who led the Millennium plot. The FBI never acted on that warning or passed it
on to the White House. On August 15, Zacarias Moussaoui was arrested on a visa
violation a week after a flight school manager in Minnesota warned the FBI of
his suspicious behavior.[32]

There was a fumble between the CIA and FBI when the former tried to pass
on information to the latter that two al Qaeda suspects had entered the country
in January 2000. Somehow the two names did not get on the terrorist watch list.

That lapse was not recognized until nearly a year and a half later. The CIA warned the Immigration and Nationalization Service (INS) on August 21 that two of the hijackers should be put on the terrorist watch list. The INS replied to both the CIA and FBI that the two had already entered the United States. The INS or the FBI should have immediately picked up both suspects, but neither acted. Two days later, the CIA asked the FBI to find one of those men. The FBI never did.[33]

Like the Bush administration, the FBI initially denied that its top echelon was aware of any warnings before September 11. Although FBI chief Robert Mueller had been in office only a week when the attack occurred and had not personally received any reports, he spearheaded his organization's subsequent cover-up of any wrongdoing. The extent of that deception was revealed when the *New York Times* published a letter that Minneapolis agent Coleen Rowley wrote to the FBI headquarters on May 21, 2002, deploring the distortion of information. Mueller finally admitted on May 29, 2002, that indeed enough information was available to thwart September 11, but that at various levels it was not understood or acted upon.[34]

Bob Woodward points to a chilling crucial lapse: "If the FBI had done a simple credit card check on the two 9/11 hijackers who had been identified in the United States . . . they would have found that [they] had bought 10 tickets for early morning flights for groups of other Middle Eastern men for September 11, 2001. That was knowledge that might have conceivably stopped the attacks."[35]

So just what did the Bush administration know about al Qaeda before September 11, 2001? Actually quite a bit, had the president and his inner circle bothered to study and act on the streams of direct briefings and intelligence reports landing on their desks. Crucial dots existed but remained unconnected. Critical information that could have prevented the attacks got lost in bureaucratic turf battles, red tape, and white noise, compounded by the Bush team's malign indifference to the al Qaeda threat. Could decisive White House leadership have shaken up the FBI and CIA bureaucracies so that they connected the array of dots and prevented the attacks? Probably, but we will never know for certain.

Ideology, Policy, and Tragedy

Why did the president and most of his advisers in and beyond the White House reject the repeated warnings by the Cassandras in the nearly nine months leading up to September 11? The reason was simple: al Qaeda was off their ideological and political radar map. Bush, Cheney, Rumsfeld, Rice, and their respective staffs were all neoconservatives. They outgunned the handful of token realists in the administration, of whom only Secretary of State Colin Powell held cabinet rank.[36] The neoconservatives were blatantly hostile to any information that refuted their cherished ideals, assumptions, and prejudices. To help ensure that ideological correctness prevailed, Bush had actually stripped realists Tenet and Clarke of their cabinet ranks.

Neoconservatism is an ideology that unabashedly calls for American military and political domination of the world. That view was perhaps best articulated in the Pentagon's 1992 "Defense Planning Guidelines" authored by Zalmay Khalilzad and authorized by then defense secretary Cheney. This document did not mince words: "Our first objective is to prevent the re-emergence of a new rival. . . . We endeavor to prevent any hostile power from dominating a region whose resources would, under consolidated control, be sufficient to generate global power. . . . We must maintain mechanisms for deterring competitors from even aspiring to a larger regional or global role."[37]

Who could argue with that? The criticisms erupted at the details. The "peace dividend" of enormous savings would be dumped in favor of ever higher Pentagon budgets. Missile defense would be the core of that military buildup. The goal would be to make America's military lead so wide that any potential rivals would never be able to catch up. And the United States would not hesitate to wield its military power against any states that defied American dominance. In reply to those who were appalled by this vision of naked American aggression and soaring Pentagon budgets, the neoconservatives insisted that the new American century and empire be a different type of imperialism. Charles Krauthammer explained that "we are not just any hegemon. We run a uniquely benign imperium."[38]

That vision was then a tough sell to informed Americans. The Soviet empire and communism had collapsed, and no other comparable state military threat lurked on the horizon. As for secondary military threats, the ambitions of Iraq and North Korea had been successfully contained by American-led international efforts, while Iran's revolutionary regime appeared to be losing support among an ever more restive population. China was focused on transforming its people from mass poverty to prosperity by embracing markets, private property, and integration with the global economy; its military was a few generations behind that of the United States. By the late 1990s a clear danger had emerged, but it came from a transnational terrorist group rather than a nation-state. The genuine critical security threats in an ever more interdependent world were not geopolitical, but geoeconomic. American power was essential in leading international efforts to prevent the collapse of financial markets and the insidious worsening ravages of global warming. So given these realities of global politics, why would Americans heed the neoconservative demands and squander crucial resources in an arms race against themselves?

The neoconservatives somehow had to find or, if need be, manufacture enemies with which to justify their military buildup. To that end, during their first eight months in power, the Bush administration deliberately exacerbated tensions with Iraq, North Korea, Iran, China, and Russia in what realists criticized as unwarranted and gratuitous conflicts. Iraq was enemy number one in the neoconservative playbook. They dreamed of destroying Saddam Hussein's regime and replacing it with a pro-Washington government that would open Iraq's oil to America's corporate petroleum giants. If nothing else, these confrontations made ideological and political sense. They helped justify the huge boosts in Pentagon spending with missile defense at their core, which neoconservatives demanded to widen the gap between America's global military and political power and that of any potential rivals. And anyone who disagreed with this vision was denounced as unpatriotic and even treasonous.

What explains the neoconservative obsession with military power and the viciousness of their attacks against those who opposed them? Psychology offers clear insights.[39] The ironies latent in such accusations ran thick. Insecure psyches lurk behind the neoconservative bluster, flag waving, chest thumping, and table pounding. Virtually all the leading neoconservatives, including Bush and Cheney, had been draft dodgers during the Vietnam era, even though they had shrilly cheered on that war from the safety of the sidelines. Ever since, they had unconsciously been compensating for that glaring moral hypocrisy and other inadequacies. They were obsessed with masculinity and the hard edge of military power with huge missiles and guns, and sneered at diplomacy, multilateralism, and peace dividends. Rather than openly question their own patriotism and manhood, they projected onto others their own inner demons by hurling accusations of weakness,

cowardice, non-patriotism, and even treason against their critics. As true believers they not only clung to their own ideals no matter how catastrophically they
collided with reality, but they dug in their heels ever deeper to "stay the course."

Ideologues, by definition, are not interested in understanding the complexities, paradoxes, and contradictions of the real world or their own psyches. They
are idealists with simpleminded visions of right and wrong, and what should be
done to champion right and vanquish wrong. They have just as simpleminded a
vision when they look in the mirror, believing themselves to personify all that is
good, while those who oppose them personify all that is evil. And that is at once
their greatest strength and weakness.

The neoconservatives believed that with implacable will and firepower, they
could impose their vision on the world. Karl Rove, Bush's senior political adviser, offered a stunningly candid insight to journalist Ron Suskind into the brutal, amoral, and deluded way in which neoconservatives judge and act:

> The aide said that guys like me were "in what we call the reality-based
> community," which he defined as people who "believe that solutions
> emerge from your judicious study of discernable reality." I nodded and
> murmured something about enlightenment principles and empiricisms.
> He cut me off. "That's not the way the world works anymore," he con-
> tinued. "We're an empire now, and when we act we create our own real-
> ity. And while you are studying that reality—judiciously as you will—
> we'll act again, creating other new realities, which you can study too. . . .
> We're history's actors . . . and you, all of you will be left just to study
> what we do." [40]

Where did al Qaeda fit in to that neoconservative agenda? It was relegated
to a footnote. To acknowledge that al Qaeda was the only genuine threat that
America faced would mean forgoing that the huge military buildup so dear to
neoconservatives. Al Qaeda could be countered by the appropriate array of spies,
diplomats, bookkeepers, and special operations teams.

Then came September 11. Suddenly the neoconservatives could no longer
ignore al Qaeda. Or could they?

5

The Post-9/11 Neoconservative War on Terror and Tyranny

Our war on terror begins with al Qaeda, but it does not end there. It will not end until every terrorist group of global reach has been found, stopped, and defeated.
—George W. Bush

This war is fundamentally religious. Under no circumstances should we forget this enmity between us and the infidels. For the enmity is based on creed.
—Osama bin Laden

The Policy Battle

On September 12, 2001, at ten o'clock sharp after the president's address to the nation, the NSC met to decide what to do and how to do it.[1] Accompanied by their deputies and other key advisers, the principals included Bush, Cheney, Rumsfeld, Powell, Tenet, Clarke, Rice, Treasury Secretary Paul O'Neill, Attorney General John Ashcroft, Chairman of the Joint Chief of Staff Hugh Shelton (soon to be replaced by Richard Myers), and White House Chief of State Andrew Card. Tenet explained that al Qaeda was undoubtedly behind the attacks and that tomorrow he would present a plan for attacking that group's headquarters in Afghanistan and its cells in scores of other countries. The principals spent hours mulling the information and their options but reached no decisive decisions that day.

For the first few days after 9/11, the shock and desire for vengeance papered over a deep division within the administration that had worsened ever since Bush had taken the oath of office. Nearly all the principals including Bush himself, Cheney, Rumsfeld, Rice, Card, and Ashcroft were diehard neoconservatives. Powell, Tenet, and Clarke were a minority of realists. Like Cassandra, the realists became frustrated as the neoconservatives repeatedly dismissed their explanations about the world's complexities, warnings of the negative results of policies rooted in neoconservative idealism, and sensible alternatives for an array of national security issues.

A glimpse of those bitter divisions was seen the next day, September 13, when Cofer Black presented a plan for attacking al Qaeda and its Taliban host in Afghanistan. The key was building up the anti-Taliban Northern Alliance with advisers, training, and equipment. The biggest challenge was diplomatic. Somehow the Americans had to divert the Northern Alliance's five factions and perhaps twenty-five subfactions from competing against each other, and instead forge them into a unified offensive against the Taliban. Black promised that he could send in his first special operations team within a week. The neoconservatives voiced skepticism that the CIA could act so quickly and demanded details in a number of areas. Tenet said that he and his staff could present a more elaborate plan within two days.

While the CIA worked on its plan, the neoconservatives prepared their case for a extreme alternative. As the NSC convened on September 15, Tenet presented an intricate plan to attack not just al Qaeda and the Taliban in Afghanistan, but also to roll up al Qaeda's cells in nearly eighty countries around the world. The CIA, however, needed the Pentagon to support its campaign in Afghanistan, in the short term with bombing and cruise missile attacks against enemy positions revealed by operatives on the ground, and eventually with enough troops to destroy the remnants of the enemy and occupy the country.

Astonishingly, the Pentagon did not have contingency plans for either mission. Shelton insisted that both of those requests would take considerable time to plan and implement. It could take weeks just to get permission from appropriate neighboring countries for overflights and bases in which to place combat search and rescue teams. It could take months to get enough "boots on the ground."

Fantasies overtook these practical concerns when Deputy Defense Secretary Paul Wolfowitz presented the neoconservative position. He passionately insisted that the United States should avoid a war in Afghanistan and instead launch an all-out attack against Iraq designed to destroy Saddam Hussein's regime as well as strike against Hezbollah bases in Lebanon's Bekaa Valley that was then occupied by Syria. Cheney, Rumsfeld, and Lewis "Scooter" Libby, the vice president's chief of staff, enthusiastically seconded that neoconservative vision.

That neoconservative vision flabbergasted the realists. Richard Clarke "realized with almost a sharp physical pain that [they] were going to try to take advantage of this national tragedy to promote their agenda against Iraq." With strained patience the realists explained that al Qaeda was responsible for the 9/11 attacks and that neither Iraq nor Hezbollah had any known links to al Qaeda, let alone those atrocities. Clarke used the analogy that to attack Iraq and Syria after al Qaeda attacked the United States "would be like our invading Mexico after the Japanese attacked us at Pearl Harbor." Striking Iraq and Syria would alienate the entire Middle East against America, except for Israel, which would enthusiastically back their unprovoked aggression. And such a strike would only strengthen al Qaeda and Islamism around the world. The neoconservative stance was all rage and ideological correctness divorced from reason.[2]

With his usual clarity, Powell explained that al Qaeda was the enemy and that defeating it required a different type of war:

> The enemy is in many places. The enemy is not looking to be found. The enemy is hidden. The enemy is, very often, right here within our own country. And so you have to design a campaign plan that goes after that kind of enemy, and it isn't always blunt force military, although that is certainly an option. It may well be that the diplomatic efforts, legal, financial, other efforts, may be just as effective against the kind of enemy as would military forces be."[3]

Only a multilateral effort of diplomats, spies, bookkeepers, and paramilitary forces could defeat al Qaeda. The administration would undermine the effort against al Qaeda if it warred against Iraq and other groups and countries that had had nothing to do with 9/11. To do so would alienate the scores of governments and peoples whose support against the terrorist organization was vital and would spread America's power thin to the snapping point.

Bush was torn. Saddam Hussein remained the leering ghost at his policy table. Bush the son was haunted by his father's refusal to destroy Saddam when he had a chance to do so a decade earlier. The ideologues were loudly demanding that 9/11 be the excuse to exorcise that ghost once and for all.

The realists finally managed to wrench the policy wheel from the neoconservatives, but only by agreeing to a Faustian pact. The neoconservatives would support the realist campaign against al Qaeda if the realists later supported the neoconservative campaign to destroy Saddam Hussein's regime.

Shortly after cutting this deal, the neoconservatives berated themselves for compromising with the realists. Within a few days they were again demanding that the United States attack Iraq instead of Afghanistan. Ego and bureaucratic politics may be as important as ideology in explaining their zeal. They complained that any war against al Qaeda would mostly be run by the State Department and the CIA. Rumsfeld protested that "they developed the Strategy. They are in charge." When CIA deputy director John McLaughlin tried to reassure him that Langley and the Pentagon would have to work as a team, Rumsfeld petulantly replied, "No, you guys are in charge."[4] This latest dust-up was resolved when both sides grudgingly acknowledged their previous deal.

Meanwhile Congress threw its support behind any policy the White House chose. By a unanimous vote in the Senate and all but one in the House on September 14, Congress granted "the president . . . all necessary and appropriate force against those nations, organizations, or persons he determines planned, committed, or aided the terrorist attacks that occurred on September 11, 2001, or harbored such organizations or persons in order to prevent any future attacks of international terrorism against the United States or any other country by such nations, organizations, or persons."

The War against Terror and Tyranny

The realists' focused, nuanced strategy against al Qaeda was not the kind of war that Bush and his fellow neoconservatives were interested in fighting. They had something far grander in mind. But to the relief of the realists, the White House did not declare a war of civilizations. Instead, to the Bush administration's credit, it was careful to distinguish Islam from Islamism and Muslims from Islamists.

During President Bush's speech on September 20, 2001, he explained that "the terrorists practice a fringe form of Islamic extremism that has been rejected by Muslim scholars and the vast majority of Muslim clerics, a fringe movement that perverts the peaceful teachings of Islam." He then addressed "Muslims throughout the world" and assured them:

> We respect your faith. It's practiced freely by many millions of Americans and by millions more in countries that America counts as friends. Its teachings are good and peaceful, and those who commit evil in the name of Allah blaspheme the name of Allah. The terrorists are traitors to their own faith, trying, in effect, to hijack Islam itself. The enemy of America is not our many Muslim friends; it is not our many Arab friends. Our enemy is a radical network of terrorists, and every government that supports them. . . . We are not deceived by their pretensions to piety. We have seen their kind before. They are the heirs of all the murderous ideologies of the 20th century . . . and they will follow that path all the way to where it ends: in history's unmarked grave of discarded lies.

If the enemy was not Islam, as the White House correctly noted, then just what were the United States and its allies warring against? Having sidestepped the fatal black hole of declaring a war of civilizations against Islam, the president and his fellow neoconservatives plunged into another nearly as grave—they declared a war against terrorism itself:

> Our war on terror begins with al Qaeda but does not end there. It will not end until every terrorist group of global reach has been found, stopped, and defeated. . . . We will starve terrorists of funding, turn them against one another, and drive them from place to place until there is no refuge or no rest. And we will pursue nations that provide aid or safe haven to terrorism. Every nation in every region now has a decision to make. Either you are with us or you are with the terrorists. From this day forward any nation that continues to harbor or support terrorism will be regarded by the United States as a hostile regime.

The president's "National Security Strategy of the United States," released in September 2002, elaborated the nature of that war: "The United States is fighting a war against terrorism of global reach. The enemy is not a single political regime or person or religion or ideology. The enemy is terrorism itself—premeditated, politically motivated violence perpetuated against innocents. . . . We must persevere until the United States together with its friends and allies, eliminates terrorism as a threat to our way of life."[5]

Realists blasted the Bush team's so-called war on terror. William Pfaff denounced the "intellectually incoherent elevation . . . of terrorism, a tactic or method of combat employed throughout the ages, to metaphysical standing as 'Terror,' a phenomenon which American arms were expected to conquer." Jeffrey Record criticized the neoconservatives for identifying

> a multiplicity of enemies, including rogue states; weapons of mass de-
> struction . . . proliferators; terrorist organizations of global, regional,
> and, national scope; and terrorism itself. It also seems to have conflated
> them into a monolithic threat, and in so doing, the administration has . . .
> subordinated strategic clarity to the moral clarity it strives for in foreign
> policy and may have set the United States on a path of open-ended and
> gratuitous conflict with states and non-state entities that pose no direct
> or imminent threat to the United States.[6]

Nonplussed by the barrage of criticism, the Bush team and neoconservatives beyond tried to promote their "global war on terror" as equivalent to the Cold War as an organizing principle for American foreign policy. That only provoked a new round of criticism. Those two "wars" bore no resemblance. The Cold War was an existential struggle between two diametrically opposed ideological blocs with the capacity to annihilate each other. In contrast the terrorist threat that al Qaeda and its affiliates pose to the United States could damage but could never destroy America and the rest of western civilization.

Neoconservatives could not refute those arguments; they could merely ignore them. For true believers the notion of a "war on terror" made perfect political and ideological sense. The concept was so vague, open ended, and scary for the average ill-informed, fearful, angry American that it could and would be used to justify virtually everything on the conservative agenda.

Bush elaborated on the kind of targets that would be included in the "global war on terror" in his State of the Union speech of January 29, 2002: "Our nation will continue to be steadfast and patient and persistent in the pursuit of two great objectives. First, we will shut down terrorist camps, disrupt terrorist plans, and bring terrorists to justice. . . . Our second goal is to prevent regimes that sponsor terror from threatening America or our friends and allies with weapons of mass destruction."

No reasonable person could disagree with that. But then Bush indulged in some name dropping that worried experts. He identified as enemies a terrorist network that included Hezbollah and Hamas, two increasingly popular Islamist movements rooted respectively in Lebanon and Gaza. Hezbollah had indeed fought and defeated the Reagan administration in Lebanon in the mid-1980s but since then had halted direct attacks against Americans. Hamas had never attacked Americans. Was the United States going to launch a war against Hezbollah and Hamas?

The president then asserted: "The United States of America will not permit the world's most dangerous regimes to threaten us with the world's most destructive weapons." He singled out Iran, Iraq, and North Korea as "an axis of evil, arming to threaten the peace of the world."

Once again the realists were stunned. No alliance bound those countries. Indeed Iraq and Iran were enemies, and each had limited ties with North Korea. The realists argued that grounding American foreign policy in the notion of a monolithic "axis of evil" would be just as deluded and ultimately disastrous to the United States as the belief in a monolithic "communist bloc" during the Cold War by earlier generations of conservatives. The Cassandras' warnings would prove to be true.

America's deterrence strategy rests on the notion that the United States would retaliate against an attack with enough force to destroy the attacker. That deterrence strategy clearly failed with al Qaeda. Neoconservatives believed that Iraq, Iran, or North Korea would likewise not be deterred from attacking the United States if they had the capacity to do so, even if they knew they would be destroyed in retaliation. According to the Bush White House's National Security Strategy, released in September 2002, the possession of WMD by Iraq, Iran, and North Korea would "allow these states to blackmail the United States and our allies to prevent us from deterring or repelling the aggressive behavior of rogue states."[7]

Yet if traditional deterrence would not work, the neoconservatives advocated something that they insisted would. Bush declared that the development and deployment of "missile defense" would "protect America and our allies from sudden attack." That puzzled the experts. None of these states had missiles capable of hitting the continental United States, nor would they acquire that capacity for the foreseeable future. Of the three, only North Korea then had nuclear bombs, but most likely only one or two crude devices possibly deliverable by aircraft, if that. And even if these three governments somehow magically acquired nuclear-tipped missiles that could destroy Los Angeles or even Washington, they would be deterred from doing so knowing that the United States would retaliate by destroying those regimes. The only realistic scenario where they might consider firing such missiles would be in the face of an American invasion.

Among the authorities that realists could cite in rebuttal was none other than Condoleezza Rice, then the national security adviser. In a 2000 *Foreign Affairs* article, Rice argued that "the first line of defense should be a clear and classical statement of deterrence—if they do acquire WMD, their weapons will be unusable because any attempt to use them will bring national obliteration." She went on to warn Americans not to "feel any panic about" the rogue states, which "were living on borrowed time." Rice abandoned realism for neoconservatism after she joined the Bush administration.[8]

There was another pillar to the neoconservative vision—what they called "preemptive war." The ideologues asserted that their pending crusade in Iraq would send a clear message to Tehran and Pyongyang. It would, but not the one the neoconservatives intended.

On March 19, 2003, the Bush administration launched an invasion of Iraq, the weakest of the so-called axis of evil, a state that posed absolutely no threat to its neighbors, let alone the United States. In stark contrast, North Korea and Iran did potentially threaten other states in their regions, if not America itself. The lesson for Tehran and Pyongyang was that the United States under neoconservative rule bullied the weak and feared the strong. So the obvious policy to counter that American threat was to become stronger. Rather than be intimidated from developing nuclear weapons, Iran and North Korea accelerated their programs. With most of America's military bogged down in Iraq and Afghanistan, neither Tehran nor Pyongyang worried that the Bush White House would launch a war against them. As political scientist Joseph Nye trenchantly observed, "Deterrence is working. The only trouble is that we are the ones being deterred."[9]

The puzzlement and worry among experts hardly began or ended with the president's various statements. Other rhetorical neoconservative assertions also complicated and confused the counterterrorist campaign. Realists criticized the neoconservative term "Islamofascism" as self-defeating. While the term helped rally America's far right, it obscures Islamism's actual nature and thus threat. An enemy can only be understood by first understanding how it understands itself. Likewise, comparing Saddam Hussein to Adolph Hitler made just as much ideological and political sense at the sacrifice of analytical sense.

The Bush administration soon compounded its self-imposed dilemmas of semantics and policy by asserting that its war against terror would be accompanied by a war against tyranny. The argument now was that terror and tyranny were an inseparable dynamic and that one could not be defeated without defeating the other. Bush devoted nearly all of his second inaugural address to promoting a crusade against tyranny that threatened the existence of America itself: "The survival of liberty in our land increasingly depends on the success of liberty in other lands. The best hope for peace in our world is the expansion of freedom in all the world. . . . All who live in tyranny and hopelessness can know that the United States will not ignore your oppression or excuse you oppressors."[10]

The public relations campaign to market that vision took off when the original justifications for invading Iraq—that Iraq was allied with al Qaeda and posed an imminent threat to attack the United States with WMD—were proven to be either blatant lies or delusions. Now the justification for invading Iraq would be to impose a revolution from above, transforming Iraq from tyranny into a liberal democracy, which would inspire similar revolutions across the Middle East and beyond. A half year after the invasion, Bush declared that in "Iraq, we are helping

. . . to build a decent and democratic society at the center of the Middle East. . . . The Middle East will become a place of progress and peace or it will be an exporter of violence and terror. . . . The triumph of democracy and tolerance in Iraq, in Afghanistan, and beyond would be a grave setback for international terrorism."[11]

Neoconservatives launched a campaign to sell their democratic crusade. Rice insisted that "much as a democratic Germany became the linchpin of a new Europe that is today whole, free, and at peace, so a transformed Iraq can become a key element of a very different Middle East in which the ideologies of hate will not flourish." In his *Time* magazine essay "Three Cheers for the Bush Doctrine," conservative pundit Charles Krauthammer asserted "that America, using power harnessed to democratic ideals, could begin a transformation of the Arab world from endless tyranny and intolerance to decent government and democratization."[12]

The Bush administration's failure to "know your war" would grossly compound the tragedies resulting from its failure to "know your enemy, know yourself."

The Real Enemy

If the enemy was not Islam, as the Bush administration correctly noted, or terror itself, as the realists asserted, then just what were the United States and its allies warring against?

Perhaps no one has more clearly articulated the essence of the war against al Qaeda and its affiliates than Lee Hamilton, the distinguished former congressman and co-chair of the 9/11 Commission:

> The United States is engaged in a generational struggle against a catastrophic terrorist threat. There is no quick fix or victory to be won. . . . To succeed, we must avoid misunderstanding the nature of the conflict. We are not engaged in a clash of civilizations, or in a war against the tactic of terrorism. Both of those definitions are too broad, and those conflicts are unwinnable. Nor are we engaged in a fight against a fixed group of terrorists or a small collection of states that sponsor terrorism. Both of those definitions are too narrow and fail to encompass the expansive nature of the threat.
>
> Our enemies are twofold: al Qaeda, a stateless network of terrorists that struck us on September 11, 2001, and a radical ideological movement

in the Islamic world, inspired in part by al Qaeda, which has spawned terrorist groups and violence across the globe. The first enemy is weakened but continues to pose a grave threat; the second enemy is gathering and will menace American people and interests long after Osama bin Laden and his cohorts are killed or captured. Thus our strategy must match our means to two ends: dismantling the al Qaeda network and, in the long run, prevailing over the ideology that gives rise to terrorism.[13]

The faith of neoconservatives in their ideology rendered them immune to such reason.

6

The War in Afghanistan
Round One

You're wounded and left on Afghanistan's plains
And the women come out to cut up what remains
Jest roll to your rifle and blow out your brains
An' go to your Gawd like a Soldier.
　　—Richard Kipling, "The Young British Soldier," 1892

Afghans cannot be bought, but they can be rented.
　　—British imperial saying

The Diplomatic Campaign

Diplomacy was crucial to the success of any war against the Taliban and al Qaeda in Afghanistan. The diplomatic campaign involved rallying the support of six key groups of supporting countries in concentric rings emanating from Afghanistan.

The first group was Afghan opposition to the Taliban, a murky world of factions, clans, tribes, and ethnic groups. Within that diplomatic snake pit, the United States had to forge a military alliance that could topple the Taliban and eventually provide a stable coalition government for the country. The second group was securing intelligence, overflight, bases, and logistics in some and ideally all the frontline states surrounding Afghanistan, including Pakistan, Iran, Turkmenistan, Uzbekistan, Tajikistan, and China. Then there was the outer ring of Islamic countries whose airspace, adjoining seas, and, in some cases, bases would be vital for American forces; Turkey, Saudi Arabia, the United Arab Emirates, Kuwait,

Oman, Bahrain, Qatar, Kazakhstan, and Kyrgyzstan were the most important of those states. The United States needed two actual diplomatic and military allies—Britain and Russia. Prime Minister Tony Blair would prove to be vital in filling diplomatic, rhetorical, and even military gaps left by the Bush team's various shortcomings. President Vladimir Putin was just as essential in providing intelligence and advice to the United States, supplying military aid to the anti-Taliban forces, and nudging the former Soviet republics to help the American cause. The White House needed at least a majority of (ideally all) members of the Security Council to issue resolutions acknowledging the justice of American retaliation and calling on General Assembly members to seize terrorists and their assets. Finally, two potential diplomatic "wild cards"—Israel and India—had to be restrained from escalating their respective conflicts with the Palestinians and Pakistanis, which could torpedo America's diplomacy with the inner and outer rings of Muslim states.

The potential support or opposition of other regions and countries varied in importance. Ideally Washington could elicit endorsements from the twenty-two-member Arab League and fifty-seven-member Organisation of Islamic Cooperation (OIC). NATO would be counted on to declare that the 9/11 attack on the United States was an attack on all of its then nineteen members. A European Union declaration of support would be helpful. Much less significant were the distant voices of Japan, Australia, New Zealand, the Latin American countries, and the rest of the non-Islamic world. Every country with al Qaeda cells would need to eliminate its dangerous presence.

While scores of countries eventually joined the United States in its war against al Qaeda after September 11, none contributed more than Britain. Indeed, Blair acted as an unofficial deputy president, making stirring speeches, conducting delicate diplomacy, and helping plan and implement grand strategy that often overshadowed the president's efforts. From September 11 through his summit with Bush on November 7, Blair met with fifty-four world leaders and traveled forty thousand miles.[1]

With all countries except Britain, the White House faced varying difficulties in coaxing them into cooperating. Many of the diplomatic obstacles the Bush team faced were self-inflicted. These efforts were haunted by the arrogant neoconservative "take it or leave it" unilateralism and disdainful "we couldn't care less" neglect of an array of vital global issues, especially the ideologues' unabashed support of Israel against the Palestinians. Anti-Americanism around the world, even among NATO allies, had risen to a fever pitch since Bush and his fellow neoconservatives had taken power.

Yet there was a window of diplomatic opportunity. The horrors of the September 11 attacks evoked widespread sympathy among people ordinarily skeptical at best, and enraged at worst, with American foreign policy. Bush had a chance to rally much of the world to America's side. But to do so, he and his players would have to display new attitudes of sensitivity, cooperation, and compromise that they had formerly scorned. Otherwise they would squander their fleeting opportunity.

The diplomacy was incredibly complex and delicate. Pushing many Third World governments too hard to side openly with the United States could destabilize them and even bring anti-American regimes to power. Nowhere was that challenge tougher than in Islamic countries. The essential challenge in rallying Muslim support in general and Arab support in particular was the conundrum that "one person's terrorist is another's freedom fighter." Moderate Muslims saw no essential difference in the attacks of Israel against the Palestinians and bin Laden's attacks on the United States, and condemned both. But the Israel-Palestinian standoff was not the only conflict that complicated American diplomacy. American diplomats had to contend with the chronic struggle between Pakistan and India over Kashmir. Virtually all Muslim governments insisted that their support would depend on the White House's ability to prove that al Qaeda was behind the attacks, and make diplomatic progress on resolving those other two conflicts.

The Bush administration took special care in forging a consensus among the frontline countries of Pakistan, Iran, Turkmenistan, Uzbekistan, and China, along with Russia. This diplomacy was eased by the common interests among them. All wanted peace restored to Afghanistan after twenty-three devastating years of war. All but Pakistan wanted the Taliban toppled from power and a moderate coalition government imposed.

Rumsfeld, rather than Powell, was the diplomatic point man in that region. On October 3 he embarked on a five-day, four-nation diplomatic offensive that included visits to Saudi Arabia, Oman, Egypt, and Uzbekistan. He made a second trip from November 3 through November 7 to prop up sagging support in Russia, Uzbekistan, Tajikistan, Pakistan, and India.

America's most important potential ally was Pakistan, with its 1,400-mile border with Afghanistan and its military bases close to that frontier. Getting Islamabad's cooperation posed several diplomatic challenges. Pakistan was a desperately poor multinational country of then 165 million people increasingly swayed by Islamism. The number of madrassas had soared from 3,000 in 1978 to 39,000 in 2001. The ISI had backed the Taliban's takeover of Afghanistan. Pakistan was one of only three countries that had diplomatic relations with that regime. It had fought three wars with neighboring India since they both achieved independence in 1947. Both Islamabad and New Delhi claimed to have tested nuclear bombs in 1974, and each definitely tested a new generation of bombs in 1998. Periodic skirmishes erupted in India's northern region of Kashmir, with its Muslim majority and separatist guerilla groups that were aided by Pakistan. And if all that that was not diplomatically daunting enough, Pakistan owed international creditors $37 billion.

The Bush administration decided to play hardball with Pakistan and issued a series of nonnegotiable demands on September 14. Islamabad was expected to supply bases, overflight rights, and intelligence to Washington and cut off all its financial, military, and diplomatic support to the Taliban. While Powell conveyed this stern message in a telephone call to President Musharraf, Deputy Secretary of State Richard Armitage delivered it directly to ISI chief Mahmud Ahmed, who happened to be visiting Washington that week. The key was to be tough, but fair and respectful. But then, with typical neoconservative bluster, Cheney complicated the diplomacy during a televised interview with Tim Russert when he repeatedly referred to the Pakistanis as "Paks," diplomatically akin to referring to the Japanese as "Japs." Bush tried to make amends on September 22, when he announced that he was waiving sanctions against both Pakistan and India that had been imposed in May 1998, after both countries tested nuclear weapons.

The subsequent signals from Islamabad were mixed. Musharraf accepted all of Powell's demands on September 14. The next day he pledged Pakistan's support for the UN Security Council resolution condemning al Qaeda but added that it would not join any military campaign against Afghanistan. He did give in to American pressure when he dismissed ISI chief Ahmed, who openly sympathized with the Taliban. But then Foreign Minister Abdul Sattar announced on September 25 that Pakistan opposed any attempt to topple the Taliban and impose another regime on Afghanistan.[2]

To nail down these concessions, Powell traveled to Pakistan and India from October 15 to 18. In Islamabad he stiffened Musharraf's wavering commitment with flattery and cash. He lauded the dictator as "a bold and courageous" leader and promised another $500 million in aid atop the $50 million that the White House had offered immediately after 9/11 attack in return for allowing the United States the right to fly through Pakistan's airspace.[3]

Musharraf continued to do what he could to curtail American involvement. After Powell left, he publicly called for an American military campaign of limited intensity and duration and warned the White House not to extend operations into the holy Islamic month of Ramadan that would begin in mid-November. On October 23 Musharraf restated that position during an appearance on CNN's *Larry King Live.*

Bush then announced that the United States would give $1 billion in aid to Pakistan. Missing from that package or other agreements were the 29 F-16s that Pakistan had originally bought in the 1980s. In 1990 Congress had withheld these fighter-bombers because of Islamabad's nuclear weapons program. The Clinton White House tried to assuage Pakistani anger at the revoked deal with a grant of $500 million in cash and commodities. But the Pakistanis desperately wanted those F-16s, which are capable of delivering nuclear bombs, to bolster the balance of nuclear terror with India. While the Bush team withheld from Pakistan any F-16s for now, it mentioned nothing about the future, thus holding out the sale of the aircraft as a carrot for Islamabad's good behavior. With all these inducements, Islamabad accepted the White House's requests.

Moscow was also reluctant at first to share its Central Asian sphere of influence with Washington. Within days of September 11, when asked about American forces having access to the Central Asian countries, Defense Minister Sergei Ivanov proclaimed that the notion held "no basis for even a hypothetical possibility." Yet a few days later Foreign Minister Igor Ivanov reversed that categorical rejection by stating that "each [Central Asian] country will decide on its own to what extent and how it will cooperate with the U.S. in these matters." Then on September 23, Putin announced that Russia was "ready to contribute to the fight against terror." To that end he promised to share intelligence, air space, and bases in Uzbekistan and Tajikistan.[4]

What accounted for this about-face? All three frontline Central Asia states resented Moscow's attempt to shove a policy down their throats; indeed they were eager to play off Washington and Moscow against each other to dilute their dependence while maximizing the trade, aid, and military benefits from both. The Russians faced their own war against Islamists in the provinces of Chechnya and Dagestan, and wanted the United States and other Western countries to switch from opposition to support of Moscow's efforts. Finally, Putin saw cooperation with the United States after September 11 as a chance to better relations with Washington, which had declined sharply since Bush took power.

Of those central Asian states, Washington had already forged close ties with Uzbekistan, which shares an eighty-mile border with Afghanistan. A small contingent of American troops had been in Uzbekistan for several years to train its army to fight terrorists and to intercept the smuggling of nuclear materials and drugs. In 1997 and 1998, units of the 82nd Airborne conducted training exercises in both Uzbekistan and Kazakhstan. On October 3 Powell got Uzbekistan's government to allow a combat search and rescue unit to operate from his country. Tajikistan joined the coalition on November 4 when it agreed to lease three abandoned Soviet air bases to the United States.

Support from the frontline state with the second longest frontier with Afghanistan was the most challenging. Washington had lacked diplomatic relations with Tehran ever since the Iranian takeover of the American embassy in November 1979. Yet both countries shared an aversion to the Taliban and al Qaeda. With naïve and rueful sincerity, Rumsfeld wondered, "How did it happen that we are on opposite sides of both Iran and Iraq? It makes no sense."[5]

Publicly the Iranians rejected Bush's war on terror. On September 20, Ayatollah Ali Khamenei at once deplored the September 11 attacks and any future American retaliation: "Islam condemns the massacre of defenseless people whether Muslim or Christian or others, anywhere and by any means. And so Iran condemns any attack on Afghanistan that may lead to another human tragedy." Both hardline Khamenei and moderate President Mohammad Khatami would both later condemn America's air strikes against Afghanistan, although the conviction behind their respective remarks undoubtedly differed greatly.

With time Tehran softened its position. When Foreign Minister Jack Straw met with Foreign Minister Kamal Kharrazi and other officials in Tehran on September 25, he was the first British minister to visit Iran since 1979. He got Kharrazi to agree to condemn and oppose terrorism. Two weeks later Mohsen Rezai, the former Revolutionary Guard commander who chaired the Expediency Council, offered to share intelligence and other duties in the war against terrorism. He explained that "if the Americans get trapped in the swamp of Afghanistan, they will definitely need Iran."[6]

Then Washington made some conciliatory gestures of its own. The Justice and State Departments jointly took Tehran's position in a lawsuit that had been initiated in 2000 by 137 Americans who sought compensation as former hostages or for their relatives. Iran did not contest the lawsuit, insisting that the District of Columbia's federal district court lacked jurisdiction. Citing that same argument, the Bush administration asked the court to throw out that lawsuit. The White House then gave the UN World Food Program ten tons of food to ship to Iran, part of which was to be distributed to Afghan refugee camps and the rest to be sent to Herat. American and Iranian diplomats held a series of private meetings in Geneva.

Starting with a unanimous vote of the UN Security Council, Washington convinced several important international organizations to condemn terrorism. On October 10, the OIC met in Qatar and released a statement condemning the "terrorist acts [that] contradict the teachings of all religions and human and moral values" while "rejecting the targeting of any Islamic or Arab state under the pretext of fighting terrorism." The Arab League committee of twenty-two foreign ministers condemned bin Laden and al Qaeda on November 4. The Arab League's secretary general, Amr Moussa, said that bin Laden "does not speak for Arabs and Muslims."[7]

Finally the White House tried diplomacy with the Taliban itself. In his September 11 address, President Bush demanded that the Taliban extradite bin Laden and others responsible for the attacks. The following day a Taliban spokesman, Rehmatullah Hashmi, said that Mullah Omar condemned the attacks and insisted that bin Laden was not involved. A few days later the Taliban repeated his denial of al Qaeda involvement but added that it might consider expelling bin Laden if the OIC formally demanded that it do so.

The White House got Musharraf to send a delegation of generals to Afghanistan on September 17 to request that the Taliban surrender bin Laden. Mullah Omar replied, "You want to please America, and I want only to please God." Nonetheless a Grand Council of seven hundred clerics presided over by Omar at Kabul on September 20 issued an edict saying that bin Laden should be prepared to leave.[8]

It appeared that the Taliban was wavering. But then Bush stiffened the Taliban's back by issuing an ultimatum that same day. The Taliban could avoid an American invasion only if they handed over all al Qaeda leaders and terrorist followers, released all imprisoned foreign nationals, and gave the United States the freedom to inspect and shut down all al Qaeda training camps. He asserted,

> These demands are not open to negotiations or discussion. The Taliban
> must act immediately. They will hand over the terrorists or they will
> share in their fate. . . . From this day forward, any nation that continues
> to harbor or support terrorism will be regarded by the United States as
> a hostile regime. . . . They are the heirs of all the murderous ideologies
> of the 20th century. By sacrificing human life to serve their radical vi-
> sions, by abandoning every value except the will to power, they follow
> in the path of Fascism, Nazism, and totalitarianism. And they will follow
> that path all the way to where it ends: in history's unmarked grave of
> discarded ideas.

Once again, the neoconservative table pounding backfired. Bush's ultimatum provoked the Taliban into issuing its final words on the American demand: "No, no, no!"[9]

Preparing for Battle

Astonishingly the Pentagon had no contingency plan for war in Afghanistan. In the days following September 11, the CIA filled that void with its plan for fighting

the Taliban and al Qaeda. Thanks to Langley's initiative and the Pentagon's inertia, the American victory came with surprising swiftness and ease. The American
rout of the Taliban and al Qaeda was largely the result of a few CIA and Special
Forces teams on the ground rallying the Northern Alliance and other warlords,
backed by massive bombing and missile attacks by the air force and navy. Had
the military taken the lead with its bureaucratic mind-set of preparing for every
worst case scenario with overkill, the war would have taken much longer to organize and implement, at a much higher cost in treasure and probably blood.

But despite the CIA's urging, President Bush refused to strike fast enough.
The neoconservative attitude of "anything but Clinton" lost the United States
opportunities to kill or destroy vital enemy targets that soon vanished. While al
Qaeda's leadership was safely tucked away on September 11, it would take time
to disperse the organization's more vulnerable assets of camps, supply depots,
and command posts. When asked when the United States would retaliate, Bush
replied, "What's the sense of sending $2 million missiles to hit a $10 tent that's
empty?" Bush was snidely referring to Clinton's decision to retaliate against the
1998 embassy bombings by launching sixty-six cruise missiles against al Qaeda's
Kili al-Badr training camp; the attack missed bin Laden and his coterie but did
kill or wound several scores of his followers. Bush's remark would come back
to haunt him.

Yet Bush's decision to delay an attack against al Qaeda and the Taliban until
overwhelming naval and air forces were in place and a coalition was built up allowed the enemy to pack up their weapons, records, and supplies and escape to
cave complexes deep in the mountains.

The United States had a large military presence in the Persian Gulf on
September 11. Since 1991, the Fifth Fleet's headquarters, with a thousand personnel, have been at Manama, Bahrain. The United States also had forty-eight-
hundred personnel split between Kuwait's Camp Doha army base and the Ahmed
al Jaber Air Base; fifty-two-hundred personnel with F-15s, F-16s, F-117s, U-2s,
and E-3 Awacs at Saudi Arabia's Prince Sultan Air Base; four hundred mostly
air force personnel in the United Arab Emirates; two hundred air force personnel
at Oman's Masirah Island Air Base; and fifty mostly army personnel at Qatar's
Al Udeid Air Base. Straddling distant approaches to the region were about six

hundred mostly navy and air force personnel at Diego Garcia Island in the Indian Ocean and two thousand personnel and F-15s, F-16s, and EA-6B radar jamming aircraft at Turkey's Incirlik air base. Each base was crammed with stockpiles of weapons and equipment.[10]

By early November the United States had massed over fifty thousand military personnel from all four services in the region and three carrier task forces in adjacent seas. Diplomacy permitted allied forces to operate from bases in Pakistan, Uzbekistan, Oman, and Saudi Arabia. U.S. Army and Air Force Special Forces units along with part of the 101st Airborne division and, most important, Predator and Global Hawk drones were deployed at Pakistan's Jacobabad, Dalbandin, and Pasni Air Bases, while one thousand 10th Mountain division and Special Forces troops along with three AC-130 gunships were located at Uzbekistan's Karshi-Khanabad Air Base.

The carrier task forces packed enormous firepower. By October the *Kitty Hawk* and *Theodore Roosevelt* had joined the *Enterprise* and *Carl Vinson*, which were already cruising the Mediterranean and Persian Gulf, respectively. The *Kitty Hawk*, based in Yokosuka, Japan, was stripped of its warplanes and packed with assault helicopters. The *Theodore Roosevelt* sailed from Norfolk, Virginia, to the eastern Mediterranean. While the *Carl Vinson* stayed, the *Enterprise* sailed back to Norfolk. Twenty-two hundred troops each of the 15th and 26th Marine Expeditionary Forces were packed aboard the *Peleliu* and *Bataan*, respectively, and two smaller assault ships. As the Pentagon funneled troops to the region, it mobilized reserves, mostly in logistics, communications, and medicine. By November over 150,000 reserves had been reported for duty, with many patrolling airports, reservoirs, and power plants in the United States.[11]

Americans were not the only foreigners mustered for the fight. Although American forces comprised well over 90 percent of the costs, troops, bombs, and missions, twenty-eight other countries contributed forces to the coalition. Eleven countries reinforced America's armada, including Australia, Belgium, Britain, Canada, Germany, France, Italy, Japan, the Netherlands, Poland, and Spain, whose combined forces totaled twenty-five warships with five thousand sailors. The largest foreign contingent came from Britain, whose task force included an aircraft carrier, assault ship, frigate, destroyer, and three nuclear submarines. Eleven countries contributed air forces—Australia, Belgium, Britain, Canada, Denmark, France, Germany, the Netherlands, and Norway—that flew 5,000 flights, 1,100 of which involved air refueling, 1,100 combat missions, and 900 reconnaissance missions. American "boots on the ground," which eventually numbered over 9,000, were supplemented by 1,200 troops from 17 other countries, including Australia, Britain, Canada, Estonia, France, Germany, Italy, Jordan, New Zealand, Norway, Poland, Romania, Slovakia, South Korea, Spain, and Turkey. Eight other countries that sent Special Forces were not identified. The Special Forces teams would eventually investigate over 120 suspected enemy sites. According to Gen. Tommy Franks, the theater commander, more than 50 countries assisted the United States either with military forces, bases, or allowing overflights.[12]

Nearly all those foreign contributions were more symbolic and peripheral than substantive. The Pentagon welcomed all but chose few to actually join operations. The reason is simple: the war would be over before most allied forces were even in the theater. Even if the fighting had bogged down, the Pentagon would still only need most of those allied forces for show rather than muscle. The war was supposed to pit the civilized world against the barbarians. Thus, the more countries that showed up for that crusade, the better. But as Napoleon once put it, "I would rather fight than join a coalition." Each ally in the field takes time to integrate and coordinate. Networking, commanding, and interfacing weapons and communications systems are all the more challenging with America's military a generation ahead of its allies in high technology warfare.

Indeed, a minor tiff broke out between the Bush and Blair governments over the sidelining of nearly all of Britain's Special Forces that had mobilized for the war. At a November 26 press conference, Defense Secretary Geoff Hoon announced that six thousand of the sixty-four-hundred British troops on a forty-eight-hour alert would stand down. He denied reports of differences over strategy between the White House and Downing Street.[13]

Just settling on a proper name for the campaign proved to be an unexpected challenge. The Pentagon originally called the operation "Infinite Justice," a name Muslims complained was blasphemous because only Allah was capable of providing that. The Pentagon changed the name to "Enduring Freedom." Western wags pointed out its unintended ambiguous and ironic meanings.

While the NSC determined Enduring Freedom's grand strategy, three men commanded the military operations. Rumsfeld, Joint Chiefs Chair Richard Myers, and Central Command's Tommy Franks coordinated the operations at least twice a day through conference calls. Central Command then spanned twenty-five countries from northeast Africa across the Middle East into Central Asia. Unable to find a diplomatically acceptable or militarily secure haven in the region, Central Command was headquartered at the McDill Air Force Base in Tampa, Florida. Decisions were primarily implemented by Gen. Charles Holland, the special operations commander at McDill, and Gen. Charles Wald, the air commander at the Prince Sultan Air Base in Saudi Arabia, seventy miles from Riyadh. Wald determined target lists from information collated by Pentagon and CIA satellites, U-2 spy planes, pilotless Global Hawks and Predators, and spotters in the field.

Locating the precise or approximate positions and numbers of the enemy was essential before any operations could begin. Satellites and drones scoured Afghanistan's landscape to pick out bases, troops, and movement, and to vacuum up enemy electronic communications. This information along with reports from spies within Afghanistan gave Langley and the Pentagon a fairly accurate picture. They concluded that the Taliban had only about 45,000 troops, 100 T-62 tanks, 250 armored fighting vehicles, 200 artillery pieces, and an air force of 10 Su-22 and 10 MIG-21 fighters. Virtually all of its military equipment was captured from the Soviets and thus was technologically obsolete and poorly maintained. Al Qaeda's forces numbered several thousand, with many of them bolstering the Taliban lines on the northern front.

What that surveillance could not determine was how well or poorly all those armed men would fight. Historically the Afghans were fierce warriors who fought for the honor, vengeance, and security of their clan or tribe. To those ends, their dedication to war varied with circumstances. Allied with other warlords, they could just as easily fight to the death or switch sides with the proper monetary temptation. The Taliban's religious zeal and hatred of foreigners made their fighting to the last bullet more likely than not. Yet many warlords were allied with the Taliban more from expediency than conviction. The loyalty and skills of al Qaeda's fighters were far superior to the Taliban's. If the Taliban were mostly ragtag militia, al Qaeda's fighters received rigorous training in weapons and tactics and were animated by fanatical loyalty to their cause.

Afghan Allies

Afghan allies were vital to the CIA plan to defeat the Taliban and al Qaeda. The CIA was certainly familiar with Afghanistan, having operated there throughout the Cold War. After the Soviet invasion, the agency did what it could to nurture ties with various tribes and militant groups fighting the invaders. That would not have been easy under any circumstances, but Mohammad Zia-ul-Haq, Pakistan's dictator, forced the CIA to use the ISI as the conduit for money, weapons, and training to the array of groups fighting the Soviets. That let the ISI take credit for delivering billions of dollars worth of weapons, equipment, and other aid, and assert varying degrees of influence over the groups by playing them off against each other, all the while skimming hundreds of millions of dollars for itself. It also mostly limited CIA operatives to superficial and fleeting meetings with mujahideen leaders. Nonetheless, the CIA managed to nurture some lasting if tenuous relationships and even directly put some arms and money in the hands of various groups.

Saudi Arabia was the third significant partner in the anti-Soviet alliance. Indeed Washington and Riyadh agreed to contribute equal amounts of money to the effort. Unlike the Americans, the Saudis insisted that its General Intelligence Presidency (GIP) rather than the ISI would directly funnel aid to the mujahideen. Some of GIP's aid went to the Bureau of Services set up by Abdullah Yusef Azzam and bin Laden, and later bin Laden's al Qaeda. Prince Turki, the GIP chief, not only knew bin Laden but for a while was a kind of father figure to him; they fell out when Riyadh turned to Washington rather than al Qaeda after Iraq's invasion of Kuwait in 1990.[14]

Contrary to a common belief, the CIA's tenuous links with the mujahideen persisted throughout the 1990s. Jim Pavitt dismissed the myth that "the CIA abandoned Afghanistan after the Soviets left and that we never paid any attention to place until September 11. I would implore you to ask . . . how we were able to accomplish all we did since the Soviets departed. How we knew who to approach on the ground, which operations, which warlord to support, what information to collect. Quite simply, we were there well before the 11th of September."[15]

During the early to mid 1990s, the most significant CIA operation in the country involved trying to buy back as many as twenty-three hundred Stinger missiles that the agency had distributed to the mujahideen during the 1980s. It was an expensive, time-consuming program, with operatives having to track down the missiles and then, depending on how the haggling went, shell out from $80,000 to $150,000 for each and, finally, somehow to get the missile out of the region to a secure location.

After bin Laden returned with al Qaeda in May 1996, trying to track, snatch, and eventually kill him became the CIA's primary mission in Afghanistan. A tribe in the Kandahar region that had been helpful in the Stinger buyback program not only supplied intelligence on bin Laden and al Qaeda but was even willing to capture or kill him. Unfortunately the tribe never had a good shot at bin Laden nor did it have enough men to play a major role in the war to come.

In all, the CIA had built up an array of assets in Afghanistan before September 11, including, according to George Tenet, "eight separate Afghan tribal networks, and . . . more than one hundred recruited sources."[16] Yet only one of those offered a viable armed opposition to the Taliban and al Qaeda, and that was the Northern Alliance, led by Ahmad Shah Massoud.

Massoud was a brilliant natural leader and warrior of quiet charisma and unsurpassed courage. His education shaped and reflected an outlook that was at once highly sophisticated, yet fervently Islamist—he had graduated from a French high school in Kabul and Cairo's Al-Azhar University, Islam's greatest theological center. After the Soviet invasion he devoted himself to studying Mao's revolutionary organization, strategy, and tactics. He put these studies to good use, becoming known as the Lion of Panjshir for successfully leading the defense of that valley against six different Soviet assaults from 1980 to 1983. A secret truce with the Soviets in 1983 allowed the Panjshir valley to sidestep the war's remaining horrors. Nonetheless he served as defense minister in the mujahideen government led by Gulbuddin Hekmatyar and Burhanuddin Rabbani after they took power in April 1992.

The CIA's relationship with Massoud began in 1984, when officers arrived with cash and guns. Over the next half dozen years, Massoud would receive only eight Stinger missiles and less than 1 percent of all the American aid dispensed during the war. Although that sliver of aid hardly reflected his worth as an ally, it was nonetheless considerable. At its peak Massoud personally pocketed $200,000 a month.[17]

Then Washington and Moscow cut a deal on September 13, 1991, whereby each would terminate aid to its respective clients in Afghanistan as of January 1, 1992. This policy appeared to make sense at the time. The Soviet empire and communism were clearly teetering and would finally collapse in December 1991. The Cold War's end promised massive peace dividends to the American people exhausted from decades of bearing onerous burdens of vast military spending and vital resources diverted from investments that would have much better enhanced national prosperity and security.

During the first half of the 1990s, the CIA maintained only sporadic contacts with Massoud. Gary Schroen, the CIA station chief in Islamabad from 1996 to 1999, reopened relations with Massoud in September 1996. His primary mission was to buy back the eight Stinger missiles held by the Northern Alliance. But ties between the CIA and Massoud strengthened as al Qaeda's threat and its dependence on the Taliban grew. With each visit Schroen would hand Massoud $250,000 and vital supplies. The policy was to keep the Northern Alliance in the fight without committing enough firepower and prestige to provoke the Taliban and al Qaeda into outright crushing it.[18]

Despite Massoud's renown, the White House and Langley were both skeptical over how helpful the Northern Alliance would be. CIA officers had visited Massoud in the spring of 2001. What they found was not encouraging. The Northern Alliance was in bad shape, with men, arms, and morale in short supply. It was composed mostly of Tajiks and Uzbeks, controlled only the northeast, and had a well-deserved reputation for terrorizing Pashtuns with robbery, rape, and murder. The Northern Alliance was split among at least five major and twenty-one minor factions. As if that political snake pit was not daunting enough, the Americans had to compete with the Iranians and Russians as suitors to Massoud and all those other leaders. Then came the word that Massoud was assassinated on September 9, 2001, by a two-man suicide squad posing as journalists and armed with a camera packed with explosives. Secretary of State Powell vividly expressed the challenge the White House faced "of marrying a First World force with a Fourth World Army."[19]

Ideally Washington could bridge the Northern Alliance with a Southern Alliance made up of the Pashtuns who inhabited much of central and most of southern Afghanistan. But there was no such alliance. Indeed the CIA had only twelve rather dubious "assets," or agents, in the entire region.

Among them was the fiercely independent Abdul Haq. He had fought against the Soviets, lost a foot to a landmine, struggled for power in Afghanistan after Moscow retreated, and opposed the Taliban after they took control. But Haq had no significant following beyond his own tribe, and he tended to keep the CIA at arm's length. On October 21, Haq and nineteen men armed with only four rifles entered southern Afghanistan to build a coalition against the Taliban. That secret mission was compromised, most likely by Pakistan's pro-Taliban ISI. As the Taliban closed in, Haq made a frantic cell phone call to former national security adviser Robert McFarlane, who promptly relayed the plea for help to the White House. But a CIA Predator arrived too late. Haq and two others were captured and executed. An American may have accompanied Haq and escaped by helicopter.[20]

The most promising anti-Taliban Pashtun leader was Hamid Karzai. Indeed Karzai appeared to be exactly what the White House was looking for in a resistance leader. He was from a wealthy, powerful Kandahar family that fled to Quetta, Pakistan, following the 1979 Soviet invasion. There he helped send military supplies to the mujahideen and humanitarian supplies to the Afghan people. He soon became a prominent figure in the *loya jirga*, or council of chiefs, among the Pashtun people. In 1993 he became the deputy foreign minister in the mujahideen government. After fighting broke out between mujahideen factions, Karzai was arrested on charges of working for Pakistan. While he was being interrogated, an explosion rocked the prison, and he managed to escape in the confusion. He eventually made it back to the relative safety of his family compound in Quetta. He would soon be called back into the political field.

The Campaign

The ground war began on September 26, when the CIA's first Special Activities team, codenamed "Jawbreaker," reached the Northern Alliance headquarters.[21] Gary Schroen (soon to be replaced by Gary Bernstein) led the seven-man team, whose members represented an appropriate array of sharply honed paramilitary, linguistic, and diplomatic skills. Schroen met with Mohammad Fahim, who had succeeded Massoud as the commander; Arif Sawari, the intelligence chief; and

Foreign Minister Abdullah and assured them that the United States was fully committed to their victory. To back that assertion, he spread a million dollars in thick bundles on the table. After eagerly scooping up the money, the Afghans declared that they would need much more than that to defeat their enemies. Schroen asked Langley for another $10 million.

Meanwhile the other team members fanned out through the Northern Alliance territory to assess the situation. What they found was highly encouraging. On October 1, Schroen reported to Tenet that "a Taliban collapse could be rapid, with the enemy shrinking to a small number of hardcore Mullah Omar supporters in the early days or weeks of a military campaign."[22] The key to that collapse would be the sustained bombardment of the Taliban forces. The CIA operatives began creeping near those front lines to get the exact coordinates of the Taliban's positions with global positioning systems.

That bombing campaign would not kick off for another week. The Pentagon insisted that no manned attacks could commence until it set up a combat search-and-rescue team in the region. Uzbekistan finally agreed on October 3. It then took days for the sixty-seven flights by C-17 transport planes to convey all the equipment and personnel to the Uzbekistan base.

The bombing began on October 7 with attacks by fifteen land-based bombers, twenty-five carrier-based bombers, and fifty cruise missiles. The next day, Bush announced this action and explained that while American and British pilots had led that initial attack, they were backed by a broad coalition of nations. He was careful to emphasize that the coalition was fighting against terrorism, not against the Afghan people or Islam, and explained that the air force was dropping food and medicine to help avert mass starvation.[23]

Within hours of Bush's speech, al Qaeda's response was broadcasted by the Al Jazeera television network. Bin Laden appeared on a previously recorded videotape boasting of the terrorist attacks on the United States and rallying Muslims to his jihad. He proclaimed that "America is tasting now . . . what . . . our Islamic nation has been tasting . . . for more than 80 years, of humiliation and disgrace, its sons killed and their blood spilled, its sanctities desecrated." He ended by promising that "America will not live in peace before peace reigns in Palestine and before all the army of infidels depart the land of Mohammad."[24]

After the bombing began the Taliban made two offers to negotiate. On October 15, Foreign Minister Mullah Wakil Ahmed Muttawakil met with Gen. Ehsan ul-Haq, the head of Pakistan's military intelligence. He asked for a three-day bombing halt while the Taliban and Washington agreed on a formula for the transfer of bin Laden to a third country. The White House rejected the offer. Then on October 15, Maulvi Abdul Kabir, the Taliban's second in command, announced that "we would be ready to hand him over to a third country. It can be negotiated provided that the U.S. gives us evidence and the Taliban are assured that the country is neutral and will not be influenced by the United States." Bush angrily dismissed this offer as well: "When I said no negotiations, I meant no negotiations. We know he is guilty. All they've got to do is turn him over, and his colleagues, and the thugs he hides. And not only turn him over, turn the al Qaeda organization over, destroy all the camps—actually we're doing a pretty good job of that right now—and release the hostages they hold. That's all they've got to do. But there is no negotiation, period."[25]

As in the Persian Gulf, Bosnia, and Kosovo wars of the 1990s, the bombing eventually broke the enemy's backbone. The bombers included B-1s and B-52s based at Diego Garcia Island in the northwest Indian Ocean, along with B-2s flown all the way from their Missouri base and F-18s launched from carriers in the Indian Ocean. Cruise missiles were launched from both surface ships and submarines. In early November, the United States began dropping 5,000 pound "bunker-buster" and 15,000 "daisy-cutter" bombs that would pulverize and seal off the enemy's cave complexes. After a while the Pentagon was hard pressed to find viable places to bomb. When asked about that at a news conference, Rumsfeld replied, "We're not running out of targets, Afghanistan is."[26]

In all, the air force and navy pilots performed prodigious feats. Pilots flew over 16,000 combat sorties and dropped over 21,000 bombs, of which 58 percent were precision guided. There were 22,000 transport flights moving 177,000 people and 249,000 tons of material from 216 bases and ports into the region of Afghanistan. Over 12,000 of the bomber and transport flights involved mid-air refueling.[27]

Not all the bombs hit enemy targets. Relying on not always reliable satellite images, the Pentagon ordered many sorties flown against positions already destroyed or abandoned. Not once but twice American bombers hit Red Cross warehouses in Kabul packed with enough food to feed fifty-five-thousand people for two-hundred days. And worst of all, "allied" warlords would call for attacks on their non-Taliban enemies to settle old or recent scores. These tragedies were hardly the best way for the Americans to win hearts and minds.

These wasted and often counterproductive bombings frustrated CIA officers at the front. They begged for a sustained attack on the key Taliban and al Qaeda positions around Mazar-e-Sharif on the road from Uzbekistan and on the Shomali Plains on the road to Kabul. It was not until late October that the Pentagon finally relented and focused its bombing on those fronts.

The United States did not just rain bombs on Afghanistan. On October 15, B-52s dropped over 325,000 leaflets over northeast and southwest Afghanistan. Each was about the size of a dollar bill with a picture of an American soldier shaking hands with a turbaned fighter along with the message, "The Partnership of Nations is here to assist the people of Afghanistan" in English and either Pashto or Dari.

Wars in the third world are about stomachs as well as hearts and minds. America was the largest donor to Afghanistan before September 11, contributing 80 percent of all the food aid distributed by the UN World Food Program. On October 4, the White House announced that it would airdrop $320 million of food and medicine to the Afghans. In doing so it would boost existing programs by the UN High Commissioner for Refugees and the International Committee of the Red Cross that were trying to provide some relief to the 23 million people then living within the country along with the 1.5 million refugees in Iran and the 2.5 million in Pakistan. On October 31 the White House announced that it would immediately buy $11 million of grain from Central Asia, with half from Kazakhstan, and distribute it through the World Food Program.[28]

The CIA and Air Force worked together to bring that humanitarian relief to desperate Afghans. George Tenet recalled that from mid-October to mid-December 2001, American "aircraft delivered 1.69 million pounds of goods in 108 drops to 41 locations through Afghanistan. Each drop was tailored to the specific requests and needs of the teams on the ground.[29]

In all, the war was going better than anyone outside of Langley expected. On October 12, Bush provided a progress report during his first formal news conference since taking office. He declared that "we're smoking al Qaeda out of their caves so we can bring them to justice. . . . But success or failure depends not on bin Laden. Success or failure depends on routing out terrorism where it may exist all around the world. He's just one person, part of a network." Bush once again appealed to the Taliban: "If you cough him up and his people today . . . we'll reconsider what we're doing to your country. You still have a second chance. Just bring him in. And bring in his leaders and lieutenants and other thugs and criminals with him."[30]

The Taliban leader fought on but seemed to realize that his days were numbered. On October 17, Omar broadcast a message that mingled defiance and fatalism: "We will succeed whether we live or die. Death will definitely come one day. We should die as Muslims. It does not matter whether we die today or tomorrow. The goal is martyrdom."[31] The only way to fight such an enemy is to assist his death wish as swiftly as possible, if he can be found. And therein was a big challenge.

The bombing of the Taliban and al Qaeda foot soldiers turned into a turkey shoot. For weeks the enemy clung to fixed positions. When they fled, the country's limited roads forced the Taliban and al Qaeda to travel along a few key arteries. Thousands died in those positions or along those roads.

However, finding, let alone killing, the al Qaeda and Taliban leaders was far more challenging. A bomb strike missed Mohammad Omar by a quarter hour; two of his close relatives died in the blast. On October 23 a bombing raid killed from twenty-two to thirty-five members of the Harkat-ul-Mujahideen, a Kashmiri guerilla group that had gone to Kabul to fight the Americans. Among the dead was at least one senior member, Ustad Farooq. The most important al Qaeda leader killed was Mohammed Atef, who was among the key planners of September 11 and who died on November 16.

The northern city of Mazar-e-Sharif was crucial to America's strategy. The airfield was deliberately left unbombed. The capture of the city just forty miles from Uzbekistan would open the way for truck convoys packed with military and humanitarian supplies to spread in the wake of the advancing Northern Alliance and American forces. A second CIA team, codenamed Alpha, along with three Special Forces military units, assisted the warlord Abdurrashid Dostum in taking the city on November 9.

Five weeks of relentless pounding finally broke the Taliban's back on the front lines. The Northern Alliance surged from Mazar-e-Sharif to capture Sheberghan, Andkhvoy, Meymaneh, and Pul-i-Khumri on November 10; Qala-i-Naw on November 11; Herat, Chaghcharan, and Taliqan on November 12; Kabul on November 13; and Jalalabad on November 14.

While the Northern Alliance chalked up those victories, a small Pashtun force operated in the rear of the Taliban and al Qaeda. Hamid Karzai led 350 supporters from Pakistan into their ancestral lands in Afghanistan on October 7. Four days later they captured Tarin Kowt, the capital of Oruzgan province. Taliban forces converged and besieged the city. A CIA team extracted Karzai on November 4. This was only a brief setback. A combined CIA and Special Forces team accompanied Karzai back to Tarin Kowt on November 14. During his absence, his tribe's fighters had swelled to more than two thousand and had repelled the local Taliban. But on November 16, the Taliban returned and assaulted the town. Karzai's fighters, backed by American bombs, routed the Taliban. Karzai led his men to besiege Kandahar, the Taliban's last city, on December 5 and captured it two days later. [32]

The White House initially had mixed feelings about the enemy's rapid collapse. The military war had outpaced the diplomatic war. The Northern Alliance's capture of Kabul and other key cities and regions was at once a military victory and diplomatic conundrum. Washington, along with Moscow and Islamabad, failed in its attempt to restrain the Northern Alliance from entering the capital. The fear was that the Northern Alliance would unleash a reign of terror of murder, robbery, and rape upon the inhabitants similar to when they controlled Kabul from 1992 through 1996.

But here again the CIA officers proved their mettle. They worked closely with Northern Alliance leaders to limit reprisals. But they could not be everywhere. They did not know that hundreds of Taliban and al Qaeda fighters were locked into steel containers and smothered to death not far from Mazar-e-Sharif. Smaller numbers of prisoners elsewhere were summarily executed, although widespread murders, rapes, and robberies of noncombatants were not reported.

It may well have been fear of being executed that provoked four hundred prisoners held in Mazar-e-Sharif to revolt on November 25. Johnny Spann, a CIA officer who was interrogating them, died in the uprising. He was the first

American combat death in the war, and the 79th officer to die in the CIA's history. The prison revolt was crushed.

Unfortunately, the Pentagon tried to undercut the CIA's brilliant conduct of that war. Rumsfeld and General Franks repeatedly tried to yank the war's controls from Langley. In mid-October Franks actually visited George Tenet at CIA headquarters and demanded that "you subordinate your officers in Afghanistan to me." Tenet replied, "It ain't gonna happen Tommy." When that direct approach failed, Rumsfeld tried to undercut the agency by promoting the DIA's pessimistic views of the war. He argued that the Northern Alliance was not reliable and that Mazur-e-Sharif could not be taken, let alone Kabul, before the new year. The last time Rumsfeld asserted this position was November 9. The Northern Alliance took Mazur-e-Sharif that very same day.[33]

The only flaw in Bush's strategy was similar to that of his father's in the Gulf War a decade earlier. George W. Bush and his advisers let the enemy escape complete destruction. After CIA and Special Forces teams, Northern Alliance fighters, and air force bombs routed al Qaeda and the Taliban, Bush failed to destroy the enemy. Al Qaeda's last stronghold in Afghanistan was Tora Bora, on the frontier with Pakistan. Systematic bombing of that region began around December 1 and continued for weeks. The accuracy improved markedly after two CIA officers and three Special Forces soldiers penetrated the area and, for four days in mid-December, directed the bombing themselves. But the Bush team failed to seal off the most likely escape routes from Tora Bora and thus let bin Laden and hundreds of his fighters flee into safe havens in neighboring Pakistan.

This debacle happened because the Bush administration sent Afghans rather than American troops into Tora Bora either to kill or capture al Qaeda's remnants. In doing so, the president and most of his advisers ignored the CIA's terse explanations that in a tribal culture like that of Afghanistan, a group's alliance often goes to the highest bidder. The Afghan "allies" met little resistance and took many bribes from al Qaeda for safe passage over the mountains into Pakistan. The Afghans pocketed $5,000 for each al Qaeda member that escaped and looked the other way. Bin Laden and his closest advisers most likely escaped on December 16.[34]

By then the fighting was essentially over. In all it had taken only 110 CIA officers, 316 military Special Forces, about $70 million in bribes, and billions of dollars worth of bombs and missiles to route the Taliban and al Qaeda. Col. John Jogerst explains the vast complex of intelligence, reconnaissance, logistics, and bombing that supported these "boots on the ground": "If the only 'teeth' in Afghanistan were the few hundred SOF personnel and aviators who initially engaged the Taliban and al Qaeda, then the tooth-to-tail ratio was miniscule. Tens of thousands of U.S. personnel flew reconnaissance, ran ships, moved logistics, processed intelligence, and moved information to support those few hundred troops on the ground who were able to topple the Taliban regime in a few months with almost no [American] casualties."[35]

Putting the Pieces Back Together

During his eight years in office, George W. Bush flip-flopped on one issue after another as his administration's policies rooted in neoconservative and "anything but Clinton" ("as simple as ABC") attitudes collided with the world's harsh and unforgiving realities. Among his more notable reversals was on nation building. On September 25, 2001, Bush made his long-standing view crystal clear: "We're not into nation-building. We're focused on justice."[36] Nation building was, from the conservative point of view, for sissies. Real men fight and win wars. Bush and his fellow conservatives sneered at the idea that in reality, nation building and justice are inseparable.

It was thus not surprising that, in that red-meat, conservative White House, no one even considered the fate of postwar Afghanistan until October 4. Astonishingly, it was the president himself who raised that vital question. While meeting with Rice and Wolfowitz, Bush casually asked: "Who will run the country?" The question stunned the national security adviser and deputy defense secretary. Neither they nor apparently anyone outside of the CIA or the State Department had pondered such an essential point.[37]

The ideologically correct reply was that it did not matter—Afghanistan would take care of itself. Rumsfeld expressed this attitude during an October 9 new conference. When asked about nation building, he replied: "I don't think it leaves us with a responsibility to try to figure out what kind of government that country ought to have. I don't know people who are smart enough from other countries to tell other countries the kind of arrangements they ought to have to govern themselves."[38]

Not everyone agreed. Democrats; moderate Republicans; White House realists like Tenet, Clarke, and Powell; and Prime Minister Blair tried to explain that
terrorism brews in the toxic cauldron of a "failed state" where mass violence,
poverty, chaos, despair, exploitation, and injustice prevail. As Blair put it in an
October 12 speech, for a war against terrorism to succeed, military means alone
were not enough and indeed would likely just exacerbate the threat. Terrorism
could only wither and die after its roots had been torn out. He then released a
British government strategy paper entitled, "Defeating International Terrorism:
Campaign Objectives," that detailed a five-to-ten-year, $40 billion development
program for Afghanistan.[39]

Bush appeared finally to throw in the ideological towel that same day when
he admitted that "we've got to work for a stable Afghanistan so that her neighbors
don't fear terrorist activity again coming out of that country. . . . I believe that
the United Nations could provide the framework necessary to help meet those
conditions. It would be a useful function for the United Nations to take over the
so-called nation-building."[40]

Yet even after acknowledging that need, Bush was no more enthusiastic about
reconstructing Afghanistan than he was Lower Manhattan. Indeed he seems to
have found both realms bewildering, alien, and dangerous, and thus wanted to
avoid having anything to do with either of them after the initial intervention was
done. Though Bush mouthed support for nation building, the concept remained
ideologically incorrect for him and his administration. Instead, for the rest of
2001 the White House continued to do little more in Afghanistan than dispense
money to warlords.

Certainly any attempt to rebuild Afghanistan was daunting. The World Bank
estimated that the country would need $10 billion over five years just to prevent
mass starvation and disease and to repair its shattered transportation and communications network. When asked how much America would contribute to that
effort, Bush officials sidestepped any commitment and simply mentioned that the
United States usually provides a quarter of peacekeeping mission costs and one-
third of reconstruction, the same portion as the European Union.[41]

The criticism persisted as the weeks passed, with no end to the Bush administration's stonewalling on nation building. The bluntest prod came from Adm.

Sir Michael Boyce, Britain's military commander, who in a December 11, 2001, speech criticized Bush's "single-minded aim" of destroying the Taliban and al Qaeda with "high tech wild West" attacks as naïve and potentially self-defeating. The real war was for "hearts and minds." Denying and failing to act on that reality actually promotes the terrorists' cause.[42]

After patiently waiting for the Bush administration to announce a plan for postwar Afghanistan, Secretary General Kofi Annan finally acted on his own by appointing Lakhdar Brahimi to lead the UN mission for that task. Brahimi was eminently qualified. Since joining the United Nations, the former Algerian foreign minister had led reconstruction missions to Zaire, Yemen, Haiti, South Africa, and Angola, as well as in Afghanistan from 1997 to 1999. His "six plus two" strategy involved enlisting the surrounding countries, along with the United States and Russia, in Afghanistan's reconstruction.

Powell then acted without the president's genuine commitment. He tapped Richard Haass, the State Department's policy planning chief, to work with Brahimi on the "nation-building" effort. The first step was to forge a political coalition among prominent Afghan groups inside and beyond the country. Foreign Service Officer James Dobbins was tapped to act as ambassador to the coalition. He traveled to London, Rome, Ankara, Tashkent, Dushanbe, Islamabad, and Peshawar to rally potential allies into a coalition. To those who complained that some rather unsavory factions were being invited into the coalition, Powell asked what other choice existed: "You can't export them. You can't send them to another country. You can't ethnically cleanse Afghanistan after this is over."[43]

Only one man could possibly cement the coalition. Haass flew to Rome to talk Mohammad Zahir Shah, the former Afghan king, into giving it his blessing. Eleven UN officials, led by Brahimi, hosted the often rancorous conference among four leading factions in Bonn from November 29 to December 5. Those present included eleven delegates and fourteen Northern Alliance representatives, eleven delegates and seven advisers from Rome-based groups including that of the king, three delegates and six advisers from exiles in Cyprus, and three delegates and three advisers from Peshawar. American officials, along with representatives from seventeen other interested states and the European Union, observed.[44]

The factions signed on December 5 an agreement whereby they formed a six-month interim executive cabinet with a chair, five deputies, twenty-three ministers, and a twenty-one-person committee to convene the loya jirga. That government's authority would be rooted in the reinstated 1964 constitution. Within six months, the loya jirga would meet to choose an executive and legislature to rule for the next two years as a new constitution was being written. The agreement committed the United Nations to supply a peacekeeping force, economic aid, and training for an Afghan army and police. It also forbade the government to grant amnesty to anyone who committed "serious violations of international humanitarian law or crimes against humanity."

The loya jirga chose Hamid Karzai to chair a cabinet that included eleven Pashtuns, eight Tajiks, five Hazaras, three Uzbeks, and two from smaller groups. Karzai and his government set up shop in Kabul on December 22. He and his ministers faced a Herculean challenge.

Afghanistan was utterly devastated from twenty-two years of war that began with the Soviet invasion in December 1979 and persisted through the American rout of the Taliban and al Qaeda in December 2001. The results were catastrophic—over 1 million dead, 1.2 million wounded and maimed combatants, 3 million wounded and maimed civilians, 5 million refugees in neighboring countries, and another 2 million displaced within their own country. The economy was shattered; millions of unexploded mines littered the countryside. There was no Afghan army or national police.

Complicating any reconstruction was the reality that there is no Afghan nation, only a mosaic of mostly mutually fearful, jealous clans, tribes, sects, and ethnicities, with none composing a majority. The Pashtuns are the largest ethnic group with 42 percent, followed by the Tajiks with 27 percent, the Hazaras and Uzbek's with 9 percent each, and an array of even smaller groups. Linguistically, the speakers of Persian dialects comprise about half of the population, followed by Pashto (the official language), Turkic dialects like Uzbek and Turkmen, and then thirty other languages.

Somehow Karzai and the provisional government had to overcome decades of war and centuries of animosities among clans, tribes, and nations. They would need all the help they could get. The Bush team would deliver few of the promises it made to the neophyte government.

Bush welcomed Karzai to the White House on January 28, 2002, and promised "a lasting partnership" between the United States and Afghanistan. But he refused to put a dollar figure on American aid and adamantly opposed American contributions to peacekeeping forces. Washington was, however, able to alleviate an immediate crisis over salaries for the new government when the Treasury Department announced the release of $221 million in Afghan gold deposited for safekeeping in the United States and frozen in 1999 because the Taliban rejected the Clinton White House's demand that it expel al Qaeda.[45]

Fortunately other countries and international organizations were far more generous in trying to rebuild Afghanistan. By September 2002 various governments, along with governmental and private international organizations, had contributed $1.8 billion to Afghanistan and completed work on sixty-three schools, sixteen medical centers, twenty-five drinking water projects, eight agricultural projects, three bridges, and sixty-two other humanitarian projects. Over Bush's protests, Congress passed, and the president reluctantly signed, a bill granting $3.3 billion to Afghanistan over the next four years.

Prime Minister Blair volunteered Britain to lead temporarily the peacekeeping forces for Afghanistan, although the policy was eventually to let Muslims command that force and contribute the bulk of the troops. Germany, France, Turkey, Jordan, Bangladesh, and Indonesia also pledged troops to the mission. Yet no country would contribute more than token numbers of troops. By February 2002, there were only forty-five hundred peacekeepers in Afghanistan, and these were mostly confined to Kabul. The warlords reigned beyond. In March 2002 Washington gave Turkey $228 million in aid in exchange for agreeing to take over command of the peacekeeping mission and supply more troops. By the summer of 2002, seventeen countries had contributed twelve thousand troops to that mission.

Although the United States had eleven thousand troops in Afghanistan, they were mostly confined to their bases and did not assist the peacekeeping mission. International and domestic pressure rose on the White House to help out. In June 2002 Joe Biden and Richard Lugar, the ranking Democratic and Republican members of the Senate Foreign Relations Committee, called on the president to expand the number of peacekeepers, include substantial numbers of American troops with them, and deploy them beyond Kabul to bring peace to other regions and thus allow nation building and thwart the Taliban and al Qaeda from returning.[46]

Initially, Bush bluntly refused but after two more months of pressure finally reversed his policy. On August 29, 2002, the White House announced "a mid-course correction" by which American troops in Afghanistan would assist the peacekeeping mission but would remain outside the peacekeeping command structure.[47]

Meanwhile Afghanistan's new government appeared to be making progress. The loya jirga met in June 2002 and chose Hamid Karzai to remain as the provisional president for the next two years until a constitution could be written and implemented. On June 24, Karzai swore in the twenty-four members of his cabinet. The first Afghan army battalion, about one thousand strong, stood proudly in review. In January 2004 the loya jirga adopted a constitution that declared Afghanistan an Islamic state but had many democratic trappings, including equal protection for ethnic groups and women, a parliamentary system, and regular elections. Afghanistan had taken some initial steps in a very long and uncertain road to reconstruction and viability.

Consequences

America routed the Taliban and al Qaeda in Afghanistan with surprising speed and efficiency. What happened to that veteran army of Islamist zealots committed to fighting to the death for their version of the Koran? And how was the Northern Alliance, largely dismissed as no more than a brutal armed mob, able to rouse itself and charge to one dazzling victory after another?

The enemy collapsed quickly beneath American precision bombing and missile attacks and Northern Alliance assaults led by 110 CIA Special Activity and 316 military Special Forces operatives. American bombs and missiles systematically destroyed the enemy's military infrastructure. The strategy was first to wipe out the enemy's fragile air defense, headquarters, and communications; then supply bases and transportation; and finally fortifications. This fragmented, blinded, and deafened the Taliban and al Qaeda into isolated pockets across the country. But the enemy helped defeat itself by holing up in large concentrations rather than scattering in small forces to hit and run against their enemies. The elaborate tunnel complexes, which the Soviets had rarely breached, became tombs for many of the Taliban and al Qaeda.

That, in turn, helps explain the Northern Alliance's transformation. American bombing, supplies, and advisers at once bolstered the Northern Alliance and shattered the Taliban and al Qaeda. Although many of the Taliban died fighting, others, in keeping with the traditional culture, were happy not just to surrender but even to switch sides to the new dominant power. In contrast, the al Qaeda fighters, largely Arab and well aware of their fate if captured, mostly died to a man when they could not flee.

On the ground, cash payments rather than bullets were the decisive weapon. CIA operatives armed with extraordinary skills and lots of money took full advantage of Afghan culture in which loyalties might be rented but never bought, according to an old British colonial saying. The going rate for minor warlords was $50,000. The CIA officers hired enough warlords and knit them into a coalition that was powerful enough to push out the Taliban and al Qaeda.

What explains that mercenary approach to politics? There was, after all, no Afghan nation, only a crazy quilt of mutually suspicious and outright antagonistic clans, tribes, cultures, languages, and faiths. In such a land, loyalties naturally go to the strongest arm or highest bidder. The Taliban itself was never a professional army, it was a coalition of warrior bands with varying degrees of commitment to the cause. Only al Qaeda members could not be bought.

America's dazzling victory was won at an astonishingly light toll in treasury and blood. The war cost $2.6 billion in the fiscal year ending on September 30, 2002. Of the forty-one American combat deaths, only eighteen—or less than half—were from enemy fire, with twenty-three from "friendly fire" or accidents. No planes were shot down, but one of the technologically unreliable and strategically all-but-useless B-1 bombers malfunctioned and crashed into the Arabian Sea about sixty miles north of Diego Garcia Island; the crew safely ejected.

The number of enemy losses will never be known, but perhaps as many as ten thousand died in their trenches and caves. America's tribal allies summarily executed hundreds and perhaps thousands of Taliban and al Qaeda. The number of enemy prisoners at Guantanamo peaked at around 660, with hundreds more held in prisons in Afghanistan. Civilian deaths numbered anywhere from several hundred to several thousand.

Yet the war in Afghanistan was not flawless. Like his father, George W. Bush and his inner circle skillfully managed the diplomacy and initial military campaign but failed to score a decisive victory. Just as the father let Iraq's elite Republican Guard divisions retreat from Kuwait, the son failed to seal off al Qaeda's escape routes to safe havens in Pakistan. Bush made two glaring tactical errors at the battle of Tora Bora, the last al Qaeda stronghold in Afghanistan. Contrary to the CIA's advice, he sent unreliable Afghan allies to lead the attack and neglected to block the mountain passes with American troops. Thus the Bush administration let as many as eight hundred al Qaeda fighters—including bin Laden, Zawahiri, and most other top leaders—escape over the mountains into the Federally Administered Tribal Area (FATA) of Pakistan. While most immediately found refuge in the Kurram tribal area, bin Laden and a circle of advisers and guards slipped into Paktia. From these immediate safe havens, al Qaeda's leaders and followers dispersed to even more remote and secure locations elsewhere in that vast region. There, they would rally, replenish their ranks, and venture forth to kill Americans, their allies, and others.[48]

7

The War on Terror at Home

*Your tactics only aid terrorists, for they erode our national
unity and diminish our resolve. They give ammunition to
America's enemies and pause to its friends.*
—Attorney General John Ashcroft

*To announce that there must be no criticism of the president,
or that we are to stand by the president right or wrong, is not
only unpatriotic and servile, but is morally treasonable to
the American public.*
—Theodore Roosevelt

*It would indeed be ironic if, in the name of national defense, we
would sanction the subversion of . . . those liberties . . . which
makes the defense of the nation worthwhile.*
—Judge Ann Diggs Taylor

The National Security Debate

While there was a firm national consensus that an administrative and legal overhaul of America's national security system was essential, a bitter debate erupted
over a crucial question: Was there a tradeoff between personal liberties and
national security, or were they were inseparable? Controversies over specific
measures, whether they required congressional approval or were revealed as secret

Bush team initiatives, were usually enveloped in a broader ongoing debate over just what threats other than terrorism America faced in the twenty-first century and what policies could best secure the nation from those threats.

Conservatives view national security very narrowly, whereby the only true threat involves a violent attack on the United States by terrorists or a state, the worst of which would involve WMD. To counter these threats, the United States must do anything that will diminish or, ideally, eliminate the potential for such an attack, however remote. Vice President Cheney insisted on launching what he incorrectly called "preemptive" wars against other states even if there was only a 1 percent chance that they threatened to attack the United States. Conservatives insist that there is a trade-off between security and liberty—you can have either but not both. As the commander-in-chief, the president has virtually unlimited powers to defend America as he sees fit. The Bush administration's policies personified these conservative values.[1]

Realists and humanitarians alike completely disagree with that worldview. They argue that "national security" involves much more than deterring attacks by terrorists or hostile governments against the United States. In an ever more interdependent, crowded, and polluted world, the core dilemma facing not just Americans but all of humanity is how to at once enhance global economic wealth and environmental health. In comparison, even the worst plausible terrorist attack would directly harm only a relative handful of people and briefly disrupt the economy.

Indeed they point out that policies rooted in conservatism actually undermine American national security and play into the hands of terrorists in two crucial ways. First, the conservative obsession with terrorism since 9/11 diverts essential resources of time, money, and expertise from confronting the inseparable economic and environmental crises that actually feed terrorism as part of a vicious cycle. Second, conservatives aid terrorists because not only do terrorists want to destroy as many people and as much property as possible, but ultimately they would love to destroy America's ideals and way of life. While no enemy group or state is capable of doing that, terrorists try to provoke a conservative government and terrified public to do their dirty work for them. The terrorists win to the degree that the White House, Congress, and the courts subvert American liberties and democracy. Realists and humanitarians insist that terrorism can be contained and diminished while preserving America's highest ideals as expressed by the Declaration of Independence, Constitution, Federalist Papers, Gettysburg Address, and other documents viewed as near-sacred texts by most Americans.

The conservative vision prevailed during the eight years that the administration of George W. Bush held power. But the failure of many of Bush's policies led a majority of Americans in the 2008 election to send the pragmatist candidate Barack Obama to the White House and a majority of realists or humanitarians to Congress. Yet that shift of power hardly ended the debate, and the grip of the realists and humanitarians on Congress is tenuous. In the 2010 election, conservatives eliminated the veto-proof majority of their opponents in the Senate and recaptured the House of Representatives.

Revamping the National Security Establishment

Over the course of eight years in power, the Bush administration enacted sweeping changes to the laws, institutions, and organization of America's national security system, or at least that portion devoted to counterterrorism. Indeed the last time Washington embarked on as wide-ranging a shakeup to America's national security system was in 1947 with the National Security Act, which established the NSC, the CIA, the Department of Defense, and the Joint Chiefs of Staff to fight the Cold War.

Within six weeks of September 11, the USA PATRIOT Act passed the Senate by 98 to 1 on October 25, was approved by the House by 357 to 66 the next day, and was signed by Bush on October 27. The PATRIOT Act alleviated some of the problems clogging the flow of intelligence through the arteries of the national security community. It did so by greatly expanding the federal government's ability to investigate terrorist conspiracies or crimes while omitting several White House demands for powers that were deemed blatantly unconstitutional, such as holding suspects indefinitely without charges. Banks are required to ensure that depositors are not laundering money, must report all such suspicions, and are forbidden from dealing with unregulated offshore shell banks. Special intelligence courts can authorize wiretaps if foreign intelligence is a significant part of the investigation. Federal officials can obtain nationwide search warrants and roving wiretaps on suspects for cell phones or new phones without the need for renewals. With a warrant, agents can "sneak and peak" into a suspect's home while they are away and not only search the premises but even install a digital "magic lantern" or "sniffer keystroke logger" on computers. The government can also secretly track library, bookstore, hotel, rental agency, university, and medical records. The statute of limitations is eliminated for terrorist crimes. Illegal aliens suspected of terrorism can be held for up to seven days before formal charges are filed. Computer hacking is now considered a terrorist crime. Both suspicious people and suspicious places, including houses of worship, can be monitored. Detention without trial until deportation is allowed for foreign suspects that authorities deem too potentially dangerous to release but lack the evidence to convict. A few restrictions accompanied that array of enhanced government powers. Information gained by the government must remain secret unless it is presented as evidence in court; the government can be sued for any leaked information or abuse of its surveillance powers. Grand jury information can be shared with federal institutions. A revised version of the act in 2005 eliminated several controversial areas such as the ability to indiscriminately search library records.

An even more sweeping change was the establishment of the Department of Homeland Security (DHS). Within a week after September 11, Bush established an Office of Homeland Security (OHS) within the White House, named former Pennsylvania governor Tom Ridge to be its director, and appointed a Homeland Security Council (HSC) of principals and deputies from relevant departments and agencies to coordinate efforts. Ridge seemed to be a solid choice. His courage and patriotism were unquestionable—he would be among the very few in the Bush administration who had not only served in the military but had fought in Vietnam. He got his undergraduate degree from Harvard and his law degree from Dickinson. He had served as an assistant district attorney in Erie, was a member of the House of Representatives from 1983 to 1995, and was governor from 1995 to 2001. While critics lauded Ridge's personal integrity and public career, they lamented his lack of experience in law enforcement or the federal government. Eventually they would also have to question Ridge's integrity.[2]

Most Democrats and many Republicans did not believe that OHS was adequate to fulfill its responsible. Senate Majority Leader Tom Daschle led the drive for the creation of a cabinet-level department. The Bush administration initially condemned that proposal as "big government," but the real reason was that a department would be under congressional scrutiny, something an office in the West Wing could avoid. Bush flip-flopped when polls revealed that most Americans liked the idea. The president offered a sensible argument for creating a new department in a June 7, 2002, speech: "Right now as many as 100 different government agencies have some responsibility for homeland security and no one has final responsibility."[3]

Support for the new department was bipartisan, although the parties differed on the details. The biggest stickler was Bush's insistence that its employees be stripped of the worker protection and union rights enjoyed by the federal civil service. When Democrats tried to protect those rights, Bush and other Republicans smeared them as being unpatriotic. The Democrats caved in to that pressure and voted for the Republican version.

Congress passed, and the president signed, the bill creating the DHS on November 25, 2002. The new department was cobbled together from twenty-two existing agencies, $37 billion worth of budgets, and 180,000 people. The DHS's counterterrorist mission is clear—prevent a terrorist attack from taking place in the United States and respond to such an attack if it does. The DHS is also responsible for anticipating and responding to natural and accidental disasters like hurricanes and nuclear power plant meltdowns.

The Homeland Security Department's duties are sweeping. Although it may be years or decades before the department is fully integrated and running at full capacity, its components are certainly fulfilling its duties. The following are some of the daily accomplishments in 2008 cited by Charles Allen, the department's intelligence chief: (1) Customs and Border Protection (CBP) processes over a million passengers and pedestrians, 70,000 containers, and over 300,000 air, sea, or land vehicles; (2) The Transportation Security Administration (TSA) screens two million passengers and nearly as many pieces of checked luggage; (3) U.S. Citizenship and Immigration Service (USCIS) conducts an average of 135,000 national security background checks; (4) Immigration and Customs Enforcement (ICE) seizes over $700,000, makes 150 arrests and 61 criminal seizures, removes some 760 aliens, and participates in 20 drug seizures; and (5) The U.S. Secret

Service seizes more than $145,000 in counterfeit currency and $50,000 in illegal profits and conducts twenty arrests.[4]

Another major shakeup occurred with the 2004 Intelligence Reform and Terrorism Prevention Act, which stripped the CIA of one of its two key missions and handed it to the newly created director of National Intelligence (DNI). Under its 1947 charter, the CIA was the intelligence community's hub, and its director ran both the community and the agency as well as served as the president's key intelligence adviser. But it has never worked out that way. Politics undercut the CIA's authority to lead the community. The Defense Department controlled 85 percent of the intelligence budget through the NSA, National Reconnaissance Office (NRO), and National Geospatial-Intelligence Agency (NGA). The intelligence gathered by CIA operatives is a drop in the bucket compared to the electronic intelligence vacuumed up by those Pentagon organizations. Those turf and budget disputes were daunting enough. For a director to try to lead both the CIA and the rest of the intelligence community, and serve as the president's key intelligence advisor, was a mission impossible.

From 2004 the CIA has been just one player in the intelligence community, although it remains the most important for human intelligence and covert actions. The CIA adapted swiftly to September 11. The following year, Jim Pavitt could report that "I have more spies stealing more secrets than at any time in the history of the CIA. . . . In the Directorate of Operations [DO] alone since just five or six years ago we are training more than 10 times as many operations officers."[5] That was quite a turnaround from the nadir in 1995 when only twenty-five people entered that year's training class. In October 2005 the CIA's DO was renamed the National Clandestine Service (NCS) and given expanded duties and power to coordinate the collection of human intelligence with other institutions.

Today America's intelligence community includes sixteen different agencies. The DNI presides over fifteen other institutions in America's intelligence community, including the CIA, NGA, FBI, NRO, DNI, National Security Agency/ Central Security Service (NSA/CSS), Defense Intelligence Agency (DIA), State Department's Bureau of Intelligence and Research (INR), Energy Departmetnt, Treasury Department, and the intelligence agencies of the army, navy, air force, Marines, and Coast Guard.

Red Tape, Turf Fights, and Money Grubbing

Severe problems lurk behind this administrative and legal shake-up. Each organization within that bureaucratic labyrinth is itself a bureaucratic labyrinth. Although described as an intelligence "community," high walls, suspicions, and jealousies still separate these neighbors despite official efforts to diminish such barriers. An April 2009 internal report revealed that the DNI had worsened rather than alleviated problems within the intelligence community by entangling itself in bureaucratic tape, mismanaging finances, and failing to oversee, let alone lead, the intelligence community. Much of the intelligence community's $45 billion budget was misallocated on wasteful programs that either did not work or were duplicates, while vital areas were underfunded. The DNI was unable to get each member of the intelligence community to overcome its shortcomings.[6]

Of all the forces that can undercut a counterterrorist strategy, few match and none exceed bureaucratic politics. The phenomenon is as old as the first bureaucracies, but its antecedents are rooted in the first humans. There is a natural human drive to want more, often at the expense of one's fellow humans. This drive is exacerbated when people band together in organized groups, especially bureaucracies. Although their missions might differ, bureaucracies share a natural political drive to aggrandize their own budgets, personnel, duties, and prestige while diminishing that of their rivals. Those natural conflicts become especially acute when bureaucracies have overlapping missions, resulting in endless, ultimately self-defeating turf battles. And these rivalries are not just among but within bureaucracies, as sections battle each other for the same reasons.

Information is a crucial element of power in any political conflict. Bureaucracies tightly hoard their secrets while trying to pry out those of their rivals. Bureaucratic politics, however, are not solely behind the obsession to amass and reluctance to part with information. Security depends on protecting sources and methods of getting critical information. Regardless, the result is poor horizontal and vertical communication within government. Not only do bureaucracies talk badly with each other, but even the layers of a given bureaucracy often do little more than mumble at one another.

Theoretically the creation of new institutions like the DNI, DHS, and National Counterterrorism Center (NCTC) helped finesse these bureaucratic rivalries. In practice these new organizations and reshufflings of the bureaucratic deck may have only added to the confusion, redundancies, overlapping authorities, and rivalries. Turf battles and information hoarding are incessant. As if this was not debilitating enough, there are technical problems. Each major component of the intelligence community has its own computer and database systems that impede their ability to share information.

The fragmentation among the elements of America's dysfunctional national security community is duplicated in America's foreign missions. Ambassadors preside over rather than run their embassies. Foreign service officers make up only a diminishing portion of the personnel. All other departments and agencies with foreign policy duties post officials in the embassies, thus globalizing Washington's federal bureaucratic politics. Each department or agency has its own foreign policy that is often at odds with that of the State Department or even the White House.

The most notorious counterterrorist bureaucratic rivalry is between the FBI and the CIA. The FBI is a law enforcement agency that collects evidence with which to arrest and convict criminals for crimes that they have already committed. The CIA is an intelligence agency that collects, analyzes, and shares information crucial to national security. Their failure to work together may well have been the most important reason why al Qaeda was able to pull off 9/11.

The FBI's deficiencies remain severe despite all the negative publicity and official promises to the clean up the mess. For instance, the FBI is still only hazily connected by personnel and computers. The bureau has been described "from the inside . . . a disorganized jumble of competing and unruly power centers; from the outside, it was a surly colossus. The field offices enjoy considerable autonomy—fifty-six FBIs and fifty-six little FBI directors."[7] This disorganization had a lot to do with the success of the 9/11 attacks. In the summer of 2001, FBI headquarters ignored warnings from the Tucson and Minneapolis offices of suspicious activities by Arabs taking flying lessons. The September 11 attacks might have been thwarted had FBI director Louis Freeh recognized and acted decisively on those suspicions. But he failed to provide any strategic direction to his organization.

Ironically, this confusion came from efforts Freeh himself made to boost the bureau's counterterrorist powers. Following the 1993 World Trade Center bombing, he created a counterterrorism division at headquarters as the equivalent of the CTC. In addition, Freeh beefed up the FBI presence in embassies overseas and decentralized operations by cutting back headquarters staff and redeploying them in the fifty-six field offices, whose agents were encouraged to take the initiative. Yet somehow that policy of boosting initiatives at the district offices diminished the ability of Freeh and his staff to understand and act on the alarming field reports in the summer of 2001.

Still other problems explain the FBI's failures. Most fundamentally the FBI lacked the systematic means to collect and analyze intelligence. Only a few agents spoke Arabic; the mountains of Arabic language documents and transcripts piling up in warehouses were not translated, let alone analyzed. The bureau's computer systems were condemned as straight out of the Dark Ages. Agents had trouble retrieving and sending documents among themselves and could not securely exchange classified information with other departments and agencies.

This failure is especially glaring, since counterintelligence in the United States has been an FBI duty for most of its history since the original federal agency was founded by President Theodore Roosevelt in 1908. Counterintelligence was always a rather neglected bureaucratic backwater in the FBI, whose central focus was fighting crime. That mission did not become official until 1981 when Executive Order 12333 authorized the FBI to take responsibility for all counterintelligence duties within the United States. Despite that order, the FBI has not made counterintelligence a priority. It was not until after the September 11 attacks that the FBI established a National Security Branch to conduct all counterintelligence operations, but the organization's emphasis continues to be law enforcement.

Counterterrorism remains only one of an array of FBI law enforcement duties that include combating organized violence, smuggling, and white-collar crime with interstate or international reach, along with counterintelligence against foreign spies in the United States. In terms of budget, personnel, training, and attention, counterterrorism remained a secondary concern up through September 11. In 2000 twice as many agents were deployed to counter drug smuggling than terrorism, despite or perhaps because of the fact that the independent Drug Enforcement Agency (DEA) existed for that specific duty.[8]

As if all those bureaucratic forces were not hobbling enough, the law also entangles the FBI's ability to protect the nation. The FBI's ability to share information remains formally restricted by Rule 6(e) of the Federal Rules of Criminal Procedure (FRCP), which details how crimes are prosecuted. That specific rule restricts who can have access to evidence and where evidence can come from to avoid tainting it. Since much of the CIA's intelligence is obtained by extra-legal means, the FBI is reluctant to handle it for fear of jeopardizing the legal cases they are trying to build. In August 2001 the FBI refused to investigate two al Qaeda terrorist suspects because the information came from an intelligence source. Although the PATRIOT Act eased some of those restrictions, the practice apparently remains embedded in the FBI's culture.[9]

The final explanation for the FBI's inattention can be traced to Attorney General John Ashcroft, who, shortly after taking power, dropped terrorism as a FBI priority. Terrorism was not among the seven "strategic goals" he set for his administration. The day before September 11, Ashcroft actually called for cutting the FBI's counterterrorism budget and denied a FBI request for 149 more field agents and 54 translators to its counterterrorism team. Indeed Ashcroft angrily told his FBI briefer that he "did not want to hear this [terrorist] information any-more." That was after their second session together.[10]

Counterintelligence would logically have been entrusted to the CIA but for the fact that its 1947 charter forbids it from conducting such operations within the United States. That has not prevented the CIA from at times doing just that through the loophole of protecting its "sources and methods" of intelligence. The political uproar when its domestic spying programs were exposed in the mid-1970s has been a major block for formally ending that restriction. Yet the CIA does not have a broad foreign counterintelligence mission for American security overseas, but instead merely concentrates its efforts on "protecting its own house and mission."[11]

To help overcome all those deficiencies, President Clinton established on January 5, 2001, the Office of the National Counterintelligence Executive (ONCIX), which replaced the National Counterintelligence Center set up in 1994 after CIA officer Aldrich Ames was caught spying for Moscow. The ONCIX's mission is to provide leadership for the nation's counterintelligence operations.

Specifically, that involves trying "to exploit and defeat adversarial intelligence activities directed against American interests; Protect vital national assets from adversarial intelligence activities; Neutralize and exploit adversarial intelligence activities targeting the armed forces." Unfortunately, the ONCIX has yet to be integrated within the intelligence community. American's counterintelligence efforts remain the neglected stepchild of national security. These efforts are compartmentalized among numerous organizations with some counterintelligence duties. There remains no organization in charge of counterintelligence.

Traditionally Washington has played defense on counterintelligence by focusing on opposing the operations of foreign intelligence services in the United States. Foreign intelligence agencies and terrorist groups have tried to penetrate all public and private sources of crucial information, including America's own intelligence community. Michelle Van Cleave, the ONCIX chief, revealed that "40 terrorists had been caught trying to infiltrate U.S. intelligence agencies as of 2005."[12]

The result is a gaping hole in America's national security system. To fill that void, many have advocated creating an American version of Britain's Security Service (commonly known as MI5), which is responsible for counterintelligence and counterterrorism within the United Kingdom. MI5 keeps track of potential spies and terrorists and then passes that information along to Scotland Yard, which makes the arrests. To do so would involve stripping FBI of its counterintelligence resources and placing it under the ONCIX, which would be fully empowered to fulfill its mission. But this idea has no political support.

Nonetheless, some progress has been made on information sharing. According to Juan Zarate, the deputy national security adviser for combating terrorism, "The walls between intelligence and law enforcement, between federal, state, and local authorities, and even between foreign counterparts have fallen or been minimized in a way previously unimagined. In addition more data is being gathered, shared, and analyzed. This has meant that more dots have and can be connected to identify terrorist nodes, networks, and problematic trends."[13]

As if the array of intelligence and counterintelligence agencies and operations were not complex enough, the Pentagon recently has been trying to muscle in on the act. The DIA was originally set up in 1961 to provide a central intelligence agency for the four separate military service branches. The following year the DIA established the National Defense Intelligence College. In 1996, the DIA created the Defense Human Intelligence Service to better utilize its military attaches assigned to embassies around the world.

For its first four decades, the DIA was largely confined to analysis and had only limited intelligence collection activities. This changed on April 25, 2002, when Rumsfeld established the Strategic Support Branch (SSB) with the duty to gather intelligence with the same methods the CIA uses, including recruiting agents, stealing secrets, and conducting covert operations. Indeed Rumsfeld admitted that his motivation for doing so was to break the "near total dependence on the CIA."[14]

The SSB actually has fewer operation restrictions than the CIA. Unlike the CIA, the SSB escaped congressional scrutiny by using "reprogrammed funds" that do not require approval or oversight. The SSB works closely with and taps many of its personnel from the U.S. Special Operations Command. It has its own clandestine school to teach its recruits spy craft. It is not required to coordinate its activities with those of the CIA, only to give a seventy-two-hour notice to Langley in advance of an operation.

The result could actually degrade America's intelligence gathering abilities. The analogy is a skilled hunter in a stretch of wilderness. He knows the territory and the game that inhabits it. When he goes out, he has a good chance of bringing something back. But if another hunter suddenly appears in that same territory, he will most likely scare the game away, and both hunters will come back empty-handed. Even if the second hunter eventually gets to know the land and develop his stalking skills, the game will be wary, and the yield will be far lower than it otherwise could have been.

Yet another problem is the inability of the intelligence community's experts to keep up with threats. There is still a dearth of people fluent in the languages and cultures in countries and regions deemed essential to American national security, with the demand for speakers of Arabic, Farsi, Pashto, and an array of other languages from the Muslim world notably outstripping supply. The FBI is especially notorious for its linguistic shortcomings. Five years after 9/11, only thirty-three of twelve thousand FBI agents were proficient in Arabic. This void severely handicaps the collection and analysis of intelligence. Meanwhile, mountains of untranslated documents are piling up in warehouses, many of which undoubtedly hold information critical to American security.[15]

How can that vital need be filled? Without government funding, America's financially strapped universities cannot provide translators. And a program's existence does not mean that students will enroll in it. Only six students earned undergraduate degrees in Arabic in 2002.[16]

There are certainly no lack of speakers of these languages within the United States. The dilemma is rooted in security. The intelligence agencies are reluctant to hire native speakers who still have relatives or close community, economic, or religious ties with their countries of origin. Yet by not tapping these enormous reserves of language skills, these same agencies undercut American national security. Only a massive investment in developing language skills for the counterterrorist community can fill that void. For even the most exotic of languages, surely there are more than enough qualified teachers who can pass a background check and be hired to teach classes of intelligence community students, who enroll with aliases. Of course, more than language skills are needed, especially for field operatives. Languages and cultures are inseparable; one cannot be understood without understanding the other. This means studying the cultures along with the languages, both with formal classes and living undercover in those cultures, if possible.

Bureaucratic turf battles are debilitating enough to America's counterterrorist efforts. Corruption further degrades America's ability to prevent or respond to a terrorist attack; the worse the corruption, the worse the corrosion. Yet during the Bush administration's eight years in power, few dared expose the corruption, let alone define it as "high crimes and misdemeanors."

The most blatant corruption plagues the DHS, whose revolving door apparently has not stopped spinning since it was installed. Indeed the corruption was so egregious that Frank Rich, a *New York Times* columnist, colorfully described the department as "an empty shell, a networking boot camp for future private contractors dreaming of big paydays."[17]

A mere four years after the department was created, over ninety top officials—including secretary Tom Ridge, deputy secretary James Loy, and undersecretary Asa Hutchinson—had shamelessly jumped ship to work as executive lobbyists in the "security industrial complex." There they earn top six- and often seven-figure salaries plus bonuses and other perks to wield their connections to get the DHS to make multimillion dollar purchases of their corporation's goods and services.[18]

According to federal law, government employees are forbidden from negotiating contracts for a future job with a company they regulate, must wait a year to accept employment in that industry, and cannot lobby on any issues for which they were formerly responsible. But the Bush White House typically exploited loopholes to grant exemptions. Ridge, for instance, swiftly went to work for Savi Technology, which makes a radio frequency identification system that he pushed the DHS to adapt when he was the secretary. Hutchinson began negotiating with Venable LLP, a lobbying firm that represents defense contractors, while he was still in office and went to work for them the day after he left the government.[19]

Politics trumped security in determining who got what from the antiterrorist budget. Halliburton was not the only recipient of pork-barrel largess from its former CEO, Vice President Cheney. He did not forget his home state of Wyoming when the White House divvied up the money. Although experts would rate Wyoming as one of the least likely targets for a terrorist attack, that state got six times more money per person than New York, which had already suffered a devastating attack and remains a prime target. New York received only $1.40 per person, compared to a national average of $3.29, or the top payouts of $9.78 in Wyoming, $7.97 in Alaska, and $7.76 in North Dakota. Indeed there was a not-too-surprising correlation between how the money was split between red and blue states; conservative bastions generally received far more grants per person. For instance, in 2005 Indiana was listed as having 8,591 targets, or 50 percent more than New York with 5,687 and twice as many as California with 3,212. The DHS actually cut money for New York City and Washington, D.C., by 40 percent while boosting it for cities like Louisville and Omaha deep in the conservative heartland. [20]

The decisions that determined who got what often had as much to do with political skills as ideological zeal. The list of 77,068 sites claimed to be worthy of DHS grants included 1,305 casinos, 163 water parks, 718 mortuaries, 3,773 shopping malls, and 571 nursing homes, along with 12,019 government offices, 8,402 public health buildings, 7,889 power facilities, and 2,963 sites with hazardous chemicals or other materials. On that priority list was the Old Macdonald Petting Zoo, the Amish Country Popcorn Factory, Mule Day, the Sweetwater Flea Market, and an unspecified "beach at the end of a street." The DHS's program was larded with all kinds of political pork, which may have undermined national security by squandering scarce resources. It did, however, help secure the reelections of White House allies in Congress.[21]

Yet another controversy involved New York's reconstruction. Although Bush promised the city $20 billion in funds just after September 11, he swiftly reneged. The reconstruction bill allocated to New York only $8.2 billion. Bush threatened to veto another bill that would have added another $9.7 billion to the city. On November 14, 2001, the House Appropriations Committee killed the bill by thirty-three to thirty-one, with only two Republicans joining the Democrats in support of reconstruction. Senate Democrats tried to outflank that obstruction by attaching $7.5 billion for New York and $7.8 billion for domestic security to a $352.6 billion defense bill. But Bush threatened to veto that bill if the money for New York was not eliminated. That amendment died on December 8 when the Senate split fifty to fifty in a vote that required sixty to pass.[22] What could have possibly motivated President Bush and his fellow Republicans to deny vitally needed reconstruction and security money? Vengeance might top the list. Liberal New York State had two Democratic senators and had voted overwhelmingly against Bush and other Republican candidates in the 2000 election.

Compounding the bureaucratic and corruption problems that undermine America's counterterrorist efforts is the increased privatization of policy. Although Washington has always contracted work to businesses, the percentage and volume of the outsourcing soars whenever conservatives take power. The reason why is explained by such nostrums as Thomas Jefferson's, "The government which governs least, governs best" or Ronald Reagan's, "Government is not the solution, it is the problem." The belief is that only the magic of the marketplace can ensure that taxpayers will be responsible for the best services at the lowest price.

Alas, this ideal more often than not runs aground on the shoals of the real world. Political payback rather than free markets determines who wins contracts. Packed with political appointees, regulatory agencies act as the lapdogs of the privileged rather than watchdogs of the public. The revolving door spins between the public and private sectors. The result is overpriced, shoddy, and even unfinished projects that the public sector could have done better and cheaper.

This can happen in any administration but is notoriously common when conservatives are in charge.[23] Not only does corruption soar, but at times even the sheer bulk of government spending as a proportion of the economy increases. This was true for not only the recent administrations of George W. Bush and Ronald Reagan, but nearly all conservative presidents back to Andrew Jackson, whose administration exemplified the "spoils system" in American politics.

The reason is simple. Conservatives may celebrate the magic of the marketplace and minimal or nonexistent government when they are trying to take or keep power but rarely live up to the principles after they win elections. Once ensconced in government, their policies are guided by less crowd-pleasing principles, such as "To the winner go the spoils," "Might makes right," and "The public be damned."

The harsh and dangerous consequences of this spoils mentality are pretty much ubiquitous across the federal government, although the severity varies from one bureaucracy to the next. For instance, although the Federal Aviation Administration (FAA) oversees airport security, the contract for each of the roughly seven hundred airport security systems goes to the lowest private bid. That system has undermined American national interests and security. Securicor, the largest of the three companies that supposedly provides airport security against terrorists and thieves, was fined by the federal government for employing convicted felons, failing to do background checks on its workers, and then lying to investigators. The possible tragic consequences of entrusting national security to a private sector driven by greed rather than duty was revealed in November 2007, when one Subash Gurung, an illegal immigrant with no fixed address, successfully passed through an x-ray machine with a stun gun and seven knives. In 2007 the DHS admitted that measures to boost airline security, including the universal implementation of terrorist watch lists and air cargo inspections, were at least five years behind schedule.[24]

Dismissive of such revelations, President Bush and his fellow conservatives in Congress fiercely attacked any proposals to federalize airport security, smearing it as socialism. But their even worse fear was that the Democratic Party could more easily mobilize the votes of unionized workers. Transportation Secretary Norman Mineta justified letting often rigged markets determine the fate of public safety by pointing to the State Department's dependence on private firms to secure its embassies and consulates. That is indeed true. Private firms were "guarding" the American embassies in Kenya and Tanzania in 1998 when al Qaeda agents drove the truck bombs into them that killed 224 and wounded more than 5,000 others.

By all accounts, the no-bid or insider-bid contracts of the Bush administration grossly undermined the counterterrorist campaigns in Iraq and Afghanistan, with tragic results for American national security. Not only were billions of taxpayer dollars often squandered on development projects that never got beyond the blueprints, but even essential security and intelligence operations were ladled to the private sector.

The selling out of intelligence was especially disturbing and self-defeating. From 2002 to 2006, the number of "contractor facilities" farmed out soared from 41 to 1,265. Private contracts accounted for 70 percent of the intelligence budget. That spoils system for intelligence resulted in the same horror stories of massive corruption as with the privatized development or security programs. Projects soared in cost, never got off the ground, or finished long after promised deadlines.[25]

Even worse is the brain drain from the public to the private sector as operatives and analysts with years of training and real world experience are lured to the private sector for higher salaries and benefits. The government has to keep hiring and training new recruits to replace seasoned veterans, which makes them more dependent on the private sector for expertise. Taxpayers bear this burden as Washington leases back services that cost many times what it once provided itself. As former CIA director Michael Hayden put it, the intelligence community has become "a farm team for these contractors."[26]

Security or Liberty

Conservatives assert that there is a trade-off between security and democracy—you can have one but not both. Michael Ignatieff argued that "sticking too firmly to the rule of law simply allows terrorists too much leeway to exploit our freedoms. Abandoning the rule altogether betrays our most valued institutions. To defeat evil, we may have to traffic in evil."[27]

Realists and humanitarians alike counter that you can indeed have both, and that in a war against a country or group with an authoritarian ideology, your enemy wins if you sacrifice democracy on the altar of security. Kofi Annan offered an eloquent retort to those who would trade civil liberties for a police state:

> There is no trade off to be made between human rights and terrorism. Upholding human rights is not at odds with battling terrorism; on the contrary, the moral vision of human rights—the deep respect for the dignity of each person—is among our most powerful weapons against it. To compromise on the promotion of human rights would hand terrorists a victory they could not achieve on their own. The promotion and protection of human rights . . . should therefore be at the center of anti-terrorism strategies.[28]

Contrary to the conservative claims that a president can do anything he wants as commander-in-chief, in reality the Constitution, Federalist Papers, and hundreds of Supreme Court rulings uphold the essential American concept of a democratic government as a separation of powers in which each branch is a check and balance to the others, and none are above the law.

Just what are the "rights" that realists and humanitarians insist are essential to American national security that conservatives are equally adamant must be sacrificed to that end? Equal legal protection and due process for those accused of crimes are essential rights. The Sixth Amendment guarantees that "in all criminal persecutions the accused shall enjoy the right to a speedy and public trial by an impartial jury . . . and to be informed of the nature and cause of the accusation; to be confronted with witnesses against him; to have compulsory processes for obtaining witnesses in his favor, and to have the Assistance of Counsel for his defense." Those rights are reinforced by habeas corpus, the right of someone in custody to petition a judge to determine whether he is being held lawfully with specific charges. The Constitution's Article I, Section 9 asserts that the "Privilege of the Writ of Habeas Corpus shall not be suspended, unless when in Case of Rebellion or Invasion the public Safety may require it."

The terrorist attacks on September 11 involved neither a rebellion nor an invasion, so a suspension of habeas corpus would have been an illegal act. Under the Constitution, had one of these conditions existed, then Congress rather than the president is authorized to suspend habeas corpus until the crisis has passed. The Supreme Court unanimously confirmed this in its 1866 *Ex Parte Milligan* ruling that condemned Abraham Lincoln's suspension of habeas corpus during the Civil War.

The Bush administration contemptuously shoved aside America's constitutional heritage when it suspended habeas corpus, along with the Sixth Amendment, for over 1,100 people arrested in the days, weeks, and months after September 11. Word trickled out from prisons of massive violations of American and international law. Suspects were detained indefinitely without charges. Records of their incarcerations and hearings were sealed. The prisoners were not allowed to communicate with lawyers, family, or friends. To force confessions, they were deprived of adequate food, sleep, and heat; some were even beaten. The Bush administration claimed that "national security" and the president's powers as commander-in-chief trumped the Constitution in justifying those acts.

Human rights organizations condemned Bush's orders for those massive arrests and detentions without charges or trials as gross violations of America's constitutional rights of due process. But John Ashcroft's Justice Department stonewalled all questions about the names of the detainees and their charges. The excuse was that any information would somehow aid al Qaeda. Eventually word leaked out that the number of detainees peaked at 1,147 on November 3, 2001. Of that number only 11 were held as material witnesses, although all those charges were later dropped. Of the rest 235 were charged with violating immigration laws, and over 650 others were charged with a litany of other crimes. None would ever be charged with terrorism.[29]

Judges in every case heard in state and federal courts in Michigan, New Jersey, New York, and Ohio ruled in favor of disclosing the names of the detainees. By 2004, several cases reached the Supreme Court. In three separate rulings (*Rasual v. Bush*, *Hamden v. Rumsfeld*, and *Rumsfeld v. Padilla*), Supreme Court majorities condemned the Bush team's policies toward its prisoners in the United States as violations of the constitutional right of due process and called on the administration either to file formal charges or to release its prisoners. While these rulings simply reflected two hundred years of Supreme Court precedents and scholarly interpretations, for that very reason they were extraordinary coming from a federal court system packed with conservatives.

Judge Diana Motz of the Second Circuit Court ruled against President Bush's detention policy, arguing that he

> maintains that the authority to order the military to seize and detain certain civilians is an inherent power of the Presidency, which he and his successors may exercise as they please. To sanction such Presidential authority to order the military to seize and indefinitely detain civilians, even if the President calls them "enemy combatants," would have disastrous consequences for the Constitution—and the country. For a court to uphold a claim to such extraordinary power . . . would effectively undermine all of the freedoms guaranteed by the Constitution. . . . We refuse to recognized a claim to power that would so alter the constitutional foundations of our Republic.[30]

The most articulate and succinct condemnation of the Bush administration's policies was issued by the Sixth Circuit Court of Appeals ruling on August 26, 2006: "The executive branch seeks to take this [constitutional] safeguard away from and beyond public scrutiny. Against non-citizens it seeks the power to secretly deport a class if it unilaterally calls them 'special interest' cases. . . . Democracies die behind closed doors. . . . When government begins closing doors, it selectively controls information rightfully belonging to the people. Selective information is misinformation." That court upheld a lower court ruling that such "blanket closure of deportation hearings" was unconstitutional.[31]

Bush ignored these rulings and defiantly approved other initiatives that raised troubling questions about whether or not they violated the Constitution. The Justice Department announced on November 14, 2001, that it would seek to interrogate 5,146 mostly Middle Eastern men between the ages of eighteen and thirty-three who had entered the United States since January 1, 2000. In addition to uncovering or spooking terrorists, the "interviews" were an excellent way for intelligence officials to recruit Arabic-speaking agents. But the legal basis for the meetings was a delicate issue. Michigan's authorities came up with a novel way of interrogating about seven hundred of the suspects living in the state. They sent invitations to the suspects for an interview. No-shows would presumably be considered reasons for special concern.[32]

The Bush administration policies certainly offended many in America's Muslim communities. Following 9/11, over a thousand Muslims, mostly illegal immigrants, were rounded up and held without trial. Muslims in traditional beards and robes have been prevented from boarding flights and have suffered other indignities. Despite this, America's Muslim community has remained overwhelmingly loyal, cooperative, and patient in the war against al Qaeda and its affiliates. Unlike most of Europe's Muslim population, America's is mostly middle class, integrated, well educated, upwardly mobile, secular, and determined to achieve the American dream.

The Bush administration's violations of the Constitution did not end with the Sixth Amendment and habeas corpus. The Fourth Amendment guarantees "the right of people to be secure in their persons, houses, papers, and effects, against unreasonable search and seizures . . . and no warrants shall issue but upon probable cause, supported by Oath or affirmation, and particularly describing the place to be searched and the persons or things to be seized."

Although the American right to privacy is not explicitly cited in the Constitution, it is implicitly protected by an array of related rights, especially the Fourth Amendment. William O. Douglas asserted that "the right to be left alone is the beginning of all freedom." Louis Brandeis called the right to privacy "the most comprehensive of rights and the one most valued by civilized men."[33]

During the twentieth century, Congress and the Supreme Court clarified and broadened Fourth Amendment rights. Congress reinforced the constitutional right to privacy with a number of laws including the Communications Act of 1934, Fair Credit Reporting Act of 1970, Privacy Act of 1974, Right to Financial Privacy Act of 1978, Stored Communication Act of 1986, and Health Insurance Portability and Accountability Act of 1996. Astonishingly, until 1961, the constitutional protection against unreasonable search and seizure applied only to the federal government; state and local government could and often did violate that right with impunity. It was not until 1963 that a defendant could get a court-appointed lawyer. The Miranda right for suspects to be informed by police that they do not have to confess came in 1966. The following year the Supreme Court ruled that illegal search and seizure applied to electronic surveillance and wiretapping, and it followed that up in 1978 by ruling that illegally obtained evidence could not be used against those whose privacy rights had been violated.

The fear that these violations might jeopardize American espionage led to the 1978 Foreign Intelligence Surveillance Act (FISA), which established the three-judge Foreign Intelligence Surveillance Court (FISC) to evaluate applications for surveillance warrants to spy on foreigners or on Americans suspected of espionage or terrorism. This lets investigators secretly obtain the information they need without violating anyone's rights. FISC decisions are sealed. Suspects are never informed that they are being watched unless the information is used in court. While the judges' identities, hearings, and decisions are secret, the results are not. From 1978 through 2004, FISC granted 18,761 warrants and denied only five requests. As if that procedure is not easy enough, operations can actually begin fifteen days before a warrant is issued. Thus does FISC at once promote constitutional rights and security needs.

Despite, or perhaps because of, FISC's success, the Bush administration was determined to violate and neuter it. President Bush ordered the NSA to spy on American citizens and residences by monitoring their e-mail and telephones without warrants. In May 2002, Attorney General Ashcroft issued an order allowing the government to monitor political or religious groups in the United States, even without probable cause of wrongdoing.

The Bush team justified these policies with the conservative assertion that the president is empowered to do whatever he wants in the name of national security. The White House also claimed, contrary to the record, that FISC was too slow and thus had to be bypassed. Karl Rove led the conservative smear campaign by implying that anyone who criticized these policies was a traitor: "President Bush believes that if al Qaeda is calling somebody in America, it is in our national security interest to know who they're calling and why." No reasonable person could disagree with that. However, the issue is not one of surveillance but of whether a court has granted permission for that surveillance. Vice President Cheney claimed that the warrantless eavesdropping had somehow "saved thousands of lives." In reality, that program not only violated the Constitution but did not work. The NSA listened in on thousands of Americans without finding one terrorist. As one anonymous FBI agent put it, "After you get a thousand numbers and not one is turning up anything, you get some frustration." Indeed, Bush's program weakened the war against al Qaeda by diverting hundreds of FBI and other officials from far more productive tasks. A report by the inspector generals of five intelligence agencies concluded in July 2009 that the warrantless surveillance program did not result in any thwarted terrorist attacks or even captures of terrorists but instead diverted resources from vital intelligence gathering operations.[34]

The legal arguments against the program were just as overwhelming. Federal District judge Anna Diggs Taylor ruled on August 17, 2006, that the Bush team's warrantless wiretaps violated the American constitutional right against unreasonable search and seizure, along with FISA. Conservatives within and beyond the White House assailed her as "liberal" and "partisan."[35]

So did the Justice Department issue arrest warrants or appoint a special prosecutor to investigate the charges? Did Congress begin impeachment proceedings? After all President Richard Nixon eventually resigned in part for illegally ordering illegal wiretaps against seventeen people—Bush had authorized thousands of illegal wiretaps. Yet nothing happened. Dominated by ideological zealots, the Justice Department and the Republican-dominated Congress joined conservatives elsewhere in condemning as unpatriotic or outright treasonous those who called for investigations or impeachment proceedings against President Bush and other key officials for committing high crimes and misdemeanors. Only after Democrats retook both houses of Congress in the 2006 election did the White House make a concession. Bush declared that he would suspend, not eliminate, the warrantless program, and for the moment seek FISC warrants.

No sooner did the politicians sweep those violations of the law under the rug than revelations of new crimes arose. The FBI had issued over ten thousand "national security letters," which is a bureaucratic procedure for obtaining telephone, financial, and business records. This act is illegal unless backed by a warrant. There were no warrants. FBI director Robert Mueller did take responsibility for the policy and promised to suspend the practice.

Another scandal broke in March 2007 when news broke that Alberto Gonzales and Karl Rove had worked behind the scenes to fire eight federal attorneys for refusing to file various trumped-up charges against Democrats running in the 2006 election and for not prosecuting Republicans who had committed actual crimes. As Thomas DiBiagio, one of those purged, put it, "There was direct pressure not to pursue these investigations. The practical impact was to intimidate my office and shut down the investigations." The attempts of those eight prosecutor to be above politics contrasted with the ideologically and politically driven behavior of their colleagues. Of the 375 federal cases broken against politicians after 2000, 298 were Democrats, 67 Republicans, and 10 independents.[36]

Congress did end a program initiated by the Pentagon's Defense Advanced Research Projects Agency (DARPA), which promoted cutting-edge technologies that can be applied to weapons and intelligence gathering. John Poindexter, DARPA's head and Ronald Reagan's national security adviser who was among those convicted for the Iran-Contra scandal, set up the Total Information Awareness (TIA) program, which data mined the Internet to pick up suspicious activities. Concerned that TIA violated the Fourth Amendment, Congress shut it down in 2003.

What did the public think about the Bush administration's violations of the Constitution and other laws? A *New York Times* poll in January 2006 found that Americans were split over the illegal wiretaps. When asked whether they were concerned about losing their civil liberties, two-thirds were either "very" (34 percent) or "somewhat" (30 percent) concerned, while 17 percent were "not at all concerned." As for which was a greater worry, that the Bush team would enact laws that took away civil liberties or that they would fail to enact tough enough laws, 48 percent said the former, 40 percent the latter, and 2 percent said both or neither. Yet when asked about the warrantless wiretaps, 53 percent disapproved, and 46 percent approved. Unfortunately there was no question in the poll about whether the respondent understood just what FISA and FISC stood for or did.[37]

Like the "right of privacy," there is no explicit constitutional reference to the "right of citizens to know" what their government is doing. Yet the concept of the "right to know" is implicit and crucial to any healthy liberal democracy. Most experts agree that the right to know is among those rights referred to by the Ninth Amendment: "The enumeration in the Constitution of certain rights shall not be construed to deny or disparage others retained by the people."

Here again the Bush administration violated with impunity an implicit American right. No administration has been more obsessed with secrecy than that of George W. Bush. From 2001 to 2004, the number of classified documents nearly doubled from 8.7 million to 15.6 million, the number of pages of declassified documents plummeted from 100.1 million to 28.4 million, and the cost of securing information rose from $4.7 billion to $7.2 billion. By February 2006, the CIA alone had reclassified more than 55,000 previously unclassified documents.[38]

Among Bush's very first acts after he took power was to issue Executive Order 13233, which suspended the application of the 1978 Presidential Record Act. That law changes the status of presidential records from private to public and allows people to gain access to them five years after the president leaves office or an additional twelve years, if the departing president wishes. Thus did Bush deny access to 68,000 pages of information due to be released in 2001 from the Reagan administration for which many of his own key officials had worked.

Under the 1966 Freedom of Information Act (FOIA), the government must release unclassified information to people who request it. On October 5, 2001, Ashcroft issued an order that suspended FOIA. Henceforth, officials would be empowered to withhold any information that they believed was "sensitive" or related to an ongoing investigation. And that applied not merely to the average citizen but also to nearly all 535 members of Congress. Only 8 congressional leaders could access such designated information. Thus did conservatism trump the citizen's right to know with the bureaucrat's power to withhold.

Ashcroft also imposed stiff research fees on the information that was released. For instance the Justice Department presented a bill to the People for the American Way Foundation for $372,799 for its inquiry into the fates of American citizens and residents jailed without charges after September 11. The Bush team's attempts to stymie investigations did not end there. They viciously attacked anyone who revealed crimes within the federal government. For instance, Pennsylvania congressman Curt Weldon pointed out that the whistle-blowers of the Pentagon's illegal Able Danger data-mining program suffered a terrible fate—their "lives were ruined" and they "were threatened and intimidated because they simply wanted to tell the truth."[39]

Related to the Bush administration's war against the Constitution was its war against science. On March 19, 2002, the president asserted his power to censor any "sensitive but unclassified information" by withdrawing sixty-six-hundred technical documents from the public realm that mostly concerned chemical and biological weapons. The administration also pressured scientific associations to censor their own articles. The American Society for Microbiology, for instance, was told to limit information shared through its eleven journals. The argument was that the reports could be used by terrorists.

Scientists, however, countered that censorship would impede their ability to assess each other's work and develop new technologies and theories. The presidents of the National Academy of Sciences, the National Academy of Engineering, and the Institute of Medicine jointly issued an extraordinary declaration on October 19, 2002. Their "Statement on Science and Security in an Age of Terrorism" argued that the Bush administration's censorship policies toward "sensitive but unclassified information" threatened to "stifle scientific creativity and to weaken national security." The reason was that "experience shows that vague criteria of this kind generates deep uncertainties among both scientists and officials responsible for enforcing regulations."[40]

Nonetheless, the scientific community eventually caved in to the Bush team's policies and pressure. During a conference of the American Association for the Advancement of Science in February 2003, twenty publishers of scientific journals agreed to censor articles that might somehow violate national security. Just how those editors would determine whether an article did so was unclear. This decision sparked enormous controversy in the scientific and civil liberty communities.[41]

As conservatives would have it, the only civil liberty that they protected rather than violated was the controversial right to own arms. Contrary to the claims of the conservatives, the Second Amendment gives the "right to bear arms" only to members of federally "well regulated militia . . . necessary to the security of a free State"—today's National Guard and reserves—not individuals. The Supreme Court affirmed this reality in the 1939 *United States v. Miller*. The conservative-dominated Supreme Court reversed that decision with rulings in 2008 and 2010.

The Bush administration had been acting in the spirit of that eventual ruling since its first day in power. After September 11, Attorney General Ashcroft had no qualms about ordering the mass roundup of 1,100 people who were held without charges, sometimes for months. Yet five days after the attacks, Ashcroft rejected an FBI request to cross-check a list of 186 terrorist suspects with gun ownership applications. As a senator, Ashcroft had voted against any measures to strengthen the regulations of firearms. Now as attorney general, he had the power to partly realize his obsession with gun rights by thwarting a federal investigation into terrorism.[42]

Among the provisions of the 1993 Brady Handgun Violence Prevention Act (better known as the Brady Bill) was the ban of nineteen types of automatic assault weapons better known as machine guns; the inauguration of a five-day waiting period for handgun purchases; the establishment of the National Instant Criminal Background Check System (NICS) that is required of everyone who wants to purchase a gun; and the ninety-day retention of applications. The background checks alone have been extremely effective in sharply reducing crime. From 1994 to 2008, these checks prevented 1.8 million gun sales, of which 56 percent would have gone to convicted felons and 13 percent to fugitives from justice.

Conservatives were determined to gut and ideally destroy the Brady Bill. Two days after George W. Bush took office, Ashcroft flexed his National Rifle Association (NRA) muscles and suspended the ninety-day retention of applications rule. Henceforth law enforcement agencies could only retain these crucial records for a mere twenty-four hours. In February 2004 the conservative-dominated Congress reinforced that policy by passing a law that required all records of gun applications and purchases to be destroyed within twenty-four hours, and once again allowed people living in the United States to buy those nineteen types of automatic assault weapons banned by the Brady Bill.[43]

The result of the gun lobby's power was to undercut American national security. From February 2004 to February 2009, people on the national terrorist watch list made 963 requests to buy guns, of which 865, or 90 percent, were approved. Those on the terrorist watch list are denied seats on airplanes and visas, but nearly all of them are permitted to buy firearms, including automatic assault weapons.[44]

Securing Borders and Hardening Sites

The abbreviation WMD can stand for "weapons of mass destruction," such as chemical, biological, nuclear, and radiological bombs (CBNR), or "weapons of mass disruption," such as cyber attacks. Al Qaeda and other terrorist groups have tried to get and wield both kinds of WMD against the United States. The National Intelligence Estimate of January 2002 found a growing WMD threat against the

United States delivered by "ships, trucks, airplanes, or other means"; a missile attack on the United States, however, was remote but would more likely come via a cruise missile than a ballistic missile. The United States has so far been spared a CBNR attack, but it suffers literally hundreds of thousands of daily cyberwarfare attacks.

A key counterterrorist strategy is to determine what targets the terrorists would be most eager to destroy or disrupt, and then hardening those sites. At the top of the priority list is "critical infrastructure," which the DHS defines as those "assets, systems, and networks, whether physical or virtual, so vital to the United States that the incapacity or destruction of such assets, systems, or networks would have a debilitating impact on security, national economic security, public health or safety, or any combination of those matters."[45]

A country's critical infrastructure changes as its economy develops. In a modern economy, the infrastructure provides the skeleton, and the industries the muscles, for providing goods and services. In a postmodern economy the industries and infrastructure are increasingly virtual, since they involve the creation and flow of information. But they can never be completely virtual, since that creation and flow must happen in specific places. So a postmodern economy's strategic infrastructure and industry are vulnerable to both physical and cyber attacks. A semiconductor factory, for instance, could be devastated both by a truck bomb parked outside or by a virus fired into the computers that run it.

At times there are tradeoffs between efficiency and security. It may make sense to route the flow of goods or information through a few key ports, but the greater the concentration, the greater the vulnerability. A 2005 congressional study revealed a few of many disturbing vulnerabilities. For instance, one-third of all containers entering or leaving the United States pass through the twin ports of Long Beach or Los Angeles. More than one-third of all freight trains rumble across Illinois, most of them through Chicago. Nearly one-third of all naval shipbuilding and repair is done in or around Norfolk, Virginia.[46]

Protecting such sites involves both deterrence and defense. Ideally, the site is hardened by a series of appropriate measures that prevent an attack or, should deterrence fail, can successfully defeat an attack that does take place. Clearly, the transportation and communication systems are vital to national security and must be hardened by reasonable means. Borders must be guarded so that terrorists do not cross by legal or illegal means. Airports and shipping ports must be made more secure. The computer systems of the government, businesses, academia, and research institutions, along with other essential facilities, must harden their sites against cyber attacks. On that, virtually all Americans are in accord, although the way the Bush team went about it once more raised questions about incompetence and corruption.

Essential to American national security is determining just who enters and leaves the United States. That is a Herculean task. In 2000 alone, 67 million international travelers arrived or departed. The Aviation Security Law, passed on November 19, 2001, helped deal with this problem by requiring all airlines with flights in the United States to supply passenger lists before each flight to the Customs Service's Advanced Passenger Information System. Originally the airlines had two months to comply. Although 90 airlines with 57 million passengers on 357,000 flights in 2000 had been doing or promptly began to do so, there were some notable holdouts for financial, technological, or nationalistic reasons. To pressure compliance, customs commissioner Robert Bonner sent an ultimatum to fifty-eight foreign carriers to comply within forty-eight hours, or else customs agents would search every foreign passenger and bag disembarking in the United States. He made a point of singling out Saudi Arabian Airlines, Russia's Aeroflot, and Air China for special scrutiny.[47]

A potential terrorist attack in the United States can come from many different methods and places. The most likely way to smuggle WMD into the United States is by sea. Each year about 7.8 million (or 20,000 a day) boxcar-sized containers are unloaded across 360 public and private American ports. About 80 percent of those move through ten ports, which obviously should be security priorities. By the time the Bush administration left office, a mere 6 percent of all containers were searched, up from 2 percent eight years earlier. Further complicating port security are the over 400,000 businesses that import goods, over 4,000 licensed forwarders and customs brokers, and thousands of consolidators and freight haulers.[48]

A worst case scenario would be for a terrorist group to plant or recruit key personnel inside a shipping company that allowed it to smuggle a "dirty" or radiological nuclear bomb encased in a lead-lined container through a global shell game from port to port and ship to ship, until it is finally unloaded at one of America's busiest ports. The White House might well react to the explosion of just one dirty bomb by halting imports of new containers and searching those piled up dockside or being whizzed by tractor-trailers across the country. International trade would collapse for weeks or even longer as inspectors desperately tried to ensure that no other bombs were here or en route. That in turn would crash the global economy with panic, chaos, joblessness, poverty, and violence sweeping one country after another.

That vulnerability was highlighted in February 2006 when a controversy erupted over whether Dubai Ports World, which is majority owned by the United Arab Emirates, should be allowed to buy the right to manage twenty-nine terminals at the ports of New York, Newark, Philadelphia, Baltimore, and New Orleans. Dubai is an important center through which Islamists transfer or bank their money. It was also the city-state where Pakistani scientist Abdul Qadeer Khan smuggled equipment for making nuclear weapons to Libya, Iran, and North Korea. Critics expressed the concern that terrorists could infiltrate that corporation to gain important intelligence on operations or even doctor papers to let a container with a dirty bomb into the United States. The White House insisted that it had looked into the question and was satisfied that there was no problem. Bush suggested that the opponents were racist and swore to veto any bill that prevented the sale from proceeding.

A dirty bomb does not have to be imported. There are various potential ways to set off an explosion that would release deadly nuclear radiation. The ninety-nine operating nuclear energy plants in the United States pose a potentially catastrophic target for terrorists. An elite team could storm and take over a nuclear plant or dive-bomb a plane into a nuclear core. The result could be a Chernobyl-like nuclear meltdown that spews deadly radiation across a swath of the nation.

Yet the Bush team was indifferent to programs that helped secure America's nuclear power plants, weapons, and materials against a terrorist attack. When the Energy Department requested $379.7 million for that program in 2002, the White House cut 99 percent of the program, leaving only $2.4 million. Representative Edward Markey pointed out the president's priorities: "The administration has requested almost $8 billion for missile defense which won't do anything to prevent suicidal terrorists from attacking nuclear facilities and blowing up dirty bombs or homemade nuclear bombs."[49]

Chemical and biological weapons are far easier for terrorists to buy, steal, smuggle, detonate, and certainly to make than nuclear weapons. Indeed terrorists have already attacked the United States with chemical and biological weapons. The Islamist terrorists had two bombs in the truck they parked within the World Trade Center in 1993, one conventional and the other chemical. Fortunately the conventional bomb vaporized the chemical bomb. Shortly after September 11, a right-wing terrorist sent letters laced with anthrax through the mail to Senate leader Tom Daschle and NBC broadcaster Tom Brokaw; although those men escaped death, five others died, and a score fell ill.

Perhaps the most likely WMD that terrorists could use against the United States would chemical in nature. The most probable scenario would be for terrorists to hijack a chemical truck. It is estimated that the explosion of a ninety-ton truck filled with chlorine on the Washington Mall during the Fourth of July holiday would kill over 100,000 people. Another method would be for a terrorist to turn a chemical plant into a WMD by nose-diving a plane packed with fuel into it. The Environmental Protection Agency (EPA) has identified 123 chemical plants that, if one exploded, would endanger the lives and livelihoods of a million or more people in the surrounding area. Thousands more chemical plants could threaten smaller populations.[50]

Aided and abetted by the Bush administration, the chemical industry staved off the implementation of any proposed regulations that would have strengthened their security. Instead, the conservatives typically used the threat of terrorism to advance other items on their ideological agenda. While they refused to take the tough measures necessary to secure chemical factories, they did prevent citizens from exercising their right to know just what and how much those plants were manufacturing and whether they were in compliance with environmental laws. The state of New York sued the EPA for violating the Freedom of Information Act after it refused to release data on how much pollution chemical plants were spewing into the atmosphere and water. The EPA won that case before a conservative judge.[51]

Cyber warfare is a potentially devastating form of terrorism. An evil genius at a keyboard could theoretically launch viruses or worms that eat or burrow their way Pac-Man-like through key sectors of a nation's defense, intelligence, financial, communications, and air transportation systems. As with other types of terrorism, cyber terrorists have already launched attacks that merely hint at the havoc they are potentially capable of inflicting. With their 1999 "Love Bug," two Filipino college computer whizzes zapped $10 billion worth of data and fried the circuits of 10 million computers around the world in just twenty-four hours.

Despite spending billions of dollars on security, America remains vulnerable to cyber attacks. In 2001 a freak fire in a Baltimore tunnel through which Internet cables passed revealed just how fragile the Internet actually can be. For days the Internet was down in Baltimore and slow in many other neighboring regions. A coordinated attack against key Internet switching stations across the country could cripple the economy as tens of millions of computer screens blank out and bring the nation's research, business, and communications to a dead halt.

The Lessons of September 11

Perhaps the best way to prevent another September 11 type terrorist attack on the United States is to understand how al Qaeda got away with the first one. Finding out, however, proved to be an enormous challenge, primarily because the Bush administration fought any attempts to investigate September 11 every step of the way.

In their very meek way, leading Democrats called for more information, if not a formal investigation, of the attack. House Minority Leader Dick Gephardt said, "I think what we have to do now is to find out what the president and the White House knew about the events leading up to 9/11, when they knew it, and, most importantly, what was done about it at the time." Senator Hillary Clinton merely asked the simple question: "The president knew what? My constituents would like to know the answer to that and many other questions, not to blame the president . . . just to know."[52] These queries were exceptional. Typically the mass media and public were mostly indifferent to such pertinent questions. During most of his eight years in power, Bush proved to be as much a Teflon president as Ronald Reagan.

After September 11, the Bush administration circled the wagons and bitterly fought any congressional efforts to find out what went wrong. The White

House rejected any requests for officials to testify, including Cheney, Powell, and Rumsfeld. The president and leading officials repeatedly claimed with straight faces that an investigation would somehow distract America from the so-called war on terrorism, although they did not venture to say just how that might occur. Ashcroft offered the standard conservative response. During an appearance before the Senate Judiciary Committee, he simply smeared his critics with treason: "Your tactics only aid terrorists, for they erode our national unity and diminish our resolve. They give ammunition to America's enemies and pause to its friends."[53]

In reality, a war against any terrorist group is fought primarily with spies, diplomats, bookkeepers, and paramilitary forces rather than blue-ribbon panelists. National security could not improve unless those in charge understood and eliminated the nation's vulnerabilities. Indeed the only diversion from the war against al Qaeda and its affiliates would come when the Bush team yanked CIA and military Special Forces, along with Predators and other essential counterterrorist assets, from Afghanistan to the neoconservative crusade in Iraq.[54]

All along, the President and his fellow conservatives in and beyond the White House waged a relentless war against anyone who raised questions, let alone criticism, by attacking their patriotism. Cheney smeared the remarks of Gephardt, Clinton, and others as "incendiary" and "thoroughly irresponsible and totally unworthy of national leaders in time of war." The conservatives did not hesitate to attack anyone who raised questions, including Republicans. They blistered Richard Shelby, the ranking Republican on the Senate Intelligence Committee, whose duty is just such oversight and investigation. Republican senator Chuck Hagel was similarly blasted for suggesting that "I think they are far better to open this process up. Eventually the information will get out. You are not going to hide anything."[55]

The Bush administration's systematic attempts to cover up September 11 broke with the traditional American way of dealing with national tragedies. Presidents have appointed scores of blue-ribbon panels to investigate an array of large and small disasters. The most famous was that of Franklin Roosevelt, who ordered no stone unturned in understanding how the Japanese pulled off their "sneak attack." Bush not only refused to appoint an independent commission, but he and his fellow conservatives across the political system did everything possible to stifle congressional investigations.[56]

Bush finally succumbed to the pressure for an independent investigation a year after the attack occurred, endorsing the idea on September 30, 2002. The Senate promptly voted 90 to 8 to support an investigation. But, having grudgingly agreed, Bush soon backpedaled. He insisted that the panel be limited in just what it could investigate. He wanted an informal glimpse at carefully selected information without subpoenas, oaths, and legal liability. He only wanted the panelists to see open sources of information; nothing classified would be reviewed. He wanted an investigation concluded within a few months rather than in the proposed eighteen months.[57]

Democrats and a handful of moderate Republicans complained that Bush's stonewalling indicated a cover-up and jeopardized American security. Then moderate Republican senator John McCain reminded Americans that "no one has really been held accountable. No one has lost their job, no one has been even reprimanded, nothing has happened as a result of September 11. Unless responsibility is assigned, then we can't cure the problem." A coalition of four groups of families, whose loved ones were among the victims, issued a statement criticizing the Bush administration for claiming to want an investigation "while apparently doing everything in its power to prevent the commission from being established."[58]

The Bush administration successfully ran out the political clock in 2002. Congress ended its session without the vital testimonies from the White House. The November election occurred without the damning revelations such an investigation might have revealed. The Republicans strengthened their grip on the House of Representatives and recaptured the Senate, making any future comprehensive and credible investigation all the more unlikely.

Nonetheless, versions of the truth eventually appeared. On July 23, 2002, the Joint Intelligence Committee issued a preliminary nine-hundred-page report that concluded that the intelligence community's failure to detect the conspiracy was due to turf battles and compartmentalization in which information and strategy were not shared, exacerbated by the Bush administration's disinterest and inertia in mobilizing against al Qaeda and warnings to the CIA and FBI to avoid exploring the link between the terrorist network and Saudi Arabia. The Bush team typically denied any wrongdoing, attacked critics for being unpatriotic, and blamed the Clinton White House for 9/11.

A parallel investigation began in December 2002, the month after the mid-term election, with the formation of the 9/11 Commission Panel of twelve foreign policy experts equally divided between Republicans and Democrats, and eventually cochaired by Republican former New Jersey governor Thomas Kean and Democratic former Indiana congressman Lee Hamilton. That commission would never have existed had not the families of September 11 victims persistently demanded its creation to Congress, the White House, and the mass media.

The Bush administration did everything possible to kill that movement for a commission and then, after Congress established it, tried to undermine it by starving it of funds, witnesses, documents, and time. They evoked executive privilege to withhold tens of thousands of pages of key documents for "national security" reasons. Bush and Cheney refused to testify unless they were both interviewed together without having to take an oath to tell the truth and for no more than an hour. That joint interview prompted *Tonight Show* host Jay Leno to wonder which Cheney knee Bush would be sitting upon. The White House nearly succeeded in running out the clock on the initial deadline for the commission to complete its investigation, but Congress extended the mandate to July 26, 2004.

Despite the Bush administration's machinations, the commission managed to gather and analyze a wealth of information. In all, the commission issued seventeen reports culminating with a 567-page book, although that final report was deliberately not released until after the 2004 election. Kean and Hamilton stated in the final report's preface:

We have reviewed more than 2.5 million pages of documents and interviewed more than 1,200 individuals in ten countries. This included nearly every senior official from the current and previous administration who had responsibility for topics covered in our mandate. We have sought to be independent, impartial, thorough, and nonpartisan. . . . Our aim has not been to assign individual blame. Ours has been to provoke the fullest possible accounts . . . and to identify the lessons learned. . . . We are looking backward in order to look forward.[59]

What readers found in the final report was largely a well-written overview that addressed most of the crucial questions. Critics, however, made a good argument that the report was largely a whitewash of the Bush administration and was filled with omissions and distortions.[60]

The commission fulfilled its promise not to assign individual blame. Instead it spotlighted the failures of Washington's bureaucracies: "We learned that the institutions charged with protecting our borders . . . did not understand how grave this threat could be and did not adjust their policies, plans, and practices to deter or defeat it."[61] In doing so, the commission failed to understand a crucial reality. Those institutions were run by political appointees who were charged with implementing White House policies. The institutions failed because Bush and his inner circle failed to act decisively against a threat that they were repeatedly warned was imminent and would be devastating.

Yet, contrary to the claims of conspiracy theorists, there is no credible information that Bush and a coterie of fellow neoconservatives knew about the pending September 11 attacks and deliberately did nothing so that they could manipulate the subsequent horror, rage, and desire for vengeance to push through everything on their ideological wish list. Given all that is now known, the Bush team was guilty of serious criminal negligence, but not treason.

Ultimately the conservatives were the dupes of their own extreme creed and overweening greed. Before September 11 they were in lockstep on cramming through Congress two priorities from their agenda. They sought large tax cuts for the rich, and they also pushed for the so-called anti-ballistic missile program, which in reality is nothing more than a scarecrow defense against the genuine threats facing America. Meanwhile bin Laden and his henchmen finalized their preparations for September 11.

Befuddled by their ideological and political imperatives, the minds of the president and his fellow conservatives were far removed from the world's unforgiving realities. Their Pollyannaish views rendered them blind, deaf, and dumb not just to al Qaeda's looming threat but to the far more serious and worsening related threats posed by global warming, the population explosion, the debt bomb, failed states and economies, biocide, and global economic collapse.

Consequences

Since September 11, according to George Tenet, the counterterrorist efforts in America and around the world have thwarted at least twenty al Qaeda plots, some targeting the United States. Ayman al-Zawahiri directly alluded to at least one such plot, a 2003 attack on New York's subway system, which he canceled because "we have something better in mind." That "something better" has yet to be revealed.[62]

Although al Qaeda sleeper cells are quite likely embedded in the United States, none to date have been uncovered. The Justice Department boasted that by June 2006, 261 of 441 defendants in terrorist cases had been found guilty. None of them, however, had anything to do with September 11, and most were convicted on immigration charges.[63]

Certainly the enhanced counterterrorist efforts acted as a powerful deterrent. Would-be terrorists were well aware of the better gathering, analysis, and sharing of intelligence among government agencies, the heightened surveillance at the nation's borders and airports, the hardened protection of key government, infrastructure, and industrial sites, and similar international efforts. Terrorists want to fulfill their missions without getting caught. The greater the chance being intercepted en route to the target, the more likely a mission would be canceled.

Yet ultimately, just why no massive attack has occurred can only be explained by those terrorists who dream of doing so. Regardless, America is merely less vulnerable than it was on September 11. It may just be a matter of patience for the terrorists and negligence for those who are charged with stopping them.

8

The Global War on Terror

*People sleep peacefully in their beds at night only because
rough men stand ready to do violence on their behalf.*
　　—George Orwell

We will have to work through, sort of, the dark side.
　　—Dick Cheney

The 1 Percent Doctrine

George W. Bush and Dick Cheney vividly expressed the scope and nature of their
so called global war on terror. The president explained that "our war on terror
begins with al Qaeda but it does not end there. It will not end until every terrorist
group of global reach had been found, stopped, and defeated." The vice president
asserted that to win that war the administration would have to "work through,
sort of, the dark side." He later elaborated just what that might mean. In what
became popularized as the 1 percent doctrine, Cheney declared that the Bush
administration would attack any group or government in any country "if there's a
1 percent chance" that it is developing WMD that could be launched against the
United States.[1]

Beyond the Iraq War where the military was in charge, the CIA would lead
the global war on terror. Cofer Black discussed his marching orders: "There was
a 'before' 9/11 and 'after' 9/11. After 9/11 the gloves came off. No limits, aggressive, relentless, worldwide pursuit of any terrorist who threatens us is the only

way to go." Roger Cressey, a former deputy director of the NCTC, admitted that the result of such a policy could get legally and morally messy: "We are going to make mistakes. We are even going to kill the wrong people sometimes. That's the inherent risk of an aggressive counterterrorist program. . . . What we need is everyone to know that it is being done with the best of intentions."[2]

The hydra dilemma was embedded deep within in that "anything goes" policy. Although most of the counterterrorism measures proved to be highly effective against al Qaeda and its affiliates, some backfired by creating more enemies than were eliminated. For instance, the "enhanced interrogation techniques" wielded to squeeze intelligence from "high value detainees" may have been crucial to getting information that saved lives. Those sessions might have remained under the political radar had they not been exposed by the gratuitous and indiscriminate humiliations and tormenting of thousands of low- or no-value detainees at Abu Ghraib and other prisons in Iraq. And photos of those abuses became terrorist recruiting posters and deepened the hatred for the United States around the world.

Another casualty was American democracy. At first glance there appeared to be no American legal obstacles to conducting a no-holds-barred counterterrorist strategy wherever the enemy could be found. The 1996 Antiterrorism and Effective Death Penalty Act authorized the president to "use all necessary means, including covert action and military force, to disrupt, dismantle and destroy international infrastructure used by international terrorists, including overseas training facilities and safe houses." That act, however, did not trump the Constitution or a variety of other laws, including ratified treaties that defined what was legal and what was illegal.[3]

The ultimate result of such indiscriminate polices was self-defeating. The Bush administration ended up at once strengthening America's enemies while severely damaging American security, power, wealth, and honor.

Hearts and Wallets

A core counterterrorist strategy is to follow the money and then eliminate the links among hearts, wallets, and violence. Six weeks after September 11, a series of decrees and laws bolstered Washington's powers to do so. On September 23, President Bush issued Executive Order 13224, which reinforced the International

Emergency Economic Powers Act to blacklist and freeze the assets of organizations listed as providing material support to terrorist groups. On September 24 the
White House announced that it was freezing the assets of twenty-seven individuals and groups involved in terrorism and asked other countries to do the same or
risk retaliation. On October 12 the White House added thirty-nine more individuals and groups to that list. Part of the Patriot Act, which the president signed into
law on October 27, strengthened the federal government's power to prosecute
individuals and groups accused of funneling money to terrorists. In 2004 the
Treasury Department set up the Office of Terrorism and Financial Intelligence
(TFI) as Washington's lead agency trying to eliminate funding for terrorism. That
mission includes shutting down the money-making activities of terrorist groups,
trying to deter people from contributing to terrorist groups, and eliminating the
pipelines by which money is circulated.

Essential to that policy was getting as many other countries as possible to
mop up the financial assets of the terrorists. The UN Security Council boosted the
Bush administration's efforts when, on September 28, 2001, it passed Resolution
1373, which evoked Chapter VII to require all United Nations members to deny
money-laundering services, travel, residence, recruitment, fund-raising, and any
other aid to terrorists; freeze any financial accounts belonging to a list of terrorist
groups; and cooperate with each other by sharing information and indicting or
extraditing suspects

The Security Council authorized the UN Counter-Terrorism Committee
(UNCTC), to monitor compliance with that resolution. The UNCTC began work-
ing closely with the al Qaeda and Taliban Sanctions Committee that was set up be-
fore 9/11, along with such international organizations as Interpol, the International
Monetary Fund (IMF), the World Customs Organization (WC), the Organisation
for Economic Co-operation and Development (OECD), the Financial Action
Task Force (FATF), the Basel Committee on Banking Supervision (BCBS), the
International Civil Aviation Organization (ICAO), the International Maritime
Organization (IMO), and the Organisation for the Prohibition of Chemical
Weapons (OPCW).

The Bush administration in turn aided those efforts when, on December
19, 2001, it submitted to the United Nations a report detailing its financial war

against terrorism. The report was presented as a global standard that all other countries were urged to adopt. By then 19 countries had actually frozen such assets. Another 111 countries promised to modify their banking laws to ease the identifying and tracking of suspected terrorists and criminals, although such leading sources of money to terrorists as Saudi Arabia, Egypt, Kuwait, Qatar, and Jordan were notably absent from that group. These efforts initially yielded modest results—the governments were able to find and freeze only $24 million in accounts suspected of being linked to terrorism.

To pressure the laggards into cooperating, Amb. John Negroponte bluntly stated that the United States

> put $1.5 billion into the coffers of the United Nations this year, basically paying off our arrears and current dues. We're working on counterterrorism issues. We've ratified 10 of 12 UN conventions on terrorism. We've moving to ratify two remaining ones. . . . Our attitude toward the United Nations is one of pragmatic commitment. We believe it has a very useful role to play, and does that mean we don't reserve the right to act on a unilateral, bilateral, or regional basis when this best advantages our interests? That I can't tell you.[4]

With an array of existing counterterrorist programs and organizations, and more yet to come, terrorism was clearly an important United Nations issue. There were thirteen existing international laws concerning terrorism, including the 1997 International Convention for the Suppression of Terrorist Bombings and the 1999 International Convention for the Suppression of the Financing of Terrorism. Those efforts were further boosted in 2004 with Security Council Resolution 1523, which established the Counter-Terrorism Executive Directorate (CTED) as a secretariat for the UNCTC. Security Council Resolutions 1540 and 1566, which passed in 2004, prohibited the transfer of WMD or their components to non-state groups, required members to do everything possible to impede or intercept any illicit shipments, and requested yearly reports on their efforts to comply with those resolutions. That was followed up by the 2005 International Convention for the Suppression of Acts of Nuclear Terrorism.

As for specific counter measures to terrorist financing, the FATF, that was setup by the Group of Seven in 1989, has spearheaded international efforts against money laundering. In October 2001 the FATF added terrorism to its list of proscribed activities. Yet the FATF has only the power to track, not to intercept illegal activities or arrest suspects. So it shares its intelligence with the appropriate organizations or governments that can. The FATF now includes thirty-four members. Another international organization is the Egmont Group, which was set up in 1996 and today has over a hundred countries. Egmont is the international network for the Financial Intelligence Units of governments that track illicit financial flows. Finally the UN Office on Drugs and Crime has a Terrorism Prevention Branch and Global Program against Money Laundering.[5]

A few key holdouts, most notably Saudi Arabia, have undercut the international financial counterterrorist efforts. Perhaps the biggest blow to money for al Qaeda and other Islamist groups came when Saudi Arabia agreed to prohibit charities from sending money out of the country and forced mosques to remove their collection boxes. In October 2007 Sheikh Abdel Aziz al-Asheikh, Wahhabism's leading cleric, issued a fatwa prohibiting Saudis from traveling abroad to commit jihad and warned everyone to take care that their charity was not being used to harm fellow Muslims. These policies crimped the ability of the largest jihadist charities like the International Islam Relief Organization and the al-Haramain Islamic Foundation to disperse funds to al Qaeda and other terrorist groups

In all, Washington and its allies have made significant progress in draining al Qaeda's money swamp. By 2007 the Treasury Department had frozen the accounts of over 460 organizations affiliated with al Qaeda and other Islamist groups like Hamas and Hezbollah.[6] The result, according to DNI chief Michael McConnell, is that "al Qaeda has had difficulty raising funds and sustaining themselves." Formerly it was al Qaeda that dispensed money to its affiliates; now it is passing the hat to its affiliates to sustain itself. The CIA intercepted a revealing letter dated July 2005 from Zawahiri to Abu Musab al-Zarqawi, who headed al Qaeda's affiliate in Iraq. Zawahiri requested "a payment of approximately one hundred thousand dollars" because "many of the lines have been cut off." That desperate need for cash had not been alleviated two years later. In May 2007 Sheikh Mustafa Abu al-Yazid, who headed al Qaeda in Afghanistan, explained that of all "the needs of the Jihad in Afghanistan, the first of them is financial. The mujahideen of the Taliban number in the thousands but they lack funds. And there are hundreds willing to carry out martyrdom-seeking operations, but they can't find the funds to equip themselves. So funding is the mainstay of Jihad."[7]

The Pitfalls of Multilateralism

Multilateral counterterrorist efforts may seem impressive on paper but have been criticized for producing "overlapping mandates, turf battles, duplication of work, and multiple and sometimes confusing reporting requirements for states. In general, information sharing and other forms of cooperation between and among these groups have been inadequate and often redundant, which has inhibited the overall UN effort."[8]

Like people, governments often say one thing and do another. Just because they sign treaties does not mean that they follow them. They may want to appear to be going along but either cannot afford the compliance costs or might secretly support the groups and activities that the treaties are designed to thwart. There are certainly no concrete sanctions for noncompliance, and with so many unwilling or unable to act, the political impact of any criticism from the United States and others is diluted, while retaliation is rare and mild.

International organizations can be unwieldy bodies for dealing with a long-term problem like global terrorism. The UN Security Council, for instance, is notorious for deadlocks or compromises that water down initiatives for dealing with divisive issues. When the Security Council does act, it tends to address a specific crisis in a country or region. Regional organizations like the Organization of American States (OAS), the Association of Southeast Asian Nations (ASEAN), and the Asia-Pacific Economic Cooperation (APEC) have formed counterterrorist task forces, but none have done anything beyond recognizing the problem.

Among the regional international organizations, only the European Union (EU) can point to any significant counterterrorist programs and successes. Many members, most notably Britain, France, Germany, Italy, and Spain, had battled domestic terrorism for decades before September 11. They treated these groups as criminal rather than military threats. The Europeans have been working together on counterterrorism since 1976 when they set up Terrorisme, Radicalisme,

Extrémisme et Violence Internationale (TREVI) to coordinate intelligence, investigation, police, and judicial efforts. The 1992 Maastricht Treaty then absorbed TREVI's legal, organizational, and operational powers.

Nonetheless the EU's efforts frequently fall behind the threats. For instance, Brussels agreed to create a European-wide arrest warrant in December 2001; it was not implemented by all members until 2004. In reviewing the compliance with the new warrants, Brussels found that eleven of the then twenty-five members had not properly integrated them with their national laws.

The March 2004 attack on Madrid's train station did briefly inspire Brussels to renew its efforts to forge a European counterterrorist strategy. The position of counterterrorism coordinator was created, and Gijs de Vries, a former Dutch deputy interior minister, became its first head. Although he was equipped with only a token staff and powers, Vries did succeed in getting Brussels to develop its Action Plan on Combating Terrorism in December 2005. But the failure of Brussels to follow up that plan eventually led Vries to resign in March 2007. Brussels took five months before appointing Gilles de Kerchove, a former Belgium justice minister, as Vries's successor.

Nonetheless there have been some counterterrorist successes. British authorities responded vigorously to the attacks in London and Glasgow in July 2007 and quickly rounded up the terrorists. German authorities thwarted a plot to explode airliners flying from Europe to the United States over the Atlantic Ocean. But these coups appear to have been largely national, rather than European-wide, efforts.

The elimination of barriers to the movement of goods or people within the European Union has clearly accelerated economic growth while exacerbating security problems. Europe's integration demands that Brussels integrate the counterterrorist operations of its members. Those challenges are compounded by swelling Islamism among European Muslims. Although Muslims comprise only 3 percent of the EU's half a billion people, their numbers are rapidly growing. The proportion of Muslims varies greatly from one country to the next, with seventeen members having 2.5 percent or fewer. The top five countries are Cyprus with 17.8 percent, Bulgaria with 12.0 percent, France with 8.3 percent, the Netherlands with 6.3 percent, and Denmark with 5.1 percent. Germany and Britain have Muslim populations of 4.3 percent and 2.7 percent of their respective totals. European

Muslims have diverse ancestries, with most of France's originating in North Africa, Germany's in Turkey, and Britain's in Pakistan or India.[9]

Although the proportions and origins of Europe's Muslims vary greatly from country to country, the problems are similar. Muslims complain that they are discriminated against and marginalized within each country and thus prevented from enjoying the same opportunities of jobs, housing, and political representation that natives enjoy.

A tiny sliver of European Muslims are so frustrated and enraged by what they perceive as injustices against Muslims in Europe and beyond that they are committed to jihad and Islamism. A study of 242 Islamist terrorists apprehended in Europe found that 40 percent were born in Europe and another 55 percent had either been raised there from childhood or had spent much of their lives there.[10] Unless the EU and each member implements its own drain-the-swamp policies, the numbers of Islamists and terrorist attacks will undoubtedly swell in the years ahead.

One international organization that the Bush administration did not enlist in its war on terror was the International Criminal Court (ICC). The ICC's origins go back to June 1998, when the General Assembly gathered for a special assembly in Rome to negotiate a treaty that would create an international organization to investigate and, if the evidence merited, prosecute violations of the international law of war, including genocide, crimes against humanity, war crimes, and the crime of aggression. The ICC would have jurisdiction only when national courts were unable or unwilling to act. The final draft was approved on July 17 by a vote of 120–7, with 21 abstentions. Although the United States was among the signatories, President Clinton did not submit the treaty to the Senate for ratification because he knew that conservatives would kill it. The treaty came into force on July 1, 2002, when the sixtieth state ratified it. The ICC officially opened for business on March 1, 2003. By January 2009, 108 states were formal members, while another forty had signed but not ratified the treaty.

The United States was not among the members. The Bush administration not only avoided using the ICC in its war on terror, but it did everything possible to denigrate that organization. Indeed, President Bush expressed conservative hatred for the ICC when he actually "unsigned" the treaty.

What explains that animus? Conservatives vehemently oppose any international organizations, laws, or other arrangements that appear to diminish the sovereignty of nation-states. Defenders of the ICC replied that no well-functioning liberal democracy need ever fear the ICC, since it would only have jurisdiction over governments that were unable or unwilling to investigate and prosecute those accused of war crimes. The sovereignty excuse only partly explains the conservative's theoretical hatred for the ICC. There was also a very practical fear. During their eight years in power, President Bush and his administration blatantly committed a series of gross violations of various international laws, and resisted, with varying degrees of success, investigations by Americans in Congress and beyond who sought to uphold the Constitution and rule of law. That certainly would have rendered the Bush administration susceptible to ICC scrutiny, if not outright prosecution, if the United States were a member.

The Unlawful Combatant Controversy

Under international law, different types of due process should prevail, depending on whether those locked up are prisoners of crime or war. Prisoners of crime, including terrorists, are charged and tried according to that nation's laws. Prisoners of war can be held for the war's duration but then must be released; during their incarceration, they are required to give nothing more than their name, rank, and serial number, and they must be treated humanely. War prisoners accused of having committed crimes must be charged, tried, and found guilty before they receive any punishment. Those who fight without wearing uniforms or openly carrying arms are illegal combatants and can be tried as war criminals. Any question of a prisoner of war's status must be determined by a legitimate military or civil court. Regardless of the designation, international law forbids the humiliation, torture, or murder of any prisoner.

The Bush administration first expressed its prisoner policy on November 14, 2001, when it declared that any captured al Qaeda, Taliban, or other terror suspects would be treated as unlawful combatants rather than as prisoners of war or criminals. Conservatives claimed that international and American laws, including the Constitution, do not apply to unlawful combatants. Instead, the accused would be tried in secret military tribunals that would allow as admissible evidence hearsay, illegally obtained information, and even confessions extracted from torture. Defendants would be denied access to the prosecutor's information. Capital punishment could be decided with a two-thirds rather than a unanimous decision. Appeals were forbidden.

International and American legal experts condemned this policy on both legal and practical grounds. They explained that international law entitled both lawful and unlawful combatants to due process. Whether unlawful or lawful combatants threaten or unleash violence against noncombatants, they are equally guilty of terrorism and can be prosecuted in a civilian or military court with jurisdiction.[11]

Foreign critics warned of severe consequences if the Bush administration violated these international laws and principles. Mary Robinson, the UN high commissioner for human rights, lamented that with the Bush team's violations of international law, "We risk the values that we fought to preserve." The Paris-based International Federation for Human Rights condemned the Bush policy as "a mere parody of justice." An editorial in France's leading newspaper, *Le Monde*, tried to remind the White House that "the difference between al Qaeda and democratic civilization is the respect for fundamental values, as set for in the U.S. Constitution." Jack Straw, Britain's foreign secretary, demanded that any British detainees be transferred to British custody for trial. Christopher Patten, the European Commission's vice chair, warned the Bush team that "having won the campaign, it would be a huge error if the international coalition were to lose the peace." Charles Grant, the director of the Center for European Reform, expressed the "European concern that America does not believe in international law, doesn't believe in submitting itself to rules, organizations, or norms that limit its freedom of action." In response to White House claims that its treatment of prisoners met Red Cross standards, that organization begged to differ, announcing that on February 8, 2002, that its forty-five legal experts had agreed that the Bush team's treatment of prisoners violated international law.[12]

The Bush administration's prisoner policy weakened America's moral and practical power to root out and destroy al Qaeda and its affiliates. That policy displayed the United States as hypocritical by at once espousing and violating fundamental human rights and democratic institutions. On November 8, 2002, a British appeals court ruled in a case involving a Briton held at Guantanamo that the Bush administration had violated both international law and habeas corpus. On January 14, 2003, Human Rights Watch listed the United States among those governments that systematically violate human rights. Spain, France, Belgium, and Germany were among countries that adamantly refused to extradite terrorist suspects to the United States as long as the Bush administration trampled fundamental democratic procedures and rights. When the White House refused to supply witnesses from its Guantanamo prison, a German court actually released for lack of evidence Abdelghani Mzoudi, who was a member of the al Qaeda cell that helped plan the September 11 attack. These are only a few examples of the tragic collisions between conservative ideology and American national security, and the resulting international reaction.

American critics were just as scathing, no one more so than the usually conservative pundit William Safire. He blasted the administration for setting up kangaroo courts or a Star Chamber that assumed the guilt of those charged, a "fiat that turns back the clock on all advances in military justice through three wars in the past half century." Bush's policy was "an assumption of dictatorial power to ignore our courts" and a gross violation of the Uniform Code of Military Justice (UCMJ), which requires public trials, proof beyond reasonable doubt, the accused's ability to select his lawyer, unanimity in death sentences, and appellate court review by civilians confirmed by the Senate. He pointed out how severely this hypocrisy would damage America's interests: "On what leg does the U.S. now stand when China sentences an American to death after a military trial devoid of counsel chosen by the defendant?"[13] Joining this chorus of critics were the voices of Colin Powell and other military leaders who argued that enemies would use the Bush policy to justify treating American prisoners with the same brutal injustice. Polls indicated that ever more Americans were troubled by the administration's policy.

This pressure eventually caused the White House to slightly adjust its policy. On February 7, 2002, the White House announced that it would uphold the Geneva Convention for the Taliban but not for al Qaeda, although neither would be granted prisoner-of-war status, and both would be tried by military courts. However, the Taliban would now be allowed the rights of presumption of innocence, counsel, public trial, silence without the inference of guilt, freedom from double jeopardy, and appeal to a higher panel of judges. Convictions would differ from civilian courts in that there would be no jury, hearsay would be accepted as evidence, and suspects would be held indefinitely.[14]

These concessions did little to mollify legal experts. Bush did not consult Congress over the tribunals, even though both the UCMJ and the Court of Appeals for the Armed Forces required him to do so. The tribunals themselves still violated the 1949 Geneva Convention that requires the status of a prisoner to be assessed by a "competent tribunal," not by the military prosecutors themselves. Once officially designated as prisoners of war, the captives can be held for the war's duration but then must be released unless charged with a specific crime. Prisoners cannot simply be persecuted for being on the losing side, a notion derisively known as "victor's justice."

The Bush policy got a boost in early 2003 when it was approved by two appeals courts. On January 10, the Richmond federal court ruled that the administration could indefinitely detain prisoners accused of terrorism. On March 12, the U.S. Appeals Court in Washington, D.C., denied a suit by sixteen Guantanamo prisoners that they were being held under American custody on land formally under American control and thus deserved American legal protection. These rulings, however, made ideological rather than legal sense, since the courts were packed with Bush appointees. Legal experts assailed these decisions.

To the astonishment of many, Anthony Kennedy, one of the conservative five Supreme Court justices, actually ruled with the four centrists against the Bush administration. Salim Ahmed Hamdan was Osama bin Laden's driver who was charged with terrorism. On June 29, 2006, the Supreme Court ruled 5 to 3 in *Hamden v. Rumsfeld* that the Bush White House had no authority to set up special military commissions for al Qaeda suspects and by doing so had violated four separate Geneva Conventions, along with the UCMJ. The specific violations included using evidence obtained under torture, admitting hearsay, and denying the accused an array of other legal rights.

Conservatives within and beyond the White House reacted with outrage and insisted that as commander-in-chief, the president could do anything he wanted. Justice Department official John Yoo, who was among the torture policy's key architects, angrily attacked the Supreme Court ruling as "attempting to suppress creative thinking."[15]

The Bush administration's attempts to weather the political storm only intensified it. So on July 11 the White House grudgingly conceded that prisoners in the
United States did have rights after all, but it would try to get Congress to pass a law
rescinding them. In August 2006, the White House submitted to the Republican-
dominated Congress a bill that essentially repudiated the Constitution, federal
laws, and the Geneva Conventions that the Senate had ratified. Then, to pressure
Congress, the president announced on August 6 that he had authorized the transfer of fourteen top al Qaeda prisoners who were being held in secret overseas
prisons to Guantanamo, and charges were being prepared against them. He then
demanded that Congress pass his bill without delay. Unstated but obvious was the
extra pressure just three months before that year's midterm elections. Then, when
protests arose, the president and his fellow conservatives accused any opponents
of being in league with America's enemies.

This bullying failed to intimidate several prominent moderate Republicans,
who united in opposition against the bill. Powell, who was now retired, argued
that the bill and the Bush policy would encourage the world "to doubt the moral
basis of our fight against terrorism" and "put our own troops at risk." In the
Senate, John McCain, John Warner, and Lindsey Graham stated their opposition
to the bill with the realist and liberal argument that America's enemies win when
the White House violates and sacrifices America's core values. Like Powell, the
three were veterans. Indeed McCain himself suffered torture as a war prisoner
during the Vietnam War. Graham had been a military lawyer. Warner used his
own experience as a veteran to chair the Armed Services Committee.

That set off several weeks of negotiations between the White House and
the moderate Republican senators. They finally cut a deal and announced it on
September 22, 2006. The compromise bill essentially provided a rather transparent legal fig leaf for the Bush administration to do all the illegal acts that it had
been doing all along. While the bill claimed to uphold the Geneva Convention
by forbidding torture, cruel or inhumane treatment, and intentional serious bodily
harm, it empowered the president to determine which interrogation techniques he
believed were lawful. Thus the president could continue to use the standard that
only techniques that resulted in "organ failure, impairment of bodily function, and
even death" were illegal; anything else was permitted and thus was not torture.

That would presumably include confessions obtained by waterboarding, sleep deprivation, forced standing or crouching for prolonged periods, and exposure to deafening and continual music. The Bush administration considered none of these actions torture as long as it did not cause, say, a heart attack, kidney failure, or death. Finally, the bill stripped the courts of their power to hear habeas corpus petitions, thus preventing the accused from challenging their own incarcerations.

In all, the Bush administration mishandled the prisoner issue in ways that damaged American security. By denying the captives prisoners-of-war status, they lost a legal means of holding them indefinitely without trial. The legal rationale would have been that prisoners can be held for a war's duration, and a war against terrorism can never be won as long as at least one person committed to threatening or using violence against innocent people remained at large. As for high-ranking al Qaeda suspects, by outsourcing their torture to foreigners in foreign lands, the United States obtained critical evidence without directly or clearly violating international or American laws. But by insisting that Americans directly torture many of the suspects, the Bush administration violated an array of American and international laws. Finally, by trying al Qaeda members in illegal tribunals, the administration set itself up for the Supreme Court rebuke that to do so violated international and American law.

Civilian courts have proven not merely far more just, but more efficient in prosecuting terrorist suspects. From September 11, 2001, to December 31, 2009, only three low-ranking al Qaeda suspects were tried in military tribunals; one was acquitted, and two are now free after serving short sentences. In stunning contrast, during that same period, federal courts convicted 195 international terrorists, while 348 international and domestic terrorists were being held in federal prisons.[16] Yet conservatives insist that only military tribunals should deal with apprehended terrorist suspects.

The Prisoner Abuse Controversy

In their global war on terror, the Bush administration incarcerated tens of thousands of suspects in prisons in Afghanistan, Iraq, the United States, Guantanamo Bay, Cuba, and dozens of secret "black sites" in other countries. Amnesty International offered a succinct summary of the numbers and locations:

Guantanamo is just the tip of the iceberg. . . . In Iraq alone . . . in early May 2005 there were more than 11,350 detainees held in U.S. custody in Abu Ghraib, Camp Bucca, Camp Cropper and in holding centers elsewhere. . . . At least 500 detainees are believed to be held in the U.S. air bases in Bagram and Kandahar in Afghanistan. An unknown number are held in other U.S. holding facilities elsewhere in the country. Several dozen "high value" detainees are believed to be held in secret CIA facilities in these countries or elsewhere. In addition, there are hundreds if not thousands of "war on terror" detainees held in other countries, allegedly at the behest of the USA, or with its knowledge and access for its agents.[17]

Word trickled out of the prison system that the White House was acting on its assertion that it would be unbound by international or American law, including the Constitution, in treating the prisoners in its hands. Human rights groups soon began documenting the systematic abuse of prisoners. The treatment of suspects in two of those prisons became especially notorious.

Hundreds of those "unlawful combatants" ended up in a prison built especially for them at the American military base at Guantanamo Bay, Cuba. From a practical point of view, Guantanamo was a good choice to warehouse prisoners. As a military base with a permanent lease in an island foreign country, the base could hardly have been more remote and thus removed from anyone who was not granted permission to enter. Legally, however, it would still be subject to both international and American law.

At its peak the prison held over 650 prisoners. Most of those suspects were rounded up not by U.S. Special Forces but by the Northern Alliance or Pakistani or other allied tribal groups. The motive for apprehending someone was often a mix of greed and vengeance. The Americans offered a bounty of $5,000 for each terrorist. What they often received were not hardcore al Qaeda operatives but the losers in private feuds. Thus did the arresting party at once pocket a small fortune and dispose of a personal enemy. Determining the difference between al Qaeda operatives and others caught in various nets was no easy matter. The only way to get even a hazy distinction was to conduct prolonged series of interrogations with constant cross-referencing.[18]

The Torture Controversy

President Bush and other leading administration spokespeople consistently and categorically denied any allegations of torture. Typical was the statement of Secretary of State Rice in December 2005 that "the United States does not permit, tolerate, or condone torture under any circumstances. . . . The United States has not transported anyone, and will not transport anyone, to a country when we believe he will be tortured. Where appropriate the United States seeks assurances that transferred prisoners will not be tortured."[19] In the light of a growing mountain of contradictory evidence, Rice's denials were disingenuous to say the least.

In reality, the White House and Pentagon statements were all lies. Shortly after September 11 the Bush administration authorized the CIA to use what euphemistically became known as enhanced interrogation techniques for al Qaeda suspects. The White House then expanded that practice to include any prisoners held in Iraq, Afghanistan, Guantanamo, or black sites elsewhere around the world. On August 1, 2002, Attorney General Ashcroft not only declared that policy legal, with arguments grounded in secret Justice Department memorandums written by John Yoo, Steven Bradbury, and Jay Bybee in January and February 2002, but he asserted that as commander-in-chief, the president could authorize torture along with anything else he thought necessary in war. Rumsfeld's Defense Department echoed its support for torture in memorandums of March and April 2003. Finally, Alberto Gonzales, the White House legal counsel who would replace Ashcroft as attorney general, advised Bush that as president, he held virtually unlimited powers, including these of torture. The only limit was torture that resulted "in serious physical injury such as organ failure, impairment of bodily functions, or even death." That certainly gave those who would carry out the policy a lot of wiggle room. Bush enthusiastically signed that executive order.[20]

Not everyone on the Bush team embraced torture. On January 26, 2002, Secretary of State Powell protested the policy, arguing that for legal, moral, and practical reasons, the White House should uphold rather than violate various Geneva conventions on war and the 1996 War Crimes Act, along with the Constitution and an array of other federal laws and statutes. Powell's view would be upheld on July 13, 2006, by the top lawyers from the army, navy, air force, and Marines who, during testimony before the Senate Armed Forces Committee, called on the Bush administration to obey international and American law.[21]

Enhanced interrogation techniques were eventually used on about thirty al Qaeda members. Waterboarding, or simulated drowning, was reportedly used on three prisoners—Khalid Sheikh Mohammed and Abu Zubaydah were respectively waterboarded 183 times and 83 times, and Abd al-Rahim al-Nashiri an undisclosed number of times. Most of the CIA and FBI professionals charged with waterboarding Zubaydah condemned the policy. They revealed that he actually was cooperating by providing critical information before the White House ordered waterboarding but shut down or provided misinformation after the torture began. Ali Soufan, one of the FBI interrogators, admitted that "there was no actionable intelligence gained from using enhanced interrogation techniques . . . that wasn't or couldn't have been gained from regular tactics."[22]

The torture ceiling that ended at waterboarding also sabotaged its success. The terrorists soon learned that there were strict limits to how often and how long they could be waterboarded. So they simply learned to endure. Meanwhile the interrogators were stranded. They were denied the array of far more fiendish devices wielded by authoritarian regimes that at times yielded genuine information. Yet the repeated waterboarding of the three terrorists forever destroyed any possibility of returning to the sophisticated psychological methods that actually extracted critical intelligence. So, with no other tools in their torture toolbox, the interrogators simply repeated the process that only hardened the resolve of the terrorists to resist.

The Bush administration tried to keep their torture policy secret. When it was revealed, the president and other officials simply denied that they had authorized torture while stonewalling any congressional attempts to investigate the policy's ultimate source. The administration claimed that it had nothing to do with the abuses, knew nothing about them until the story broke, and blamed a few low-ranking "bad apples" for the problem. The Pentagon investigation concluded that there were no orders from above and that the abuses were sporadic and spontaneous, not systematic.

In retrospect, the Bush administration's policy of gratuitously tormenting or outright torturing thousands of prisoners (as opposed to the very selective en-

hanced interrogation of key terrorist suspects) should have come as no surprise
to those who understood the nature of conservatism. To Bush and his fellow conservatives within and beyond the White House, it did not matter that torture was
illegal and did not work. Torturing prisoners fulfilled some of their deepest and
most perverse pathologies. Torture was just one of an array of illegal acts committed in the name of their guiding principles that "might makes right" and "to
the victor go the spoils." And they did not blush from acting on those principles.
Ever since they took power, the Bush administration had warred against both the
Constitution and international law by word and deed. The Iraq crusade itself was
a gross violation of international law. Bush's torture policy clearly violated the
1948 Geneva Convention, the 1984 Convention against Torture, the 1996 War
Crimes Act, and a variety of American laws. And they mercilessly attacked anyone who questioned the legality of their policies as unpatriotic and even treasonous. These attitudes flowed downward to poison the Pentagon's entire pyramid
of power to the lowliest of privates. Clearly the widespread abuse of prisoners
was not the result of a few bad apples but of the bad barrel that contained them.[23]

Unlike the array of other scandals pockmarking the Bush team's eight years
in power, the torture policy did result in charges and convictions. When denials
no longer worked, the Bush team responded to the growing national and international condemnation of its torture policy by hurriedly finding those few bad apples to scapegoat. By March 2005 there were official investigations of evidence
that Americans had tortured to death or swiftly murdered twenty-six people. By
February 2006 the number of murder cases had risen to thirty-four. Eventually,
twelve people were found guilty. None, however, received a sentence longer than
five months. By April 2006, of 410 investigations of about 600 American military and civilian personnel accused of torture, the cases against 260 were dismissed, while 150 received disciplinary actions of various kinds. Of those found
guilty, only ten were sentenced to more than a year in prison, thirty received
terms of less than a year, and the rest were reprimanded. As for the abuses at Abu
Ghraib, eventually seventeen low-ranking personnel were charged with derelic-
tion of duty, maltreatment of prisoners, and aggravated assault and battery, and
twelve were actually convicted. Only one high-ranking officer was penalized;
Gen. Janis Karpinski, who commanded the prison system in Iraq, was demoted

to colonel. The CIA inspector general conducted his own investigation of twenty allegations of torture and eventually cleared everyone except a contractor who was convicted of murder and received an eight-year sentence.[24]

So the judicial trail ended far short of the White House, where the torture policy originated when the commander-in-chief authorized it. Al Gore spoke for many when he declared that "in Iraq, what happened at that prison, it is now clear, is not the result of random acts of a few bad apples. It was the natural consequence of the Bush administration policy."

As commander-in-chief, Bush was legally responsible for the violation of American and international law that he had so eagerly authorized. Should he have been brought to justice for his alleged crimes? After all, his predecessor was actually impeached for lying under oath about having sex with someone other than his wife. By that standard of impeachment, what should have been done with a president who stood accused of ordering the torture of thousands of prisoners? And this is only one of the more serious charges. "Should," of course, is always subject to politics. For that invincible reason, Bush and others of his inner circle who stand accused of an array of high crimes and misdemeanors will never be brought to justice.

There is absolutely no question that torture is illegal under an array of American and international laws. The Constitution clearly outlaws torture. The Fifth Amendment protects suspects from being "compelled in any criminal case to be a witness against himself, nor be deprived of life, liberty, or property, without due process of law." The Eighth Amendment forbids "cruel and unusual punishment." Evidence obtained illegally or under duress is inadmissible in American courts. Under the Constitution, ratified treaties become part of the law of the land. The 1948 Universal Declaration of Human Rights bans torture. The 1949 Geneva Convention elaborates that ban by forbidding the torture, use of violence, and "cruel, inhuman, or degrading" methods of questioning prisoners "at any time and in any place." The 1984 Convention against Torture defines the practice as "any act by which severe pain or suffering, whether physical or mental, is intentionally inflicted on a . . . non-consenting, defenseless person" to obtain a confession, to obtain information, to punish, and/or to coerce the sufferer or others to act in certain ways; Article 3 forbids the transfer of prisoners to third countries where they may be tortured. The U.S. War Crimes Act of 1996 makes any violation of the Geneva Convention a felony. A federal law (18 USC sec 2340) enacted on January 26, 1998, defines torture as "an act committed by a person acting under the color of law specifically intended to inflict severe physical or mental pain or suffering (other than pain or suffering incidental to lawful sanctions) upon another person within his custody or physical control." The UCMJ, which originated with an act of Congress in 1775 and since then has been repeatedly updated, forbids the "unlawful detection" and "cruelty and maltreatment" of prisoners.

The Bush administration did succeed in legally sidestepping a sliver of that vast legal system. The Military Commissions Act of 2006 retroactively rewrote the War Crimes Act so that detainees could not apply for habeas corpus or other rights for criminal suspects.

If torture is legally wrong, can it ever be morally right? Many people believe that torture is justified in certain circumstances. The authorities know that a terrorist has planted a bomb somewhere in a densely populated area and that the bomb will soon detonate. They nab the terrorist who planted the bomb. It would be illegal to torture the terrorist. But would not torturing him prevent a much worse evil if he confessed? If a jury subsequently found authorities guilty of torture, would a judge then be morally as well as legally correct in suspending the sentence?

The ticking bomb scenario aside, most experts believe that torture is usually counterproductive. Nearly everyone cracks under torture and will confess anything to stop the pain. The result is disinformation that, if made the foundation for policy, would most likely harm rather than enhance national security. Two interrogators with decades of experience explain that harsh techniques "are rarely useful in eliciting useful intelligence and often serve to harden a detainee's resistance." Historically kindness rather than coercion has yielded nearly all crucial information from interrogations. The key is "establishing the kind of relationship—one based on trust—that is almost always necessary to win a detainee's cooperation."[25]

When it came to torture, Bush and his administration were not interested in such legal, moral, or practical dilemmas and ambiguities. While reasonable people could debate the merits of torturing high-value al Qaeda operatives, none supported the gratuitous abuse of prisoners at Abu Ghraib and other prisons. There the moral arguments for torture did not apply. Not only were no high-value al Qaeda operatives held there, but, according to General Karpinski, 90 percent of the prisoners were not even insurgents or terrorists. It is questionable whether any significant intelligence was extracted from the beatings and other abuses of thousands of prisoners. Two things were clear: Those prisoners will bear an enduring hatred and zeal for vengeance against their tormentors and the country whose government had them tormented. And, like America's invasion of Iraq, the prison abuse scandal was a dream come true for all of America's enemies, Islamist or not.[26]

The lack of any apparent practical and moral justifications for the mass abuses at Abu Ghraib and elsewhere did not prevent conservatives from rushing to excuse them. "Hate radio" king Rush Limbaugh compared the abuse to a fraternity prank in which people are "having a good time, these people, you ever heard of emotional release?"[27] Such rants, of course, empower America's enemies everywhere. Other justifications of torture by conservatives were a bit less crude but boiled down to "might makes right" and "the lesser of two evils" assertions.

The consequences of the Bush administration's torture policy were disastrous for American national security and honor. As if the conservatives had not already enflamed Islamism enough, the photos of prisoners who were humiliated and tortured at Abu Ghraib have sullied America's national image and acted as recruiting posters for countless enraged people to join Islamist and other terrorist groups and seek vengeance against America.

The Rendition Controversy

A rendition is the apprehension and transfer of someone from one country to another country. Ordinary renditions usually involve a joint operation between appropriate officials of the host government and the foreign government that wants that suspect. With extraordinary renditions, the foreign government captures and carries away a suspect without the host government's official permission, cooperation, or knowledge. Extraordinary renditions can occur when there is no extradition treaty with the host country; the host country is hostile; or the host country may be willing to help but is weak and beset by terrorists and insurgents, and public knowledge of it aiding a rendition would swell the enemy's ranks. Regardless, extraordinary renditions tend to break that foreign nation's laws. So a rendition can happen either with the host government's connivance or defiance.

As if America's rendition policy were not controversial enough, some of those nabbed were handed over for harsh interrogations in third countries, a process that has been called "torture by proxy."[28] That type of rendition usually occurs either when the information a suspect might yield is deemed far more valuable than a conviction, or there is not enough hard evidence to arrest and convict a suspect through the judicial system, but there is enough circumstantial evidence to make getting him behind bars and interrogating him an essential step in a counterterrorism campaign.

Each extraordinary rendition involves a crucial decision at the highest level over whether it is worth the risk. An array of things can go wrong. The apprehenders themselves might get caught and charged with various crimes. Injury or even death might occur to those involved, to host government officials, or to innocent bystanders. The rendition might become public knowledge with embarrassment to the government or governments which committed it. That embarrassment can become especially acute if the suspect is taken to a third country whose government may have no qualms using enhanced interrogation techniques to gain confessions. The host government may be split between those who support and those who oppose the rendition, and those differences might be made public. The suspect might be completely innocent. A failed rendition makes future renditions all the more difficult to pull off. In all, a bungled rendition can provoke a diplomatic, public relations, and legal crisis.

America's official rendition policy dates to the mid-1980s. The first publicly known rendition was the apprehension of the SS *Achille Lauro* hijackers in 1985. President Reagan made that policy official when in 1986 he issued a directive that authorized the CIA to apprehend terrorist suspects anywhere in the world. That policy was elaborated by President George H. W. Bush with National Security Directive 54, issued as a classified document in January 1991. On June 21, 1995, President Bill Clinton signed unclassified PDD-39 that authorized the rendition "of terrorists by force," which "may be affected without the cooperation of the host government." The justification for such extraordinary renditions was that when "terrorists wanted for violation of U.S. law are at large overseas, their return for prosecution shall be a matter of the highest priority. . . . If we do not receive adequate cooperation from a state that harbors a terrorist whose extradition we are seeking, we shall take appropriate measures to induce cooperation. Return of suspects by force may be affected without the cooperation of the host government."

Before September 11, the United States rendered about seventy terrorist suspects; since then, about one hundred. Although the rendition policy's official original intent was to bring suspects back to the United States for trial, this happened in relatively few cases, as the intelligence gleaned from a suspect from harsh interrogations was deemed more vital than a conviction. The general procedure is to apprehend, sedate, hood, and shackle a suspect, and drive him to a plane waiting on a nearby airport tarmac. The plane is usually leased by the CIA from one of its front companies. The suspect can end up in any one or more of a range of secure locations, from American jurisdiction in the United States or military bases at Guantanamo Bay in Cuba or in Afghanistan or Iraq, to prisons in countries like Egypt, Morocco, Jordan, Thailand, Poland, Romania, and Syria, or an array of black sites around the world in other cooperative countries.[29]

CIA Director Tenet explained the crucial importance of renditions to counter-terrorism: "These renditions have shattered terrorist cells and networks, thwarted terrorist plans, and in some cases even prevented attacks from occurring."[30]

This undoubtedly is true. It is also true that extraordinary renditions violate the sovereignty and laws of other countries, along with international law including the International Convention for the Protection of All Persons from Enforced Disappearances, which was adopted by the UN General Assembly and opened for signature in December 2006. Renditions to third countries for harsh interrogations violate the 1984 Convention Against Torture.

Ironically the actual transport of suspects is allowed through an international legal loophole. The Convention on International Civil Aviation lets private non-commercial flights fly over and even land in a country without prior notification or authorization. Among the better known of the private and often front companies the CIA has used for renditions and an array of other operations are Southern Air, Evergreen International, Tepper Aviation, Premier Executive Transport, and Aero Contractors. As one carrier becomes too well known, the agency will switch to others. The flights often land at American bases overseas for refueling and other purposes.

There is, however, a catch. This convention also empowers host government officials to require that flights land only at designated airports and be inspected if "there are reasonable grounds to conclude that it is being used for any purpose inconsistent with the aims of the Convention." Since renditions as kidnappings in general and specifically for torture violate international law, this would empower local officials to board and inspect flights suspected of carrying terrorist suspects. The fact that there are no publicly recorded cases of such inspections reveals that the CIA has secret agreements with host governments to allow these flights without hindrance.

Some powerful voices object to this "blind eye" policy. On February 14, 2007, the European Parliament endorsed a report that claimed that the CIA had made 1,245 flights that touched down at one or more European airports, and insinuated that those all involved illegal activities somehow connected with renditions. The European Parliament then condemned those activities, demanded that they end, and called for further investigations.

State Department officials condemned this report as a gross and uninformed distortion of the nature of these flights. In reality, perhaps several score of these flights involved renditions, and most were likely approved by the host governments. Secretary of State Rice offered this terse comment: "Rendition is a vital tool in combating trans-national terrorism. Its use is not unique to the United States or the current administration."[31]

The controversy over renditions reached a peak when the details of two operations, one in Italy and the other in Germany, were publicly exposed and the participants indicted. Appropriate officials in both the Italian and German governments knew of the renditions and had agreed either to aid or turn a blind eye to them. The trouble came when other officials became aware of the rendition plans and opposed them.

The Italian case received far more publicity. There a rendition team nabbed Hassan Mustafa Osama Nasr, an Islamist mullah and terrorist suspect, in Milan on February 17, 2003; drove him to America's nearby Aviano Air Base; and flew him to Egypt, where he was held in prison until his release on February 11, 2007.

Nasr claims to have been tortured at Aviano and in Egypt. The rendition came to light because of sloppy tradecraft and the resentment in at least part of Italy's government against the Bush administration's array of policies. The counterterrorist section of Italy's Military Intelligence and Security Service (SISMI) approved and aided the rendition. The American team came under scrutiny from other segments of Italy's security community when its members used cell phones to communicate with each other and lavishly spent over $140,000 for the operation, largely by eating at expensive restaurants and staying at expensive hotels.[32]

Eventually an Italian court indicted twenty-six Americans and SISMI's counterterrorist director, Nicolò Pollari, and another Italian for Nasr's rendition. The court rendered its judgment in November 2009. Five suspects were acquitted—the two Italians because of state secrecy laws and three Americans because they had diplomatic immunity. But twenty-three Americans were found guilty. While it is unlikely that any of those found guilty will serve any time, clearly American interests have suffered.[33]

Obama Policies and Dilemmas

Unlike his predecessor, President Barack Obama understood that any successful counterterrorist campaign against al Qaeda and its affiliates depended on winning hearts and minds around the world, especially among those most susceptible to Islamism's allure. In a sharp break with Bush, Obama launched a public diplomacy campaign that tried to counter enemy propaganda by promoting American values and visions. He began by talking directly, candidly, and respectfully to Muslim leaders through interviews with Muslim journalists and a speech before Egyptian university students in Cairo. He tried to align American policies more closely with American values by vowing to end the gratuitous abuse of prisoners, torture of terrorist suspects, and confinement at Guantanamo Bay. Finally, he tried to restore the rule of the Constitution and related laws to America by ending illegal warrantless wiretaps, violations of habeas corpus and the public's right to know, and the "imperial presidency."[34]

The Guantanamo prison has become a symbol to the world of the Bush White House's contempt for and gratuitous violations of international and American law. Shortly after taking office, Obama declared that he would close that prison within a year. Human rights advocates cheered, but realists were among those concerned by that plan.

Obama announced his policy without considering the consequences. For instance, where would the 242 prisoners at Guantanamo go? Transferring them to prisons in the United States or other countries and holding them without trial would hardly be a human rights improvement. Prosecuting them under civil or even military law could result in mistrials and releases of dangerous terrorists, since much of the evidence was obtained illegally. A year after Obama's announcement, only 44 of the prisoners had been transferred or released, while 198 remained.[35]

Can terrorists be rehabilitated? Since 2004 Saudi Arabia's government has tried to do just that. The Saudis believe that alienation and a misunderstanding of Islam drives people to terrorism. Thus terrorists can be rehabilitated by educating them about Islam's true nature and reintegrating them into society. The theological key is getting terrorists to understand the difference between appropriate and inappropriate jihad—it is appropriate only when cleric leaders approved by the Saudi government say so. Ties are renewed between the students and their family and friends. But perhaps the best motivation for giving up terrorism is material. New students are given a suitcase filled with clothes, computer games, and self-help guides. Graduates are supplied with jobs, cars, and even wives. The final exam includes signing a pledge rejecting terrorism. Most students graduate within a couple of months. Others might take years to graduate. Hard cases who refuse to repent may be held indefinitely. Meanwhile, Riyadh is trying to preempt people from becoming terrorists in the first place by trying to get the madrassas to conduct classes and outreach programs with similar messages and techniques. Impressed with the overall results, other countries are setting up similar rehabilitation programs, with Egypt, Yemen, and Singapore leading the way.[36]

Although the Saudi program has been lauded for successfully rehabilitating hundreds of former terrorist group members, it has not been foolproof. Riyadh admitted that 14 of the 218 rehabilitation program graduates had rejoined al Qaeda.[37]

That is hardly surprising. Quite likely a burning desire for jihad and vengeance animates the vast majority of the thousands of detainees, whether or not they were originally terrorists. A Pentagon report issued in May 2009 revealed that of the 534 men released from Guantanamo, 74 were "confirmed or suspected of reengaging in terrorist activities," a recidivism rate of 14 percent. One former Guantanamo prisoner, Said Ali al-Shihri, exemplified the potential danger in letting them go. Shihri was released to Saudi Arabia in 2007, passed through Riyadh's terrorist rehabilitation program, and then hurried to Yemen, where he became deputy head of al Qaeda's affiliate there. He is suspected of having been behind the deadly bombing at America's embassy in Sana'a, the capital, on September 16, 2008.[38] How many other released prisoners will trod similar paths? In all, the catch, torture, and release policy may not be the most efficacious counterterrorist strategy.

International law may hold a more practical solution. Under the laws of war, prisoners of war may be held for the war's duration but must always be treated humanely. The prisoners have already been wrung dry for intelligence, so there is no need for any more harsh interrogations. They can be legally warehoused indefinitely as long as their designation is changed from "unlawful combatants" to "prisoners of war."

Of course international law would also demand the prosecution of those who authorized and carried out various crimes against those prisoners. If justice were truly served, this would ultimately bring former president Bush to trial, since he signed off on those policies. Obama has said repeatedly that his White House will not prosecute members of the previous administration for their alleged crimes. CIA director Leon Panetta declared that CIA officers "should not be investigated, let alone punished," since they were simply following Bush's orders.[39]

That no-prosecution policy may complicate the Obama White House's efforts to promote cooperation on other pressing global problems. While his predecessor's administration was notorious for cherry-picking laws as well as intelligence, the Obama administration will be held to a higher standard.

Likewise there may be some problems with Obama's no-torture policy. Not just the law, but the weight of practical experience, backs this policy. Experts condemn the gratuitous abuse of prisoners; most experts believe that torture is rarely effective and often counterproductive. Whether the repeated waterboarding of high-ranking terrorists like Khalid Sheikh Mohammed or Abu Zubaydah yielded information is hotly debated. Regardless, should torture be banned in all cases? What about the ticking bomb scenario where the terrorist has been nabbed but refuses polite requests for the bomb's location? Most people would argue that torture is the lesser evil in that dilemma.

And then there is the controversy over renditions. Without doubt Americans break a variety of laws when they commit renditions without the support of the government in the country where they take place. Mistakes have been made, and innocent people have been imprisoned and tortured before being released. Yet should all renditions be banned?

If renditions are wrong, would not targeted killings be ethically worse? Ideally, terrorists are captured and interrogated rather than killed, but often that is not possible. Obama has authorized scores of targeted killings in Pakistan's Northwest Territory, tribal regions, and, spectacularly, the raid that killed Osama bin Laden and three of his followers in May 2011. Is there an ethical inconsistency in his policies? If targeted killings are justified, then why not the less-brutal actions of rendition and torture? There are no easy answers to these policy questions. To his credit, Obama gave himself some wiggle room. In a March 2009 press conference, he explained that "there could be situations . . . where . . . we have a well known al Qaeda operative that doesn't surface very often, appears in a third country with whom we don't have an extradition relationship or would not be willing to prosecute, but we think is a very dangerous person."[40] That situation applied perfectly to bin Laden.

Yet even a "decapitation strategy" can pose counterterrorist dilemmas. Expert David Kilcullen argues that the policy can backfire if the efforts "to kill or capture insurgent leaders inject energy into the system by generating grievances and causing disparate groups to coalesce. . . . Moreover, although leaders are key nodes, their destruction would do little damage to the linked but separate groups in the global jihad. Rather, their martyrdom would inject energy into the system and allow a new class of leaders to emerge."[41]

These possibilities do not appear to have followed bin Laden's killing. Indeed, his death appears to have dealt a massive blow to al Qaeda. Yet even if it had fulfilled Kilcullen's fears, killing the world's most deadly and influential terrorist certainly helped bring a sense of justice and closure to the countless people around the world, especially in the United States, enraged by his crimes against humanity.

Who is Winning?

The killing of Osama bin Laden triumphantly capped a nearly decade-long global war against the terrorists, networks, and funds of al Qaeda and its affiliates. In that struggle, the United States has racked up victories from the beginning. As early as November 2002, CIA Director Tenet reported that over three thousand known or suspected al Qaeda operatives had been arrested and hundreds of safe houses raided or shut down in ninety-eight countries. Cofer Black explained that by the end of 2003, "most of [Al Qaeda's] leadership is dead or in custody, its membership is on the run, and its capabilities sharply degraded. More than 3,400 . . . suspects have been arrested or detained worldwide."[42]

Although bin Laden and Ayman al-Zawahiri escaped, the United States had captured or killed three of the four top leaders at the time of September 11. The greatest kills came in November 2001, with Mohammed Atef, al Qaeda's military commander in Afghanistan, and Qaed Salim al-Harethi, who planned the attack on the USS *Cole*, and four companions in Yemen.[43] But far more important were the captures of Zubaydah, who planned the thwarted Millennium bombing in Amman, and Khalid Sheikh Mohammed, who masterminded September 11, in Pakistan on March 23, 2002, and March 1, 2003, respectively. Under vigorous interrogation, both yielded intelligence that helped thwart plots and eliminate cells around the world.

Zubaydah's confessions were especially intriguing. He was shot during his capture and was somehow made to believe that he was safely in Saudi hands. He revealed that key members of the Saudi ruling elite had conspired with al Qaeda. Not long after, three of those he named died under mysterious circumstances.

Overall bilateral rather than multilateral counterterrorist measures have worked better. After September 11, Washington worked openly with twenty-three foreign intelligence agencies and covertly with scores of others. Among the covert relations were Syria, Libya, and Sudan. All three countries had already cut back their own nurturing of terrorists, or freedom fighters, depending on one's perspective. Sudan had actually harbored bin Laden from 1992 to 1996, before expelling his group and severing ties. Yet with their radicalized societies, none wanted to associate openly with America's counterterrorist campaign.

In all, the United States and its allies mastered a virtuous counterterrorist cycle whereby the more terrorists they took, the more intelligence they received, which led to more suspects being taken, and so forth. That intelligence let America and its allies to stymie several dozen terrorist plots since September 11, the most potentially serious of which was the Heathrow Plot to set off bombs on seven airliners over the Atlantic Ocean.

With time journalists' questions about when Bush would fulfill his promise to take bin Laden "dead or alive" became ever-more embarrassing to the White House. The Bush administration increasingly played down the importance of bin Laden and al Qaeda and emphasized its broader war on terrorism. To reinforce that message, the Bush administration pointedly ordered the CIA to shut down its special bin Laden unit in 2006.

But the Bush administration was no more successful in its war on terror. Statistics belied White House claims that they were making steady progress.[44] In reality, the number of terrorist attacks around the world has soared since the American invasion of Iraq:

Year	2001	2002	2003	2004	2005	2006	2007
Global Attacks	348	198	190	1,907	11,153	20,573	14,499
Global Dead	3,572	725	307	9,321	14,618	14,552	22,685

Source: Patterns of Global Terrorism, State Department annual reports, www.state.gov.

But from the neoconservative perspective, what was important was not these hard statistics of failure but the administration's ability to spin the illusion of success for most Americans. In contrast to the neglect of Bush and his fellow neoconservatives, Obama promised that he would focus on destroying bin Laden and al Qaeda. Obama was as good as his word. Bin Laden is dead, and al Qaeda is dying a prolonged death.

9

The War for American Hearts and Minds

Whenever the people are well informed they can be entrusted with their own government.
—Thomas Jefferson

Democracies die behind closed doors. . . . When government begins closing doors, it selectively controls information rightfully belonging to the people. Selective information is misinformation.
—Judge Damon Keith, U.S. Sixth Circuit Court of Appeals

The Puppet-Masters and Dereliction of Duty

The Bush administration's foreign policies may not have won many hearts and minds overseas, but they largely succeeded at home. Although the president's approval rating steadily declined from 90 percent shortly after September 11 to around 25 percent when he left office, along the way the conservatives managed to push most of their agenda through Congress, the bureaucracy, and the courts. Many reasons explain those victories. Among the most vital was the brilliance with which the conservatives manipulated the mass media and public opinion.

Yet that feat was not as difficult as it might seem. The average American is generally more naïve, ignorant, fearful, hateful, and credulous than people in other democracies. Unable to understand the complexities of the array of problems facing the nation and the relations among them, most succumbed enthusiastically to the fear-and-smear tactics of conservatives in and beyond Washington.[1]

The mainstream media, which has the professional and moral duty to inform the public of critical issues and perspectives, largely failed to do so.[2] For nearly all eight years that the Bush team held power, the mainstream media was a lap-dog rather than watchdog because they put profit before professionalism. The Bush administration's fear-and-smear campaign intimidated the mass media to the point where it sacrificed professionalism on the altar of profits. To that end, on one vital issue after another, the media pulled its punches or outright buried stories.

The mainstream media's tilt toward Bush and the conservative agenda did not begin after September 11. That conservative bias was actually well estab-lished by the 2000 presidential candidate debates when Al Gore was held to a far higher standard. All Bush had to do was stay in the ring with Gore, who needed a knockout punch to be named the victor. Then the mainstream media accepted without question the Supreme Court's 5 to 4 ruling in *Bush v. Gore* that handed the election to the conservative candidate. That ruling followed a 7 to 2 ruling that declared the Florida election a gross violation of the rights of equal protection and one person/one vote. The logical next step should have been to declare the Florida election invalid, which would have allowed Al Gore, the candidate with the most electoral votes, to be the president. The mainstream media ignored these blows to American democracy. Instead, as presidential scholar Fred Greenstein explained, "the media coverage of Bush's inauguration focused on the dignified pomp of the occasion, not the legitimacy of the process that led up it."[3] The main-stream media's honeymoon with the new president extended for months longer than for his predecessor and was only gently waning by late summer.

Then came the horrors of September 11. Conservatives immediately launched an all-out offensive against their critics that would persist through the Bush team's years in power and beyond. They ruthlessly pounded the mainstream print and electronic media for any stories that put professionalism before shallow patriotism and blatant propaganda. The rhetoric they wielded was as skilled as it was intellectually and morally dishonest. They asserted that objective report-ing and tough questioning was not just unpatriotic but outright treasonous. They demanded whether the "right to know" was greater than "somebody's right to live." In other words, anyone who believed that a transparent government was

an essential foundation of a liberal democracy was actually allied with terrorists. Questioning the president and his advisers for their behavior leading up to
or following September 11, or showing dead, wounded, or displaced civilians
in Afghanistan and elsewhere—collateral damage, as the Pentagon called it—
became an act of collaboration with America's enemies. Peter Jennings, ABC's
news anchor, provoked conservative table pounding and name calling when he
dared to suggest that "the country looks up to the president and on occasions like
this to be reassuring to our nation. Some presidents do it well, some presidents
don't." The conservatives accused Jennings of criticizing Bush even though the
news anchor never mentioned which presidents he meant.[4]

The Bush administration stepped up its bullying by demanding more self-
censorship. The White House insisted that the press not publish or broadcast full
texts of al Qaeda statements. In a coordinated offensive against the mainstream
media, National Security Adviser Condoleezza Rice attacked television while
Press Secretary Ari Fleischer assaulted newspapers. Rice claimed that broadcasting unedited statements by bin Laden and other al Qaeda spokesmen was unpatriotic and allowed the terrorists to send secret messages to their foreign agents.
The Bush team did not stop there. White House adviser Karl Rove attacked presidential historian Robert Dallek for daring to criticize Bush's immediate handling
of September 11.

As if that onslaught was not intimidating enough, the mainstream media faced
even fiercer competition from the right-wing mass media. Fox News, the jewel in
the crown of Rupert Murdoch's media empire, was the flagship for hundreds of
conservative television and radio stations. Fox unashamedly marketed the Bush
administration's policies and the broader conservative agenda, thus making an
Orwellian mockery of its slogan "fair and balanced." Roger Ailes, who founded
Fox News in 1996 and served as its president, was a frequent White House guest
and consistent adviser. Fox spiced up its programs with tabloid sensationalism
and the bellowings of such far right–wing ranters as Bill O'Reilly. That "big time
wrestling" approach to news was enormously popular. After September 11, Fox
surged past CNN in the number of viewers.[5]

Thus the four mainstream television private news networks—CNN, CBS,
NBC, and ABC—faced a terrible dilemma. Should they cling to professional

standards and watch helplessly as their viewers, along with their advertisers and profits, steadily eroded? Or should they "Foxify" to quell that erosion? A Pew Research Center survey of fifteen hundred adult television viewers offered an encouraging finding. Only 30 percent claimed that they preferred biased to balanced news. But that figure was not reflected in the actual television market, as Fox's share steadily swelled.[6]

The mainstream broadcasters knuckled under to the bullying and announced self-censorship on October 11, 2001, exactly a month after the attack. During the next half dozen critical war years, they proved incapable of providing their usual balanced coverage as they literally rallied around the flag. With the Stars and Strips fluttering behind them, newscasters reinforced their softball presentations of Bush administration policies. CNN went so far as to require that any reports about American bombings of enemy positions be accompanied by reminders of September 11, as if the average viewer was too thick-skulled to make that connection on his own. ABC News president David Westin actually apologized for suggesting that reporting the attack on the Pentagon should be objective. Just as the mainstream media had turned a blind eye to the legitimacy of the Supreme Court's rulings that handed the 2000 election to Bush, it just as studiously avoided raising any questions over the Bush administration's responsibility for the September 11 attacks, despite all the warnings by Richard Clarke, George Tenet, and other experts. Thereafter the Bush administration would be beyond serious criticism for several years until the utter ineptness of its handling of the Iraq War, Hurricane Katrina, and dozens of other problems, caused shifts in public opinion that proved impossible to ignore.[7]

Even satiric comic strips did not escape censorship. New York's *Daily News* banned Aaron McGruder's *Boondocks* comic strip after dialogue suggested that President Ronald Reagan's policies were partly responsible for anti-American terrorism. Other satirists censored themselves. After the September 11 attack, Gary Trudeau withheld a week's worth of strips mocking President Bush's ignorance and disinterest in the world.[8]

The Bush administration even tried to pressure Hollywood to join its propaganda machine. On November 11, 2001, Karl Rove met with about fifty Hollywood executives in Los Angeles. Several possible Hollywood contributions were discussed, including films and television shows, along with movie stars making public announcements about the war. Little came from the meeting. A group of producers, directors, and actors formed the Hollywood 9/11 committee. Their first project was a montage of patriotic images gleaned from scores of films and shown before features. Muhammad Ali was enlisted to explain the war to Muslims in a short film. But the initial war in Afghanistan was over before other schemes could be realized.[9]

The biggest conservative Hollywood coup came with the six-hour, made-for-television movie *The Path to 9/11* that ABC aired without commercials on two nights in September 2006. The screenplay was written and produced by right-wing activist Cyrus Nowrasteh in a way that blamed the Clinton administration for September 11 and whitewashed the Bush administration. To these related ends, the movie included made-up scenes and excluded actual events like the warnings that Bush and his key officials received from the outgoing Clinton administration, Clarke, and Tenet that al Qaeda posed an imminent and dangerous threat to the United States. This blatant propaganda provoked impotent outrage among former Clinton White House officials and experts within and beyond government.

In the mainstream media only those few with backbones and an undying devotion to the First Amendment resisted. MSNBC president Erik Sorenson lamented that "any misstep and you can get into trouble with these guys and have the Patriotism Police hunt you down. These are hard jobs. Just getting the facts straight is monumentally difficult. We don't want to wonder if we are saluting properly. Was I supposed to use the three-fingered salute today?"[10]

There was a definite double standard between what the White House and the press could report. For instance, Bush promised after September 11 to "follow the money as a trail to the terrorists. . . . We're putting banks and financial institutions around the world on notice—we will work with their governments, ask them to freeze or block the terrorists' ability to access funds in foreign accounts." In doing so, the president put the terrorists on notice that they had better find more secure means of saving and transferring money. But then, more than four years later, Bush blasted others for doing what he himself had done: "There can be no excuse for anyone entrusted with vital information to leak it—and no excuse for any newspaper to print it." Although he singled out the *New York Times* for his attack, the *Wall Street Journal* and the *Los Angeles Times* had also reported on the government's SWIFT Program that tracks the financial transactions of cooperating banks. In reality, al Qaeda and other terrorist groups were undoubtedly well aware that the United States and its allies would cooperate in wielding the most sophisticated possible means to track their money, even if Bush had not informed them shortly after September 11.[11]

While no reasonable person would object to tracking terrorist funding, the SWIFT Program had a much more controversial side. The federal government investigated the financial transactions and accounts of Americans without warrants to do so. Critics blasted the *New York Times* for its reporting—conservatives were incensed that the story was aired at all, and progressives that the story was not aired sooner. Indeed Bill Keller, the *New York Times* executive editor, had learned of the program as early as the summer of 2004 but withheld it until December 15, 2005, more than a year after the 2004 election. Keller claimed that he buried the story so he would not affect the election, but of course in doing so he helped Bush and the conservative movement.[12]

Among the mainstream media, the conservatives faced a lone holdout that maintained strict professional standards of journalism and ethics—PBS, which conservatives mobilized to destroy. For the hatchet man, Bush appointed Kenneth Tomlinson as PBS's chair. Tomlinson in turn packed the ranks with ideologues including Patricia Harrison, the former co-chair of the Republican National Committee, and Cheryl Halpern, a Republican Party fundraiser. They cut back Bill Moyers' Now Program of tough, in-depth investigative journalism from an hour to thirty minutes and gave the half hour to Paul Gigot, the editor of the *Wall Street Journal*, to propagate that newspaper's right-wing editorial slant.

As if bullying the mainstream media were not egregious enough, the Bush administration actually planted false news stories and false reporters in the mass media. During the ten months leading up to April 2006, at least sixty-nine television stations actually broadcast "news" segments that were packaged by twenty federal bureaucracies. And then there was the revelation about "Jeff Gannon" (real name James Guckert), an accredited member of the White House press club who lobbed softball questions at Bush officials from 2003 until he was outed in 2004. He worked for a website called Talon News, which was a front company for the Republican Party, but he was outed for more than false journalism. Apparently, he was a gay porn star and a two-hundred-dollar-a-night escort with his own website. The Gannon scandal was only the most tawdry. Five other pseudo-journalists were exposed as Bush team propagandists planted in the news media.[13]

The conservatives were not content merely to eviscerate the mainstream media for exposing their foibles. Bush joined the chorus calling for prosecuting under the Espionage Act of 1917 the *New York Times* journalists who received a Pulitzer Prize for revealing the administration's system of secret prisons in Europe and elsewhere around the world. Under that law it is a felony for someone to release "information the possessor has reason to believe could be used to the injury of the United States." The law clearly violated the constitutional rights to freedom of the press and speech.

The mainstream media was hardly the only target of right-wing rage. On October 9, 2001, Bush condemned certain members of Congress for leaking what he claimed was critical, secret information. Like Joe McCarthy, Bush never revealed just who was behind the alleged leak or just what was leaked. Congressional leaders were just as puzzled with Bush's allegations as their predecessors were over those of McCarthy. Nonetheless the president threatened not to provide any more information to anyone in Congress. Meek suggestions by Democrats and moderate Republicans that Bush's refusal to share information would violate the Constitution, along with various other laws, provoked more condemnations from conservatives. However, Bush did take a step back when he declared that he would share information only with the eight senior majority and minority members of Congress, known as the Gang of Eight. More grumblings from prominent Republican moderates got Bush finally to agree to obey the law and share relevant information with the full Senate and House foreign relations, intelligence, and armed service committees.[14]

The practice among conservatives in general, and the Republican Party in particular, of making unsubstantiated and inflammatory accusations that slander the patriotism of their opponents has become known as swift boating. The term came from the "Swift Vets and POWs for Truth, a conservative group that, during the 2004 election year, accused Democratic presidential candidate John Kerry of having lied about his war record in Vietnam and thus being undeserving of the Silver and Bronze Stars he was awarded there. Kerry was not the only prominent Vietnam War veteran that the conservatives Swift Boated. After Kerry, the most notorious target was Max Cleland, a Democratic senator from Georgia who had won Silver and Bronze Stars and lost three limbs in Vietnam.

As always, irony lurked in the conservative accusations. Virtually all the leading neoconservatives had dodged the draft to avoid serving in the Vietnam War, including Bush himself. Throughout Bush's political career, his backers had promoted him as some sort of all-American hero, even though his father's political connections had wrangled him a spot in the Texas Air National Guard and thus enabled him to avoid possibly being drafted and sent to Vietnam.

At times it was difficult to determine whether such slander campaigns were deliberate lies or a lesser crime of willful ignorance and self-delusion. For instance, was Bush lying when he offered this justification for ordering the invasion of Iraq: "When the inspectors first went into Iraq and were denied, finally denied access, a report came out of the Atomic—the IAEA—that they were six months away from developing a weapon. I don't know what more evidence we need."[15] Each segment of that sentence was not only wrong, but the exact opposite was true.

The Bush team's crusade against freedom of the press and speech was most viciously wielded when it deliberately leaked information that Valerie Plame, the wife of career diplomat and former deputy chief of mission to Iraq Joe Wilson, was an undercover CIA operative. On July 6, 2003, an essay of Wilson's called "What I Did Not Find in Niger" was published on the *New York Times* editorial page. Wilson revealed that the CIA had sent him to Niger in 2002 to investigate the allegations that Iraq was purchasing uranium yellowcake from that country. In reality the rumor was a hoax, complete with crudely forged documents. Nonplused by the revelation, the Bush administration continued to claim that Iraq was buying uranium for a nuclear weapons program.

Although it is a felony to reveal the name of a clandestine CIA officer, the only person to go to jail in that case was Judith Miller, a *New York Times* reporter who refused a court order to reveal who within the White House leaked the information about Valerie Plame to her. Miller spent eighty-five days in prison before she was let out after Scooter Libby, Vice President Cheney's chief of staff, agreed to release her from her pledge of confidentiality. Judge Thomas Hogan, a conservative appointee, also threatened to lock up Matthew Cooper, a *Time* magazine reporter. Fortunately Cooper's source let him off the confidentiality hook before the reporter was thrown in prison. To pile irony upon irony, Miller never even wrote about the leak, while Cooper merely wrote about the various theories over why the administration leaked the information and who leaked it. Not surprisingly, the right-wing pundit Robert Novak, who originally revealed Valerie Plame as a CIA operative in his newspaper column, escaped prison.[16]

Federal prosecutor Patrick Fitzgerald did announce on October 28, 2005, an indictment containing five counts against Libby, the point man in leaking that information to at least a half dozen reporters. The charges, however, did not address the felony of revealing a CIA operative. Instead Libby was indicted for obstruction of justice, perjury, and related crimes. No charges were issued against Cheney, Rove, or Deputy Secretary of State Richard Armitage, even though they had also participated in the leaks. On July 13, 2006, Joseph Wilson and Valerie Plame sued Cheney, Libby, and Rove for conspiring to destroy Plame's career by leaking her identity as a CIA operative, but the issue died because the Bush administration refused to release the information that would have proven their case.

That was not the Bush administration's only obstruction of justice in that case. Although a jury did find Libby guilty on four of the five counts on March 6, 2007, Bush commuted Libby's prison sentence on July 2, 2007. That was the first and last felony conviction for a member of Bush's inner circle. For eight long years, most members of Congress, the courts, the mainstream media, and the public either ignored or covered up rather than prosecuted an outrageous array of the Bush administration's high crimes and misdemeanors.

Capturing American Hearts and Minds

Perhaps the most chilling result of the conservative movement's propaganda and violation of civil liberties is that so many Americans supported it. That was not surprising in the immediate aftermath of September 11. A *New York Times*/CBS survey in November 2001 found that Bush's approval rating had soared from 55 percent to 90 percent. The majority of Americans also embraced Bush's policies that violated the Constitution, with 77 percent agreeing that it was a good idea to detain suspected terrorists indefinitely without trial, while 16 percent were opposed; 72 percent agreed it was a good idea to eavesdrop on conversations between jailed terrorist suspects and their lawyers, while only 22 percent disagreed; and 64 percent thought it would be a good idea to curtail civil rights guaranteed by the Constitution to fight terrorism while 29 percent were opposed. Only half of Americans supported their nation's judicial system—they preferred trying terrorist suspects in civilian over military courts by 50 percent to 46 percent. Americans were similarly split over whether restrictions on civil liberties would directly affect them, with 13 percent not concerned, 22 percent not very concerned, 32 percent somewhat concerned, and 33 percent very concerned. They were just as equally divided over whether the antiterrorist laws were excessive or weak, 45 percent to 43 percent. The conservatives were able to maintain that support during the run up to the Iraq War and during the rapid destruction of Saddam Hussein's regime.[17]

An anthrax scare atop September 11 undoubtedly affected those results. The first reports of a biological attack appeared in late October when traces of anthrax were found in the mail center serving the CIA, Supreme Court, and Walter Reed Army Medical Center. Anthrax-laden letters were sent to Senate Majority Leader Tom Daschle and NBC news anchor Tom Brokaw, who shared centrist political beliefs. With such targets the most likely suspect is an extreme right-wing American. The types of anthrax varied, with the most sophisticated strain sent to Daschle. Although only five Americans died, that scare undoubtedly made most Americans all the more willing to give unquestioned support to the Bush administration.

In all, George W. Bush and his fellow conservatives won a decisive victory for the hearts and minds of the American people.

10

The War for International Hearts and Minds

If we turn this into a PBS documentary—seesawing on every
side and being balanced—that's not promoting democracy.
—Rep. Ileana Ros-Lehtinen (R-Fla.)

Soft Power

Image matters. One's image is part of the soft side of one's total power. Those
with favorable images are more likely to attract, and those with disreputable images are more likely to repel, potential followers. Thus those who understand
the nature of power do what they can to favorably manipulate their image in the
hearts and minds of others.

More than any other type of war, a revolutionary struggle is generally won by
the side that can mobilize the majority of a targeted population against the other.
Since September 11 the United States and al Qaeda have been engaged in a global
tug-of-war for Muslim and non-Muslim hearts and minds. To destroy al Qaeda
and its affiliates, the United States must rally as many people as possible to its
side. Although al Qaeda is mostly focused on trying to mobilize over 1.5 billion
Muslims around the world into a revolution against a global system dominated by
modernity and Western civilization, it is certainly well aware of the importance
of public opinion in non-Muslim countries, even if it can do little to shape those
outlooks.

Virtually no policy of the Bush administration's so-called global war on terror has escaped criticism. Some of the harshest condemnation has slammed the

193

White House's mishandling of that global struggle to win over hearts and minds, especially on such issues as the Iraq War, Abu Ghraib, Guantanamo Bay, renditions, and torture. Public opinion polls during the Bush administration's eight years in power revealed a plunge in the proportion of people with favorable views of the United States not just in Muslim countries but all around the world, including countries that are traditional allies. And that matters because the more a country and its policies are despised, the more likely that in a war its potential allies may sit on the fence or join the other side.

Unlike his predecessor, Obama understands how crucial capturing hearts and minds is for success in any revolutionary war, and he has made repairing America's sullied image a key policy. Yet to date, that effort has regained little lost ground.[1]

Heart, Minds, and the War against Al Qaeda

The September 11 atrocities initially stirred widespread sympathy for America around the world. Nonetheless the Bush team faced a tough challenge in capitalizing on that empathy in the struggle against al Qaeda and its affiliates. During their first nine months in power, the president and his fellow conservatives had alienated countless governments and peoples with their bellicose table-pounding, chest-thumping attitudes and behaviors on crucial global security, economic, legal, and environmental issues, which defied and offended allies and friends, went against common sense, and hurt American interests abroad. As a result, most people, even within allied countries, remained skeptical or even hostile toward the Bush administration.

To its credit, the Bush administration did recognize the importance of that global tug-of-war war for hearts and minds. The White House launched a public relations campaign that preceded, accompanied, and followed its initial war in Afghanistan. The key battleground in that struggle was the global twenty-four-hour news cycle. To favorably spin that cycle the Bush team set up round-the-clock news war rooms in the White House, vice president's office, and Departments of State, Defense, and the Interior. In late October 2001 the Bush and Blair administrations set up a Coalitions Coordination Center (CCC) to choreograph the American and British hearts and minds offensive. Blair's communications director, Alistair Campbell worked with Karl Rove and Bush advisor Karen Hughes to promote as favorable an array of news as possible.

Yet, at the same time, the Bush team committed nefarious acts that, when revealed, alienated countless people around the world. For instance, they tried to convert the Voice of America (VOA), the United States' overseas broadcasting institution, from balanced to biased reporting. In doing so, they deliberately reversed the policy of the Clinton administration. The result was to harm rather than enhance American power and honor.

To protect the VOA's integrity and thus the perceived credibility and legitimacy of its broadcasts, the Clinton White House had reconstituted the governing board so that it was autonomous from its parent organization, the U.S. Information Agency (USIA). The VOA's charter proclaims its mission to be "a reliable and authoritative source of news" based on "accurate, objective, and comprehensive" reporting. The VOA programs in fifty-three languages are often the only source of objective information beleaguered peoples can get about their collective fates. Two out of three Afghans listen to VOA broadcasts on a daily basis.

The Bush administration tried to force the VOA to conform to its ideological line by accusing it of siding with al Qaeda. The excuse was that the VOA Pashtun and Dari services had used some excerpts from speeches of Taliban leader Mohammad Omar. The point man in that attack on the VOA's credibility was Robert Reilly, the network's newly appointed director and an outspoken conservative. He tried to revive a policy that he had initiated two decades earlier when he had worked for the Reagan administration, based on the idea that "it is time that we recaptured the words 'balance' and 'objectivity' from the rhetorical excess of the left and reestablished them to stand for the full truth about this country—the last and best hope of freedom in the world." Reilly's crusade drew enthusiastic support from congressional conservatives. Florida representative Ileana Ros-Lehtinen, who chaired the Subcommittee on International Operations and Human Rights, made the Orwellian assertion that "if we turn this into a PBS documentary—seesawing on every side and being balanced—that's not promoting democracy." The conservatives partly got their wish.

The Pentagon joined the battle for international hearts and minds in 2002 when it proudly unveiled the Office of Strategic Influence, whose chief duty would be to plant propaganda stories in mass media around the world. That announcement at once made suspect any story favorable to the Pentagon or United States. The criticism by realists on practical grounds and humanitarians on moral grounds of such a blatant policy was deafening. Within days, the Pentagon sheepishly declared that it had abolished the propaganda office. But the damage had been done. It was assumed that the Pentagon had simply renamed and hidden the office. Indeed that was the case. Recognizing that the Pentagon's propaganda office was a counterterrorist liability rather than an asset, President Obama actually did close it in April 2009. Or at least the White House said it had.[2]

The Bush White House faced a news organization that could either be a formidable rival or source of power in the global war for Arab hearts and minds. With its twenty-four-hour broadcasts, 350 editors, 35 bureaus around the world, 40 million viewers, the Al Jazeera television news network (based in Doha, Qatar) is a Middle East version of Fox News—as popular as it is biased in its reporting. Founded in 1996, Al Jazeera is among the rare Arab networks that is not a mere government loudspeaker. Yet, like Fox News, Al Jazeera has the trappings, but lacks the substance, of a professional news organization. The distinguished scholar Fouad Ajami dismissed Al Jazeera as little more than a forum for radical Islamic and anti-Western propaganda.[3]

Within days of the bombings, Al Jazeera became an essential arena in the propaganda war between al Qaeda and the United States. Several videotapes of bin Laden and other terrorist leaders exhorting their followers to jihad were slipped to Al Jazeera and broadcast in full, including one that Al Jazeera agreed not to air until immediately after the United States began bombing.

Despite Al Jazeera's slant, it did provide airtime for alternative views. It took several weeks before realists in the White House could convince their dominant conservative colleagues how vital Al Jazeera could be for broadcasting the Bush administration's positions to the Arab world. Colin Powell was the first to be interviewed by Al Jazeera, followed by Donald Rumsfeld and Condoleezza Rice. Rumsfeld explained the central message: "This effort is not against Afghanistan, it's not against any race or any religion. It is against terrorism and terrorists." When bin Laden's fifth message appeared on Al Jazeera, a State Department spokesman, Christopher Ross, refuted him point by point in fluent classical

Arabic. While those belated efforts on Al Jazeera are to be commended, the Bush White House neglected opportunities to present its views on more moderate Arab mediums such as the London-based Middle East Broadcasting Center and the Lebanese Broadcasting Corporation International.[4]

America received an unexpected ally when a panel of five prominent Islamic scholars issued a fatwa on September 27, 2001, that not only denounced terrorism but asserted that Muslims had a duty to apprehend terrorists. The scholars rendered that opinion in response to a plea for guidance by American army captain Abdul Rasheed Muhammad, a Muslim chaplain. The fatwa was especially surprising since one of the panel's members was Sheikh Yusuf al-Qaradawi, an adviser to Egypt's militant Muslim Brotherhood who was outspokenly anti-American. The other clerics were the Syrian Haytham al-Khayyat and three Egyptians, Tariq al-Bishri, Muhammad al-Awa, and Fahmi Houaydi. The fatwa stated:

We find it necessary to apprehend the true perpetrators of these crimes, as well as those who aid and abet them through incitement, financing, and other support. They must be brought to justice in an impartial court of law and punish them appropriately, so that it could act as a deterrent to them and to others like them who easily slay the lives of innocents, destroy properties, and terrorize people. Hence it's a duty on Muslims to participate in this effort with all possible means.[5]

But the fatwa of those scholars and the broadcasts of moderate Arab stations were tiny islands of reason in a sea of countless Muslim newspapers, television and radio stations, pamphlets, books, and websites that spewed torrents of the most outrageous conspiracy theories. It was widely reported and believed that Israel actually attacked the World Trade Center and the Pentagon; supposedly all four thousand Jews working in the Twin Towers stayed away on September 11. Ibrahim Nafie, editor of the semi-official Egyptian newspaper *Al Ahram*, declared that the United States was deliberately dropping poisoned food in mine fields to kill the Afghan people.[6]

America scored a victory in the propaganda war when an unedited videotape of a November 9 meeting of bin Laden and some associates was found in a

Kandahar safe house. This was the smoking gun proving bin Laden's complicity in September 11. The terrorist leader is by turns boastful, modest, relaxed, and assertive, but confident throughout. If he was at all nervous about fighting the world's sole superpower, he did not show it. Most incriminating were his statements that the attack's death toll surpassed his expectations and that most of the terrorists did not know their exact missions until that morning.[7]

The White House released the tape on December 14, following more than two weeks of debate over whether to do so. The neoconservatives feared the tape might contain hidden messages or enhance bin Laden's popularity, be dismissed as a fake, or, worst of all, cater to what they insisted was a false public right to know. The realists recognized the propaganda equivalent of a fifteen-thousand-pound bomb when they saw it. In all it took months after September 11 before the Bush administration got traction in the global propaganda war. Yet here, too, was the inevitable dilemma. The lawyerly talking-heads approach whereby Powell, Rice, Rumsfeld, and other officials stated America's case on Al Jazeera and other television networks was vital, yet it simply could not compete with the image of devastated villages and dead children in Afghanistan and Palestine beamed around the world. That daily parade of horrors overcame the images of the World Trade Center's destruction in the minds of not just Muslims but people everywhere. The videotapes of a reposed Osama bin Laden, cradling a Kalashnikov, sipping tea, and calling on the faithful to jihad contrasted with the terse statements of White House officials.

Two forces briefly turned the tide in the global propaganda war. Most important was the devastating impact of American military power on routing the Taliban and al Qaeda. While that victory won few converts, it did convince many terrorist sympathizers in the futility of their cause. Then there was that image of an unguarded, callous, at times even frivolous bin Laden. Although most Muslims dismissed the tape as fake or doctored, these imaged eroded some of the leader's mystique.

But then, typically, the Bush administration committed acts that squandered this public relations coup. Bush and his fellow conservatives were not just openly contemptuous of international law, but they repeatedly and gleefully violated it with impunity, most blatantly in their humiliation and torture of prisoners and with the war against Iraq. These policies appalled law-abiding governments and publics around the world. Surveys indicated not just increasing opposition to the Bush administration but ever more virulent anti-Americanism. Like the boy who repeatedly cried wolf, the United States under the Bush White House suffered an widening credibility gap as discerning people noted the contrast between America's ideals and policies. The Pew Global Attitudes Project (PGAP) revealed that countries' favorable views of the United States plummeted during the Bush years, although there were some exceptions. The approval of America's three key European allies all dropped sharply from 2000 to 2008, with Britain's falling from 83 percent to 53 percent, Germany from 78 percent to 31 percent, and France from 62 percent to 42 percent. As a result, many formal allies either limited their support or shuffled along reluctantly and red-faced with White House demands.

Hearts, Minds, and Hypocrisies

Among the more formidable obstacles Washington faces in winning hearts and minds around the world are America's own double standards. For instance, until the Iraq War, no issue enraged Arabs in particular, and Muslims in general, more than the Israeli-Palestinian conflict. Today most Arab and other Muslim states accept officially or unofficially Israel's right to exist but demand that the Palestinians have their own state. Indeed, this two-state "solution" appears to have won over virtually all governments except the two that count the most— Israel and Hamas.

Washington could alleviate considerable rage in the Middle East by brokering a viable two-state solution to the Israeli-Palestinian conflict. But the Bush administration abandoned the traditional "honest broker" role that the United States had pursued since the 1973 Yom Kippur War. Instead Bush and his fellow conservatives openly embraced their fellow Israeli conservatives.

Obama has made negotiating a two-state peace between the Israelis and Palestinians a priority. But any peace seems remote as the number of Israeli settlers and settlements swells in the West Bank, while the anti-terrorist barrier around the West Bank appears to be Israel's de facto boundary. Meanwhile the Israeli population is marching further to the political right. Tel Aviv has rejected any notion of dismantling its settlements or barrier. Peace between the Israelis and Palestinians appears to be as remote as ever.

A related dilemma has been Washington's inability to resolve the dilemma that one man's terrorist is another man's freedom fighter. For most Muslims, Hezbollah and Hamas are freedom fighters, while Israel is a state that conducts terrorism. When Washington unconditionally backs Tel Aviv, the United States is seen as collaborating with terrorism. Virtually all Muslims and much of the rest of the humanity viewed Israel's wars against Hezbollah in southern Lebanon and Hamas in Gaza as blatant terrorism. Tel Aviv argued that it did everything possible in those campaigns to minimize civilian deaths

The American double standard over nuclear weapons angers countless numbers of people around the world, not just Muslims. Washington has consistently turned a blind eye to Israel's nuclear arsenal and since 9/11 has accepted the nuclear arsenals of Pakistan and India while condemning the nuclear ambitions for "rogue" or "axis of evil" states like Iraq, Iran, and North Korea.

And then there is Saudi Arabia. Experts puzzle over just how to categorize America's relationship with the kingdom. Although Washington and Riyadh call each other allies, the Saudis clearly play both sides of the political fence as suits their interests. Meanwhile, billions of Saudi dollars, both official and unofficial, have been invested overseas in mosques and madrassas that expound Islamism. Hundreds of millions of dollars have been passed to al Qaeda and an array of other Islamist terrorist groups. Within Saudi Arabia itself, the schools indoctrinate children with a fervent Islamism that condemns modernization and America. But the global economy's addiction to oil prevents any president from confronting those realities.

Neoconservatives champion democracy as the solution to the Middle's East's vicious cycle of problems. They believed that their crusade in Iraq would not only impose a democratic revolution from above on that country, but that in turn it would inspire democratic revolutions across the Middle East and beyond. Meanwhile the Bush administration pressured governments across the regions to hold elections and release political prisoners.

Alas, in trying to realize that ideal, Bush and the conservatives gave democracy a bad name. After failing to find WMD and al Qaeda links in Iraq, the Bush administration switched the justification for its war into a crusade for democracy.

The result was to lose countless more hearts and minds to Islamism and anti-Westernism.

That was no paradox. Few people around the world failed to notice the glaring gap between the Bush administration's democratic rhetoric and its autocratic practices. The notion of imposing democracy at gunpoint on Afghans and Iraqis was derided as hypocritical, either cynical or naïve, and ultimately self-defeating. Here again the conservatives mistook style for substance. Elections do not equal democracy. Indeed an election can destroy a democracy if it brings to power those determined to do so.

Realists would have been appalled by the Bush team's democratic crusade even had it not been accompanied by such glaring hypocrisy. They blasted the conservatives for their ignorance of history and for the belief that America's unique experiences, culture, values, and institutions could be universalized.

That old adage "be careful what you wish for" certainly rings true for the Bush administration's pressure on authoritarian but friendly Muslim states to hold elections. More often than not the results did not bode well for democracy or American interests, especially as Hezbollah strengthened its popularity in Lebanon, Hamas took over the Gaza Strip, and the Muslim Brotherhood made gains in Egypt. Then came the Arab Spring of 2011, in which mass demonstration against dictatorship and for democracy erupted in Tunisia, Egypt, Bahrain, Yemen, Libya, and Syria. It remains to be seen whether genuine democracy, Islamism, or secular authoritarianism will triumph in each of those countries.

What has been clear to the world are the flaws embedded in America's version of democracy. The Supreme Court's five-justice conservative majority declared Bush the winner of the 2000 election despite the reality that more people across the United States and in the disputed Florida count turned out to vote for Democratic candidate Al Gore. The Bush administration then used the excuse of the September 11 terrorist attacks to violate the Constitution, along with an array of American and international treaties, for the purposes of warrantless wiretaps, detentions without charges, and torture. Atop that was the conservatives' spoils-system and carpetbagger approach to government, whereby they used their power to reward their corporate sponsors with no-bid contracts, inside information, vast giveaways of money or public lands, and the violation, degradation, or elimination of laws and regulations to prevent such abuses. Most recently, the ultra-conservative Tea Party movement captured the Republican Party and helped them win a majority in the House of Representatives in the 2010 mid-term election. Republicans then went on to push the United States to the brink of financial default in the summer of 2011.

Hearts, Minds, and the Muslim World

To its credit, the Bush administration was able to distinguish Islam, the peaceful faith of a billion and a half people around the world, from Islamism, the revolutionary anti-Western movement. During several speeches the president tried to explain that difference. During his 2002 State of the Union, he explained: "The enemy of America is not our many Muslim friends; it is not our many Arab friends. Our enemy is a radical network of terrorists, and every government that supports them. We are not deceived by their pretences to piety."

Unfortunately the Bush team's behavior did not match the president's rhetoric. Nothing Bush and his colleagues did alienated more Muslim hearts and minds than the conservative crusade in Iraq. For Richard Clarke, the former counterterrorist chief, the consequences are severe: "We invaded and occupied an oil-rich Arab country that posed no threat to us, while paying scant time and attention to the Israeli-Palestinian problem. We delivered to al Qaeda the greatest recruitment propaganda imaginable and made it difficult for friendly Islamic governments to be seen working closely with us."[8]

The PGAP revealed differences within the Muslim world in reaction to Bush administration policies and other global events and trends. In the half-dozen years after September 11, America's standing fell in Egypt from 30 percent to 22 percent, in Turkey from 52 percent to 12 percent, in Jordan from 25 percent to 19 percent, and in Indonesia from 75 percent to 37 percent. But positive views of the United States actually rose in Lebanon from 36 percent to 51 percent and in Nigeria from 46 percent to 64 percent, although the span of Bush years varied.

The World Public Opinion survey published in 2007 found deeply entrenched anti-Americanism in four key Muslim countries whose governments generally work closely with the United States.

Nonetheless al Qaeda and its affiliates did have some vulnerabilities as revealed by surveys of select Muslim countries. The same survey found mixed attitudes toward al Qaeda in particular and terrorism in general.

TABLE 10.1

Views of the Current (2008) U.S. Government

	Favorable	Unfavorable
Morocco	16%	76%
Egypt	4%	93%
Pakistan	15%	67%
Indonesia	20%	66%

U.S. Goal to Weaken and Divide Islam

	Definitely/Probably	Definitely Not/Probably
Morocco	78%	11%
Egypt	92%	4%
Pakistan	73%	9%
Indonesia	73%	15%

U.S. Goal to Spread Christianity

	Definitely/Probably	Definitely Not/Probably Not
Morocco	67%	22%
Pakistan	64%	14%
Indonesia	61%	21%

Primary Goal of U.S. War on Terror

	Weaken, Divide Muslims	Political, Military Domination of Middle East Oil	Protect Itself from Terrorism
Morocco	33%	39%	19%
Egypt	31%	55%	9%
Pakistan	42%	26%	12%
Indonesia	29%	24%	23%

Approval of Attacks on U.S. Troops in Iraq

	Approve	Mixed Feelings	Disapprove
Morocco	68%	11%	14%
Egypt	91%	2%	4%
Pakistan	35%	13%	35%
Indonesia	19%	11%	61%

Approval of Attacks on U.S. Troops in Afghanistan

	Approve	Mixed Feelings	Disapprove
Morocco	61%	14%	17%
Egypt	91%	2%	4%
Pakistan	34%	14%	33%
Indonesia	19%	10%	59%

Approval of Attacks on U.S. Troops in Persian Gulf

	Approve	Mixed Feelings	Disapprove
Morocco	52%	19%	17%
Egypt	83%	3%	10%
Pakistan	32%	14%	57%

TABLE 10.2

Groups Favor al Qaeda Using Violence against Civilians

	Agree	Disagree
Morocco	66%	19%
Egypt	88%	7%
Pakistan	30%	35%
Indonesia	65%	21%

Support for Suicide Attacks against an Enemy

	Often Justified	Sometimes Justified	Rarely Justified	Never Justified
Morocco	16%	19%	19%	34%
Egypt	41%	19%	8%	28%
Pakistan	6%	11%	11%	62%
Indonesia	3%	12%	13%	68%

Attacks on Civilians in America

	Approve	Mixed Feelings	Disapprove
Morocco	7%	8%	78%
Egypt	6%	2%	91%
Pakistan	5%	13%	67%
Indonesia	4%	7%	75%

Attacks on Civilians in Europe

	Approve	Mixed Feelings	Disapprove
Morocco	6%	7%	82%
Egypt	4%	2%	93%
Pakistan	6%	14%	63%
Indonesia	3%	5%	78%

Attacks on U.S. Civilians working for U.S. Companies in Muslim Countries

	Approve	Mixed Feelings	Disapprove
Morocco	7%	13%	73%
Egypt	6%	2%	90%
Pakistan	7%	16%	58%
Indonesia	3%	7%	76%

Feelings toward Osama bin Laden

	Positive	Mixed	Negative
Morocco	27%	26%	21%
Egypt	40%	34%	20%
Pakistan	27%	24%	15%
Indonesia	21%	32%	19%

(continued on next page)

Table 10.2 continued

Effects of 9/11 on Islamic World

	Positive	Mixed	Negative
Morocco	12%	13%	62%
Egypt	23%	3%	70%
Pakistan	8%	6%	50%
Indonesia	19%	4%	56%

Support for Groups that Attack Americans

	Disapprove of Some	Approve of All	Approve
Morocco	44%	35%	3%
Egypt	26%	51%	15%
Pakistan	43%	10%	5%
Indonesia	52%	18%	6%

	Average	Morocco	Egypt	Pakistan	Indonesia
Views of al Qaeda	15%	9%	25%	9%	15%
Support Attacks on U.S. and Share its Attitudes Toward U.S.	23%	31%	31%	7%	24%
Oppose Its Attacks but Share Many Attitudes Toward U.S.	26%	26%	31%	17%	29%
Oppose Its Attacks and Do Not Share Its Attitudes	37%	35%	14%	66%	32%

As for general values, the respondents overwhelmingly valued traditional Islamic values and rejected Western values.

Goal to Keep Western Values Out of Muslim Countries

	Agree Strongly	Agree Somewhat
Morocco	33%	31%
Egypt	80%	11%
Pakistan	45%	22%
Indonesia	40%	38%

Goal for the Strict Application of Sharia in all Muslim Countries

	Agree Strongly	Agree Somewhat
Morocco	35%	41%
Egypt	50%	24%
Pakistan	54%	25%
Indonesia	17%	36%

These results mostly reveal an enormous gap in values along with distrust and outright aggression toward the Western world. Yet three attitudes offered the chance for some common ground. The trouble is just how the respondents interpreted the concepts. When most claimed to favor democracy, they clearly had an Islamic rather than a liberal version in mind, given their overwhelming support for a strict application of sharia in every Muslim country. Likewise it is unlikely that the prevailing notion of globalization was the free flow of ideas and lifestyles along with shiny new gadgets and satellite television. Of these three, perhaps the most heartening was the belief that a clash of civilizations was not inevitable if common ground were somehow found. Yet after pondering the implications of the other results, a Westerner might wonder whether common ground is a chimera.

TABLE 10.3

Views of Democracy

	Good	Bad
Morocco	61%	16%
Egypt	82%	14%
Pakistan	61%	21%
Indonesia	65%	24%

Views of Globalization

	Good	Bad
Morocco	62%	23%
Egypt	92%	5%
Pakistan	65%	14%
Indonesia	80%	11%

Clash of Civilizations?

	Inevitable	Possible to Find Common Ground
Morocco	28%	54%
Egypt	45%	49%
Pakistan	21%	43%
Indonesia	13%	66%

The PGAP revealed two significant counterterrorist bright spots—the support both for bin Laden and suicide bombing had plunged, with approval in five of six Muslim countries surveyed dropping for the former and all six for the latter.

TABLE 10.4

Favorable views of Osama bin Laden

	2002	2008
Jordan	56%	19%
Indonesia	59%	37%
Lebanon	20%	2%
Turkey	15%	3%
Pakistan	46%	34%
Nigeria	44%	58%

Favorable Views of Suicide Bombing

	2002	2008
Jordan	56%	19%
Indonesia	59%	37%
Lebanon	20%	2%
Turkey	15%	3%
Pakistan	33%	5%
Nigeria	47%	32%

Source for Tables 10.1–10.4: "Views of the U.S. and American Foreign Policy" and "Attitudes toward American Culture and Ideas," Pew Research Global Attitudes Project, June 13, 2012

These statistics undermined Samuel Huntington's argument that there is a "clash of civilizations" between the Western and Islamic worlds. Huntington asserted that Islam itself, rather than its fundamentalist fringe, was the problem: "It is Islam, a different civilization whose people are convinced of the superiority of their culture, and are obsessed with the inferiority of their power." He also noted that throughout its thirteen-hundred-year history, "Islam has had bloody borders."[9]

The Muslim world is composed of 1.5 billion people who are split by how they interpret and follow their faith, as well as by nationality, class, ethnicity, experience, aspirations, jobs, status, and the array of other ways in which people can define and express themselves.

The surveys reveal that opinions vary from country to country and time to time and change in reaction to international events and trends. Both the Bush administration and al Qaeda did things over the last decade that alienated many more people than they inspired. That is a vital counterterrorist lesson—hearts and minds can be lost as well as won. Although just as many Muslims hated America for what it did, these Muslims might begin to respect America for policies that at once promote American and international interests.

The fight for the hearts and minds of the Muslim world has been among the weaker elements of the counterterrorism strategy of the United States and its allies. Michael Leiter, the NCTC's director from 2007 to 2011, stated that "no Western state has effectively countered the al Qaeda narrative" of the West as Islam's enemy and itself as Islam's salvation. The United States and its allies can counter that by revealing that actually the opposite is true, that "it is al Qaeda, and not the West, that is truly at war with Islam." Juan Zarate, the deputy national security adviser for counterterrorism from 2005 to 2009, pointed out "the challenge" in "shifting this paradigm so that the myth of such a conflict is debunked. Part of this is explaining that Muslims are a part of the West and breaking the notion of a clash of civilizations."[10]

Consequences

What a difference a war can make. Most people around the world responded with outrage and sympathy when terrorists flew jetliners into the World Trade Center towers and the Pentagon on September 11, 2001. *Le Monde*, a frequent critic of Washington's policies, famously declared that "we are all Americans now." Scores of governments around the world enthusiastically pledged to work with the United States to identify and eliminate al Qaeda cells in their midst. For the first time since it was founded in 1949, NATO declared that an attack on one of its members constituted an attack on them all, and later joined the American war in Afghanistan against al Qaeda and the Taliban. Of course, not everyone mourned the death and destruction of 9/11. All of America's enemies, Islamist and non-Islamist alike, rejoiced in those attacks.

Then came the conservative crusade in Iraq. American spokespeople have been mostly on the defensive ever since, fending off accusations of committing war crimes and being anti-Muslim. The White House never played up the reality that during the 1990s, the United States sacrificed blood and treasure to save Muslims in Somalia, Kuwait, Bosnia and Herzegovina, and Kosovo, or that half of all of al Qaeda's victims have been Muslims. In all, the Bush administration was ham-fisted in its attempts to market its wars and the measures it took to fight them.

What goes down can go up. Just as Bush administration policies deeply offended many people around the world, different policies might begin to reverse the devastation to American prestige and popularity.

Obama has tried to repair or construct relations between the White House and Muslim governments. In July 2009 he journeyed to Cairo, where he called for "a new beginning between the United States and Muslims around the world, one based on mutual interests and mutual respect." To that end he elaborated ways to resolve the conflict between Palestinians and Israelis, the wars in Iraq and Afghanistan, and development in Muslim countries. In another speech, he eloquently described "the children of Adam" as "limbs to each other, having been created of one essence."[11]

Yet these and similar words have had little discernable effect on Muslim hearts and minds, which are shaped above all by deeds. No matter how beautiful the phrases or noble the sentiments that are expressed, public relations are only as progressive as the policies it attempts to market. And then there are those problems without viable solutions. Terrorism feeds off both the White House's self-destructive policies and chronic problems that will only worsen with time.

In the vicious socioeconomic, social, religious, environmental, and political cycle that afflicts the Arab and most of the Muslim world, the demographic time bomb is perhaps the most malignant. The populations of those countries are growing faster than the economies, which means that poor people are becoming poorer. More than half of that population is well under twenty years old, and those young people are growing into economies that not only fail to provide them with jobs but also basic needs like adequate schools, health care, housing, electricity, sewage disposal, water, and recreation. Meanwhile the governments are growing more corrupt, brutal, and inept, and they deliver to the people little more than promises.

The result is worsening desperation. The only hope for a large segment of the Muslim population is a radical version of their faith. Islamism explains the reasons for their poverty and despair as the result of Western imperialism that has planted Israel in their midst and imposed corrupt apostate government atop them. If only true Muslims could rise up and drive out the Western imperialists, destroy Israel, and overthrow the corrupt apostate governments, then a new caliphate ruling through sharia would arise and resolve all problems.

What, if anything, can the United States and other wealthy countries do to break that vicious cycle? The Bush and Obama administrations both insisted that over the long-term, nation building offered the only possible solution. And publicizing progress in transforming those countries in turn would win over more hearts and minds and thus boost that transformation. However, the two administrations differed sharply in their approach to nation building and its importance to their counterterrorism strategies.

Bush and his fellow conservatives called for democratic revolutions across the Muslim world. But they ended up blackening the concept of democracy by trying to impose it by authoritarian and imperialist means overseas while violating many of its essential elements like freedom from arbitrary arrest, surveillance, and imprisonment without charges or trial within the United States.

The Obama White House is trying to clean up that mess by quietly dropping the notion of a democratic crusade. As students of history, Obama and his advisers know that economic development almost invariably precedes democracy. Secretary of State Hillary Clinton asserted that the "bottom line for any action has to be that it is in the best interests of the United States" to which end "we need to focus on the three Ds, defense, diplomacy, and development." She pointedly left unsaid a possible fourth "D"—democracy. The president explained that democracy can develop only after a government proves that it "is actually delivering a better life for people on the ground." He also promised that when his White House did promote democracy, it would "be less obsessed with form, more concerned with substance." That was an obvious rebuke to the Bush administration, which appeared to equate elections with democracy.[12]

The Obama administration also understands the broader context in which al Qaeda in particular and Islamism in general flourishes. Former defense secretary Robert Gates explained that in "recent years, the lines separating war, peace, diplomacy and development have become more blurred and no longer fit the neat organizational charts of the twentieth century."[13] So Obama initiated a long-term drain-the-swamp strategy that hopefully would transform poverty- and war-devastated Muslim lands into stability and peace. He pledged to boost American aid to $50 billion a year by 2012 and to counter the Islamist madrassas with a $2 billion education program for children.

These efforts would be paid for by ending the Bush administration policy of no-bid contracts to its political allies and the rampant corruption that it either tolerated or outright encouraged. On March 4, 2009, Obama attacked government spending, which was "plagued by massive cost overruns, outright fraud, and the absence of oversight and accountability. . . . In Iraq too much money has been paid for services that were never performed, for companies that skimmed off the top." He then signed an executive order requiring all subsequent contracts to be open to competitive bids with no favoritism allowed. Those firms that do win contracts would be held liable for the results. Firms that failed to fulfill their contracts would be fined and prevented from participating in future projects. Cleaning up corruption in government contracts would annually save American taxpayers at least $40 billion.[14]

The drain-the-swamp strategy faces a bleak future. The 9/11 Commission noted that the "combined gross domestic product of the 22 countries in the Arab League is less than the GDP of Spain. Forty percent of adult Arabs are illiterate, two-thirds of them women. One third of the broader Middle East lives on less than two dollars a day. Less than 2 percent of the population has access to the internet. The majority of older Arab youths have expressed a desire to immigrate to other countries, particularly those in Europe."[15] As if that these wretched conditions were not formidable enough, the populations of the Arab countries are growing faster than their economies, which means that the average Arab is getting poorer rather than wealthier, and the demand for jobs, housing, schools, health clinics is greater than the supply. The result will be more desperate people willing to do anything to alleviate their plight. Islamism provides desperate people with enemies.

The 9/11 Commission explained that any progress of that strategy must "be measured in decades, not years. It is a process that will be violently opposed by Islamist terrorist organizations, both inside Muslim countries and in attacks on the United States and other Western nations. The United States finds itself caught up in a clash within a civilization."[16]

11

The War in Afghanistan
Round Two

*Afghanistan has been known over the years as the graveyard
of empires. We cannot take that history lightly.*
—General David Petraeus

*This is a war of perceptions. This is not a physical war in
terms of how many people you kill or how much ground you
capture. . . . This is all in the minds of the participants.*
—General Stanley McChrystal

*Afghanistan is where the war on terror began and that is
where it must end.*
—President Barack Obama

How to Empower the Enemy

For experts, the efforts of the United States and its allies to win the war in
Afghanistan against the Taliban and al Qaeda appeared to reached a nadir in early
2009 as George W. Bush left the White House. Gen. David Petraeus admitted that
the strategic position had "deteriorated markedly in the past two years" and that
the "downward spiral of security" would continue unless decisive measures were
taken. He reminded those familiar with history that "Afghanistan has been known
over the years as the graveyard of empires. We cannot take that history lightly."
Richard Holbrooke, the special envoy to the region, put it even more bluntly:
"I've never seen anything remotely resembling the mess we've inherited."[1]

By the time the Bush administration left office, over six hundred American troops had been killed in Afghanistan. As in Iraq, roadside bombs accounted for a large portion of those deaths. The number of roadside bombs soared from 782 in 2005 to 3,200 in 2008. Suicide bombings are also steadily increasing, with none in 2002, two in 2003, five in 2004, and nine in 2005, but then the number soared to 97 in 2006, 142 in 2007, and 148 in 2008. In 2008, 3,611 bombs were located, and most were defused before they could be detonated. That was twice as many bombs as in the previous year. Some of these bombs did explode. More than 175 Americans were killed in 2008, twice the previous year's losses.[2]

Why was America losing that war? The comeback of al Qaeda and the Taliban was not inevitable. As in Iraq, the Bush administration's policies in Afghanistan tended to feed rather than starve America's enemies.

Bush and his advisers made crucial decisions that saved al Qaeda and the Taliban from the brink of destruction. In early December 2001 they chose not to send in American troops to cut off al Qaeda's retreat from its Tora Bora fortress, thus allowing bin Laden and hundreds of fighters to escape into nearby Pakistan. These blunders were compounded by Bush administration policies for "postwar" Afghanistan. Rather than blanket Afghanistan with troops and aid workers to secure and rebuild that shattered country, the Bush administration diverted key military, intelligence, and development assets to the buildup for and execution of its crusade against Iraq.

The fourteen thousand American troops that remained in Afghanistan were largely confined to bases, while NATO was entrusted with ensuring that the Taliban and al Qaeda did not return. NATO proved to be inadequate for that mission. No NATO member matched America's operational, logistic, and intelligence power. Each member has its own rules of engagement. The result was a frayed patchwork quilt of different national commands presiding over different regions, capabilities, strategies, and tactics. Gradually American troops got out of their bases and conducted their own patrols over larger swaths of the country. But by then it was too late. The Taliban and al Qaeda had regrouped and were steadily infiltrating villages and cities across Afghanistan.

No matter what was being done or not done, there were simply too few boots on the ground to protect the population from the Islamists. American or allied patrols might periodically pass through a district to collect information and search for enemy forces but would then swiftly withdraw into their bases. Animosity against the foreign troops in general and American troops in particular swelled steadily through the years. Clans and tribes are very territorial. Many attacks on the Americans and other foreign forces were provoked simply because the intruders did not ask permission to enter the territory of an especially sensitive group. The Taliban and al Qaeda took advantage of these blunders and steadily expanded into the vacuums.

The Bush administration had plenty of dire warnings that al Qaeda and the Taliban were regrouping. The first came in early February 2002, when Tenet delivered to Bush a classified report predicting that Afghanistan would once again fall into violence and anarchy among the warlords while the Taliban and al Qaeda spread their influence unless Washington committed itself to a massive, systematic nation-building program for the country. The report criticized the peacekeeping forces as too small and largely confined to Kabul and called on the White House to boost the Afghan army to at least one hundred thousand troops. This would take many years, most likely decades. Yet much as they closed their ears to warnings about an al Qaeda attack in the United States, the Bush White House ignored the subsequently troubling reports about Afghanistan.

Since the rout of the Taliban and al Qaeda in December 2001, the American and international aid efforts in Afghanistan have done little to rebuild, let alone develop, a country shattered by three decades of almost incessant war. An Afghan government, army, and police force have been established. Roads, bridges, and schools have been built, and tens of billions of dollars have been spent. But most Afghans have not significantly benefited, and these efforts are merely a sliver of what needs to be done.

The self-defeating incompetence, corruption, and violence that characterized America's occupation of Iraq is also present in Afghanistan, although on a smaller scale. For instance, the Pentagon lost track of eighty-seven-thousand firearms, mortars, and other weapons, or over one-third of what was shipped over to supply the Afghan army that it was trying to build. The Pentagon did not even bother to record the serial numbers of forty-six-thousand firearms of that arsenal. Just how these arms disappeared and where they ended up remains unknown. It is safe to say that many and perhaps most are in the hands of those determined to kill Americans and other Westerners in Afghanistan and beyond.[3]

The battle for hearts and minds in Afghanistan could not be more challenging. Afghanistan is twice the size of Iraq in territory and, with 32 million people, has 4 million more to secure and develop, compared to 28 million Iraqis. Despite those far greater strategic challenges, in January 2009 when Barack Obama took the presidential oath, the total number of foreign troops in Afghanistan was 75,000, of which 33,700 were American, compared to 146,000, of which 120,000 were American, in Iraq. The disparity between native forces was even wider: Iraq had 560,000 police and 260,000 troops, compared to Afghanistan's mere 132,000 police and 82,000 troops.

The cultural obstacles to development alone are overwhelming. Afghanistan essentially remains a feudal culture woven into a crazy quilt of thousands of clans and hundreds of tribes led by fiercely independent warlords. In some ways Afghanistan is even more traditional today than it was before the Soviet invasion in December 1979 (ironically and primarily, to supplant one communist faction in power with another closer to Moscow), which began three decades of nearly nonstop warfare. With what little modern economic and political infrastructure that once existed shattered, Afghans have burrowed like turtles even deeper into their hard shell of tradition. As in Iraq, clan and tribe trump religion as the focus of identity and loyalty. Thus when there is violence between any of the eight of ten Afghans who are Sunnis and the two who are Shiites, the primary cause is usually not religious. Traditional societies not only do not value literacy and the learning it can inspire, but they actually fear it; only 28 percent of Afghans can read and write (43 percent male and 13 percent female).

Afghanistan is a rural country. As many as eight of ten people live in the countryside, and half of all Afghans live in villages with three hundred or fewer people. Paved roads remain few and are mostly so potholed that they reduce traffic to a bone-jarring crawl. The country is almost equal parts desert and mountain, with scattered patches of arable soil and flowing water.

The government that the United States constructed to rule Afghanistan has failed to do so. That is only partly the fault of the man whom the Bush White House backed to be president. Hamid Karzai has been accused of doing nothing to unify the country or curb rampant and worsening corruption, instead skimming millions of dollars into his own pocket and stealing the August 2009 election by massive ballot-box stuffing.

Periodic pressure by the White House and congressional delegations have failed to inspire Karzai to assert progressive policies. Karzai's invariable response has been to deny such allegations and then criticize the United States either for not giving enough aid or for the indiscriminate shootings and bombings that kill innocent civilians. A typical exchange occurred in February 2009. Obama stated his belief that Karzai was "unreliable and ineffective," while Secretary of State Clinton declared that Karzai was "presiding over a narcostate." Karzai replied by blasting the United States: "Our demands are clear—to stop the civilian casualties, the searching of Afghan homes, and the arresting of Afghans. And, of course, the Americans pressured us to be quiet and to make us retreat from our demands. But that is impossible. Afghanistan and its president are not going to retreat from their demands." That exchange of rhetoric reveals a disturbing and potentially fatal weakness in the war against al Qaeda and the Taliban.[4]

To worsen matters, Karzai decreed that the election scheduled for August 20, 2009, be moved to April of that year, apparently to limit the campaign time for his opponents. He justified that policy by pointing to two constitutional requirements, that he step down on May 21, when his five-year term ended, and that a presidential election be held from thirty to sixty days before that transition in power. Opposition leaders criticized him for doing so and failing to take measures that would make any election transparent. Although Karzai agreed to the August election date, he refused to give up power to a provisional government before the election. His play for more power further eroded his legitimacy.[5]

When the election was held on August 20, 2009, Karzai and his henchmen blatantly stole it. The Election Complaint Commission (ECC), composed of three foreign and two Afghan observers under UN auspices, estimated that over one million votes, or one-third of those cast for Karzai, were fraudulent, and called for a runoff election. But Karzai's rival, Abdullah Abdullah, dropped out of the race, explaining that a free election was impossible under the current system. In February 2010 Karzai solidified his control over the electoral process by announcing that henceforth he would appoint all the members of the ECC, and its five members would be Afghans.

In doing so, Karzai throttled Afghanistan's nascent democracy and essentially transformed it into a dictatorship, albeit a scrawny one with little power beyond Kabul. This posed another dilemma for the United States, succinctly explained by White House counterterrorist adviser Bruce Riedel: "The strategy requires an Afghan government that is credible and legitimate, both to get Afghans to support it, and get Americans and their allies to help. That strategy can't work around a South Vietnamese–style government."[6]

As if the president's machinations, corruption, and weaknesses were not troubling enough, his brother, Ahmed Wali Karzai, was becoming just as notorious. He blatantly reaped million of dollars from smuggling heroin. Meanwhile, the CIA paid him to deploy his Kandahar Strike Force against the Taliban and other insurgent groups, although the effectiveness of those operations has been questioned. The personality but not the underlying problem disappeared in July 2011 when a suicide bomber killed him.[7]

President Obama showed his displeasure with President Karzai in March 2010 by curtly revoking an invitation for a summit at the White House. Karzai responded by inviting Iranian president Mahmoud Ahmadinejad to Kabul. At the presidential palace the two presidents stood side by side as Ahmadinejad delivered a vicious anti-American and anti-Western speech before reporters and other guests. A few days later, on March 27, Karzai flew to Tehran to share with Ahmadinejad a second summit and Iran's New Year celebrations.

The following day, Obama flew to Kabul for a brief visit with the troops and an even briefer meeting with Karzai in which he rebuked the Afghan president for the continued corruption and the fraudulent election. The day after the visit, Karzai stepped before reporters and blamed the Americans and other foreigners for Afghanistan's problems, including the very same corruption and fraudulent election.

The dilemma of relying on Karzai and his clan to run Afghanistan was starkly explained in a November 2009 report by Gen. Karl Eikenberry, the American ambassador and former ground commander in Afghanistan. Eikenberry stated bluntly that "Karzai is not an adequate strategic partner. . . . Karzai continues to shun responsibility for any sovereign burden, whether defense, governance, or development. He and much of his circle do not want the U.S. to leave, and are only too happy to see us invest further." Yet there is no viable alternative: "Beyond Karzai himself, there is no political ruling class that provides an over-arching national identity that transcends local affiliations and provides reliable partnership."[8]

The Karzai government presides over a country split among countless warlords and an expanding Taliban movement. This poses a dilemma for the Americans. They give financial and military support to the warlords in return for information, protection for convoys rumbling through their territory, and, oc-casionally, actual attacks on the Taliban. But in doing so they undermine the Karzai government's ability to assert its influence beyond Kabul. It is also quite expensive. American and NATO contracts to warlord escorts for convoys was $2.2 billion in 2009. Many of the warlords are playing a double game, shaking down the Americans and other foreigners while collaborating with the Taliban. Finally, atop all the profits the warlords wring from the foreigners, they often use the convoys to smuggle heroin.[9]

Grossly complicating America's efforts in Afghanistan was the increasingly anti-Americans attitude of its president. Karzai has sought to deflect attention from his own inept, corrupt, brutal rule by scapegoating the United States. His remarks in March 2012 were increasingly typical: "Let's pray for God to rescue us from these two demons" as he equated the United States and the Taliban. Bizarrely, that underouts not only America's strategy but Afghanistan's own chances of surviving.[10]

The Opium War Dilemma

As if Afghanistan's interrelated cultural, social, economic, and political problems were not debilitating enough, the country is hooked on heroin and is run by drug lords—the heroin trade accounts for about two-thirds of the economy. Ninety percent of the world's heroin originates in Afghan opium fields. The narco-economy may be as much of a threat to that country's development as the Taliban and al Qaeda.[11]

The incentives for farmers to grow opium rather than other crops are compel-ling. Opium grows like a weed and demands relatively little fertilizer or water, and the profits are greater—$5,500 a hectare versus $500 for a hectare of wheat.

Fruits and grains can spoil and lose their value, while opium and its heroin derivative are much more durable.

This poses a terrible dilemma to those in charge of counterterrorism. Ignoring the narcoeconomy will allow it to eat away like a cancer at any progress toward democracy and diversified economic development. The opium trade boosts the wealth and power of the Taliban and al Qaeda, along with the warlords, at the expense of the national government. The Taliban and al Qaeda benefit from the narcoeconomy by taxing, warehousing, transporting, protecting, and laundering the profits from an ever larger cut of the trade. The Taliban alone is said to skim $300 million annually from the narcoeconomy, more than enough to pay for its recruits and weapons. The warlords further weaken the central government by corrupting its bureaucrats and forcing politicians to turn a blind eye to the narcoeconomy. As Karzai put it, "If we don't destroy poppy, it will destroy us."[12]

Yet, paradoxically, the initial strategy to eliminate the narcoeconomy aided the Taliban and al Qaeda by alienating the warlords and peasants who live off that trade. The Pentagon began a poppy eradication policy in 2002. That hurt the counterinsurgency campaign in two ways. It diverted troops from tracking and fighting the Taliban and al Qaeda. It also supplied the insurgency with recruits who had been deprived of their livelihoods. In 2005 the White House expanded the army's war against the opium trade with five counternarcotics teams run by the DEA. That campaign added interdiction to eradication, which struck directly at the warlords as well as the peasants. Although it had little effect on the opium trade—only 5 percent of the crop was eradicated—it hampered the counterinsurgency, since the warlords were the best sources of intelligence on the Taliban and al Qaeda. At the very least, those harmed by interdiction stopped talking to American intelligence officers, and they often turned their militias against the occupation. Obama shifted the strategy to eradicating warlords, but that too has been just as ineffective.

Washington has yet to promote a comprehensive policy for getting peasants to eradicate opium production and shift to other crops or livelihoods by offering credit, fertilizers, pesticides, seeds, better transport to local markets, access to international markets, and, above all, security from the warlords and Taliban who would prevent them from making that transition. A parallel cultural strategy would emphasize that Islam forbids opium along with other addictive and mind-altering drugs.

Afghanistan does have an alternative potential source of wealth, although its development is stifled by war, would take years to exploit even if the country were secure, and would be reaped by a tiny segment of the population. Deep in the earth beneath the rubble of war is an estimated trillion dollars worth of minerals, including iron, copper, niobium, cobalt, gold, and molybdenum. So far the only foreign corporation that has begun a mining operation is Chinese.[13]

The Nature of the Enemy

The Taliban rules through terror. Taliban fighters and mullahs operate at will across the countryside, murdering opponents, imposing their rule, indoctrinating the population, and mobilizing the young men to join their ranks and spread the revolution ever further. While the Taliban is as ruthless as ever, it has become more flexible and thus more effective. For instance, the Taliban banned photography and television after taking power in Afghanistan in 1996; now they use both medias to propagate their cause.

In addition to the crucial revolutionary ingredients of organization, ideology, and leadership, the Taliban has no lack of cash and guns. To pay for its operations, the Taliban has become a money-making machine. They reap "taxes" from countless households and businesses under their control. Mosques and charities around the world annually contribute tens of millions of dollars. Perhaps most alarming of all is how the Taliban, along with other warlords, skim fortunes from the heroin trade. All that income gives the Taliban plenty of money to buy weapons from willing sellers to use against the Americans, their allies, and the Kabul and Islamabad governments. Guns, munitions, bombs, and other necessities of war are diverted from Pakistan army arsenals. Others follow more circuitous routes. Russian- and Chinese-made surface-to-air missiles (SAMs) have been smuggled from Iraq's Kurdistan across Iran into Pakistan.

So what, if anything, can counter let alone crush that insurgency? Gen. David Petraeus, the author of the successful surge policy in Iraq, explains that "We just cannot take the tactics, techniques, and procedures that worked in Iraq and employ them in Afghanistan." The reason is simple. Each insurgency is unique and thus the counterinsurgency strategy for each must be tailored to that uniqueness.[14]

These caveats aside, a divide-and-rule strategy is crucial to countering the insurgency. Despite its growing power, the Taliban does have a significant vulnerability. What is called the Taliban is a broad movement composed of a loose confederation of clans, villages, and tribes, each with varying degrees of loyalty to the cause. Although the tribes and clans are all highly conservative practitioners of Islam, each has its own political and cultural prerogatives that could potentially limit or even oppose inroads by the Taliban and al Qaeda. As in Iraq, money rather than belief entices many a fighter to the Islamist cause. The Taliban pays fighters twenty dollars for every day they fight against the foreign troops. It is estimated that about seven of ten Taliban fighters joined primarily for the money. Then there are many groups and individuals who are terrorized into allegiance when the Taliban presents them with the stark choice of join or die.[15]

These mixed motives for groups affiliated with the Taliban offer counterinsurgency opportunities. The key question is whether a group joins the Taliban out of terror, cash, or conviction. A group that joins for cash can be outbid. A group that joins out of terror can be enticed away if it is protected. That strategy of providing cash and protection worked in Iraq, where it was known as the Awakening.

Securing the population is essential for a successful counterinsurgency strategy. There is no question that most Afghans crave protection from the Taliban. The brutal murders, beatings, and shakedowns by the Taliban on reluctant tribal chiefs and villages have alienated not only them but others who fear suffering the same. That may make them quiescent in the short run but potentially rebellious if they had a reliable ally who could protect them. After all, among the reasons why the Americans were able to rout the Taliban and al Qaeda in 2001 was that their extreme version of Islam had repulsed many Afghan hearts and minds. What is needed is to blanket Afghanistan's vulnerable regions with enough troops to drive the insurgents either out or underground and thus secure the population so that they can begin rebuilding and, ideally, developing their lives.

As if the Taliban were not a formidable enough enemy, there are at least two other large-scale Islamist groups fighting to drive out the foreign troops and destroy the Karzai regime. Like Mohammad Omar, Gulbuddin Hekmatyar and Jalaluddin Haqqani achieved fame and power fighting the Soviets in the 1980s.

Pakistan has at times supported both leaders and their groups. And, like the Taliban, both of those groups skim tens of millions of dollars from the heroin trade.

Hekmatyar is the better known, as he served as Afghanistan's prime minister from 1993 to 1994 and in 1996 before the Taliban toppled the regime. His Hezb-i-Islami, or Islamic Party, is dedicated to an Islamist revolution. Although Pakistan initially supported him, it switched to the Taliban when Hekmatyar and other Mujahedeen leaders proved to be too brutal, corrupt, and inept. Hekmatyar forged ties with al Qaeda when it returned to Afghanistan in 1996 and helped bin Laden and his followers escape into Pakistan in December 2001. Hekmatyar himself initially sought refuge in Iran and later in Pakistan and has received support from both countries to revive his group. He and his several thousand fighters largely operate in northern Pakistan and northeastern Afghanistan.

Another Islamabad-supported group is led by Haqqani and his son Sirajuddin, or Siraj. Haqqani was among the CIA assets fighting the Soviets during the 1980s and was a member of the Islamic Party that Hekmatyar eventually headed. Since then the relations between Haqqani and Hekmatyar have been tumultuous, and at times they fought against and then alongside each other. Although as one of mujahideen Haqqani initially opposed the Taliban movement, he allied with it soon after it took power. Haqqani's ties with bin Laden went back several decades to the 1980s, when they both fought against the Soviets. With its base in Pakistan's North Waziristan tribal region, Haqqani sheltered and reequipped the Taliban and al Qaeda after they were routed in December 2001 and has joined them in infiltrating and spreading across Afghanistan. Haqqani's forces include about four thousand fighters. Islamabad has rejected continual pressure by Washington to launch an offensive against that group. Instead, in February 2010, Islamabad insisted that the Haqqani group be included in any negotiated settlement with the Taliban in Afghanistan.[16]

Each of those insurgent groups is growing more powerful in numbers, territory, and deadliness.

Surge Redux?

During his presidential campaign, Barack Obama repeatedly stated his priorities in the war against al Qaeda and its affiliates: "Afghanistan is where the war on terror began and that is where it must end." Upon entering the White House, he and his advisers devised a policy, the core of which was the security and development of the Afghan people. That included deploying more American and NATO troops and development aid to Afghanistan, boosting the efforts to train and field the Afghan army and police, pressuring Karzai to stamp out corruption and ineptness from his government, and pressuring Pakistan to attack al Qaeda and Taliban strongholds in the North-West Frontier Province.

Many more boots on the ground were an essential element for that plan to succeed. On February 16, 2009, Obama announced that he would send 17,000 more American troops and 4,000 trainers to Afghanistan, bringing the total to 68,000 by the year's end. That was in addition to 35,000 troops from NATO and other allied countries. But were 104,000 foreign troops enough to protect the Afghan people?[17]

The standard formula for securing a population is one soldier for every 50 inhabitants. The ratio of that surge of troops to Afghanistan's 32 million people would be one to 363, far short of the ideal. The number that Obama designated was slightly over half the reinforcements that Gen. David McKiernan, the American ground commander, requested. But there were no more troops to spare. American forces were already stretched thin to the snapping point all around the world. McKiernan's request could only have been met by diverting troops already committed to Iraq.

Gen. Stanley McChrystal, a career Special Forces officer who had fought for five years in Iraq, replaced McKiernan as the commander in June 2009. Shortly after arriving in Kabul, he launched a clear-and-hold offensive in Helmand Province. As the mostly Marine force swept through, the enemy fled or hid among the population rather than fight. That did not bother McChrystal, who explained that the "measure of effectiveness will not be enemy killed. It will be the number of Afghans shielded from violence."[18]

That strategy had one glaring weakness—there were not enough American and allied troops to secure all the people in Afghanistan threatened by the Taliban. So on September 1, 2009, McChrystal sent the White House three strategic options. Each called for expanding the number of troops, and the more the better. The high-risk option would boost the ranks by 15,000, the medium-risk by 25,000, and the low-risk by 40,000. He warned that Washington had only twelve to eighteen months to turn around the war before it would essentially be lost.

McChrystal's report set off a debate within the White House mediated by National Security Advisor James Jones. Secretary of State Hillary Clinton, Defense Secretary Robert Gates, and Joint Chief of Staff Chair Mike Mullen supported the low-risk strategy. Vice President Joe Biden, along with most congressional Democrats, rejected any of McChrystal's options and instead called for reducing American and other foreign troops and using missile strikes and special operations to kill al Qaeda and Taliban leaders. On October 8, 2009, President Obama announced his decision to go with the medium-risk option that brought the number of American troops to 100,000 in 2010.

As in Iraq, the goal is gradually to replace the American and other allied troops with a steadily expanding Afghan army and police force, along with local militias. Each of these institutions was but a shadow of what was needed, with little possibility of becoming anything more.

Although McChrystal called for a 240,000-man Afghan army by the end of 2011, problems plagued the existing 90,000-man army. There was a lack of good leaders at all levels. Desertion was rife. Pay was poor—only a hundred dollars a month for a soldier, while Taliban fighters earned two or three times as much. The soldiers were poorly equipped and often sold what little they had, like arms, munitions, and uniforms, to the enemy. Spies riddled their ranks and passed on intelligence to the Taliban and other Islamist groups. Only one of three battalions was deemed capable of operating independently, and that number was declining.[19]

Police rather than soldiers are the front line of any counterinsurgency. McChrystal sought to expand the police ranks from 90,000 to 160,000 by 2011. Yet as an institution, the police were even more deficient than the army. Corruption, low morale, brutality, and ineptness permeated the police ranks. As a result, most police abetted rather than suppressed criminals and insurgents alike.

And then there is the militia. As in Iraq, the strategy of empowering militias, known as the Local Defense Initiative, is risky. Many of those groups have ties with the Taliban, and even more have conducted murderous feuds with other groups. Warlords head most of the militias and want to keep the national government as corrupt and weak as possible; many of them are deeply involved in the heroin trade. As a result, Washington's militia-empowerment policy may end up undermining its nation-building policy.

The final challenge to successfully implementing a clear-and-hold strategy is the enemy itself. Across many regions, the Taliban and its allies have created a parallel and more efficient government that mobilizes money and men, eliminates opponents, and gathers intelligence. The leaders increasingly recognize that wielding terror to intimidate clans, villages, and tribes into compliance usually backfires, as it provokes fear and hatred rather than inspires loyalty. So they are relying more on persuasion rather than coercion to rally Afghans. Taliban chief Mohammad Omar kicked off that "kinder, gentler" public relations campaign in May 2009 when he issued a directive with sixty-nine rules of war, including the ban of suicide bombings against civilians, forbidding the mutilation or beheading of those who resist, and ending the burning of schools. Commanders who violate those rules are eliminated.[20] He instructed Taliban cadres in the villages and neighborhoods to rally grassroots support by meshing preaching with problem solving by trying to find people jobs, resolving disputes, and arranging marriages.

That strategy is succeeding, as it is increasingly difficult for American and Afghan troops to achieve tactical surprise. Any patrols are preceded by locals whistling, honking horns, releasing dense puffs of smoke, or flying kites, which lets any enemy forces in the area either escape or prepare a deadly ambush.

If the Taliban has the intelligence and military edge on the ground, the Americans partly make up for that with what intelligence and havoc they can reap from the sky. The newest generation of drones includes the MQ-9 Reaper that not only flies higher, faster, and further than the smaller Predator but can carry fourteen Hellfire missiles and has thirty different cameras scanning the earth. Back at the air force or CIA operating base, four personnel are assigned to carefully watch what each camera reveals. The Reapers, Predators, and smaller types of drones are essential for finding and killing militants, especially the leaders, and forcing the survivors to disperse and lie low. Yet at best the drones can disrupt and deplete the enemy; only boots on the ground can secure the population, the most crucial step in defeating an insurgency.

A clear-and-hold operation, however, is only the prelude to the third element of a successful counterinsurgent strategy—building. A civilian surge of international aid workers must transform Afghanistan from a war-shattered, feudal realm into a modern country with schools, police, electricity, paved roads, sewers, clean running water, and viable businesses. Another key development strategy is to aid farmers to grow food rather than opium.

The obstacles to the building mission are severe. Even if the troops secure the country, it could take decades to accomplish. Karzai announced in December 2009 that he did not foresee his country being able to pay for its own security or defend itself until at least 2024. That prediction just might be optimistic, given the worsening vicious cycle of violence, poverty, and desperation plaguing the country. Even without the direct threat of a terrorist attack, corruption and outright extortion distorts, stunts, and often kills any development project. For instance, both the posts and decisions of the judicial system's key elements—police, officials, lawyers, prosecutors, and judges—are all for sale to the highest bidder. So instead, people take their disputes to the Taliban, whose judicial system grounded in sharia may be severe but at least is swift, inexpensive, and "just."[21]

That was not true everywhere. In January 2010 the Shinwari tribe's chiefs announced that they would resist the Taliban and send one man from each village to join the army or police. That was a significant victory. With more than four hundred thousand members, the Shinwari is one of the largest tribes. More importantly, they are located in eastern Afghanistan in territory surrounded by the Taliban. Money was perhaps the most important reason for the chiefs' decision. The Americans paid millions of dollars to the chiefs and promised an array of development projects that would bypass the corruption gauntlet in Kabul. Whether other tribes follow the Shinwari or continue to draw closer from fear and or hope to the Taliban remains to be seen.

General McChrystal first asserted the clear, hold, and build strategy on a massive scale against the Taliban stronghold of Marja in Helmand Province starting in February 2010. Contrary to standard procedures in which secrecy is paramount, the offensive's objectives and timing were announced weeks beforehand so that civilians had a chance to escape before the fighting erupted. The campaign included American, British, and Afghan troops that encircled and methodically routed the Taliban from their lairs. The priority was to protect the noncombatants and their property. Afghan police followed the troops and maintained order behind the lines. Allied commanders sat down with tribal councils and politely explained that this time, they were here to stay. Humanitarian and development aid was given directly to the chiefs, thus avoiding the massive corruption when it passes through the Afghan government. General McChrystal explained his strategy's essence: "This is a war of perceptions. This is not a physical war in terms of how many people you kill or how much ground you capture. . . . This is all in the minds of the inhabitants."[22]

In that battle for hearts and minds, the Taliban and the United States both appeared to be losing. From February 2005 to February 2009, the proportion of Afghans with a favorable view of the United States plummeted from 68 percent to 32 percent. Still the United States scored better than the public's favorable view of the Taliban, which fell from 9 percent to 7 percent. Unfortunately, less than half the population (48 percent) had a positive view of the Afghan government, down from 80 percent. Then, in the spring of 2012, positive views of the United States plummeted to about one in ten after American troops inadvertently burned copies of the Koran and a soldier murdered seventeen Afghan civilians.[23]

Although General McChrystal surpassed his predecessor in stepping up the war against the Taliban and other insurgent groups, in June 2010 he was ousted after a *Rolling Stone* magazine article revealed that he and his staff were openly contemptuous of Obama and his administration. Obama replaced him with David Petraeus, the brilliant theorist and practitioner of counterinsurgency warfare whose leadership was crucial in pacifying Iraq. Whether he achieves the same results in Afghanistan, however, remains to be seen.

Petraeus launched a massive clear, hold, and build campaign in Kandahar and the surrounding region in September 2010. The challenges of winning hearts and minds in Kandahar far surpass those of Marja. Kandahar's population of half a million is more than ten times that of Marja. Kandahar is the Taliban's spiritual home, where Mohammad Omar developed the movement in 1992, and the movement is deeply embedded there.

The counterinsurgency campaigns across Afghanistan went so well that Secretary of Defense Leon Panetta announced on February 1, 2012, that the United States could begin winding down its combat role there in 2013. Time will tell if that assessment was prescient or premature.[24]

The Diplomatic Strategy

President Obama readily accepted the view of experts that the war could only be won diplomatically, not militarily. Ultimately the Afghan surge is intended to provide the security and breathing space necessary to negotiate an end to the war.

The diplomatic strategy involves bringing as many different groups into the political process as possible, including those elements of the Taliban that are motivated more by fear or cash than belief. Any groups affiliated with the Taliban that gave up terror and recognized the government would be eligible for protection, aid, and participation in politics. This strategy makes sense. It is estimated that only 5 percent of the Taliban was incorrigible, and thus the other 95 percent are potentially open to varying packages of inducements. Afghan rather than American officials would take the lead in any talks.[25]

Obama explained the logic behind that policy: "If you talk to General Petraeus, I think he would argue that part of the success in Iraq involved reaching out to people that we would consider to be Islamic fundamentalists, but who were willing to work with us because they had been completely alienated by the tactics of al Qaeda in Iraq. There may be some comparable opportunities in Afghanistan and the Pakistani region." He was quick to acknowledge the differences: "But the situation in Afghanistan is, if anything, more complex. You have a less governed region, a history of fierce independence among tribes. Those tribes are multiple and sometimes operate at cross purposes, so figuring all that out is going to be much more of a challenge."[26]

Obama's negotiation policy was less of a departure from that of his predecessor than it may have appeared. Officially the Bush administration was committed to the conservative nostrum that "negotiating with terrorists" was "appeasement," and thus should never be done. But like Ronald Reagan before him, Bush did just that, and for a very good reason. The "no negotiation" stance confounded counterterrorist efforts in Afghanistan and Iraq. As a result, the handful of realists in the White House were eventually able to convince the conservatives to at least try a divide-and-conquer strategy that played off different factions against each other. That was a key reason why the surge in Iraq was a success.

Yet that strategy faces tough obstacles. The Karzai government actually began an amnesty program as early as January 2005. The program did convince over six thousand Taliban fighters and supporters to switch sides. Unfortunately, the Taliban more than made up for those losses with new recruits. Frustrated with that hydra dilemma, Karzai decided to try going straight to the head of the insurgency. On November 17, 2008, he publicly promised Mohammad Omar that his safety would be guaranteed if he opened talks with the government for peace in Afghanistan. Bush did back Karzai's offer by agreeing to rescind the $10-million price on Omar's head should he come in from the cold.[27] So far Omar has yet to take Karzai's offer. His reticence is understandable. The rules of Afghan politics are decidedly those of Machiavelli rather than Queensbury; more often than not, handshakes between enemies are followed by a stiletto in the back.

Negotiating with "moderate" Taliban leaders has proven to be far more challenging than with Islamists in Iraq. One reason is the vastly different levels of development between the two countries. Despite decades of war and sanctions, Iraq made significant progress toward modernity, with high degrees of urbanization, literacy, economic diversity, social mobility, and secularization. This softened all but the most hardened Iraqi Islamists. In contrast, Afghanistan remains a deeply traditional society, and thus Islamism's appeal to its leaders and followers is much more absolute. Another reason is that al Qaeda reinforces the Taliban's hard line. Unlike in Iraq, where al Qaeda alienated the population through indiscriminate mass murders, in Afghanistan and Pakistan al Qaeda has not conducted widespread terrorism.[28]

These moderate Taliban chiefs take a hard line at the negotiating table—they demand the immediate withdrawal of all American and other foreign troops. That, of course, is a deal-breaker for Washington and Brussels. But from a Taliban perspective, the Western demands that they renounce violence and lay down their arms are just as extreme. They swear they will do so only after the last foreign soldier leaves Afghanistan. Thus the negotiations have deadlocked.[29]

This is not the only downside to negotiating with the Taliban. The movement is largely rooted among the Pashtun people, who comprise about 45 percent of Afghanistan's total population. Peace talks with the Taliban further alienate the Tajiks, Uzbeks, and Hazaras from the Karzai government and its foreign sponsors.[30]

Wooing the Regional Players

In greatly varying ways and degrees, Afghanistan's fate depends on what happens in neighboring countries.

As in Iraq, Iran is a key player in Afghanistan and thus can help or harm America's efforts there. Among the more humiliating dilemmas that the Bush White House faced was its need for Iranian cooperation during the initial phases of its war in Afghanistan. Tehran was happy to cooperate because the Iranian Shiite revolution is theologically opposed to the Sunni Islamist revolutions led by al Qaeda and the Taliban. So after September 11, Tehran cooperated by providing intelligence and rounding up al Qaeda operatives within Iran. In August 2002 Tehran extradited sixteen Saudi members of al Qaeda to Riyadh. But having routed the Taliban and al Qaeda, the Bush team spurned Iranian offers of even greater support. Tehran's cooperation ended after the American invasion of Iraq and Western efforts to stop Iran's nuclear program.[31]

In contrast with his predecessor, Obama not only recognizes the realities of Iranian power but is willing to work with it. But cooperation in Afghanistan remains entangled with Iran's nuclear program, along with political turmoil in Iran following the rigged June 12, 2009, election. Although in October 2009 Tehran pledged to open its nuclear facilities to inspection and allow France and Russia to process some of its uranium, it has yet to do so.

Iran is steadily increasing its influence in Afghanistan. To do so, that Shiite Muslim regime has set aside theological differences with the Sunnis and forged ties with both sides of the war. Karzai openly meets with and takes cash from Iranian leaders. Tehran has also forged ties with the Taliban and al Qaeda by emphasizing their common enemies, the United States and the modern world. Tehran is an important source of money, arms, training, intelligence, smuggling, and refuge for Islamists, Sunni and Shiite alike, in Afghanistan and beyond.[32]

To the north of Afghanistan, the United States has both strategic and economic interests in Central Asia. Each of these five Central Asian states is Muslim, but for now none are Islamist. Indeed, their secular governments fear the sort of Islamist revolutions that consumed Iran and Afghanistan. Three of these states—Turkmenistan, Uzbekistan, and Tajikistan—border northern Afghanistan. While Kazakhstan and Kyrgyzstan are more remote, they too play a logistical role in America's efforts against the Taliban and al Qaeda. American economic interests in the region mostly concern fossil fuels. Central Asia accounts for about 5 percent of global oil reserves, with Kazakhstan, Turkmenistan, and Uzbekistan enjoying the lion's share. One final concern is that those countries are among the transit routes for Afghan heroin to global markets.

Moscow is the biggest obstacle impeding American interests in the region. Central Asia is to Russia as Central America is to the United States, a vital sphere of influence because of its proximity, markets, and resources. Although the United States never directly controlled Central America, Russia outright conquered Central Asia in the nineteenth century and only relinquished the five states with the Soviet Union's breakup in 1991. Both spheres of influence posed threats in the form of revolutionary movements: communism in Central America, and Islamism and nationalism in Central Asia. While Moscow disputed Washington's domination over Central America during the Cold War, it did not face a direct competitor in its own backyard until recently.

Beijing is a secondary player in the region. Although Chinese rule never extended that far west, Beijing certainly values Central Asia for the same reasons as Moscow. Given the Chinese economy's insatiable appetite for fossil fuels, Beijing's interest in tapping Central Asia's oil fields will steadily raise that region's importance. And as this happens, tensions between Beijing and Moscow will rise.

Moscow and Beijing have tried to mitigate some of their rivalry through annual summits among themselves and the heads of Kazakhstan, Kyrgyzstan, and Tajikistan, starting in 1996, and the addition of Uzbekistan and the transformation of that association into the Shanghai Cooperation Organization in 2001. Pakistan, India, Iran, and Mongolia have observer status. That group has forged agreements on border security, troop levels, and counterterrorism. They hope eventually to extend their security issues to embrace greater economic ties.

America, Russia, and China share one interest in Central Asia—ensuring that Islamist revolutionary movements are throttled there. Muslims are the majority population in the Russian and Chinese provinces bordering Central Asia and have suffered discrimination from the empires that colonized them centuries earlier. Indeed for decades Moscow and Beijing have battled their respective Chechen and Uyghur separatist movements. Both the Russians and Chinese feared the spread of Islamism following the Taliban's takeover of Afghanistan in 1996.

So after September 11, Russia and China supported America's battles against al Qaeda, the Taliban, and other Islamist revolutionary groups. To that end, Putin agreed to help the Bush administration gain temporary base rights in some of the former Soviet republics of Central Asia. That welcome quickly faded after American forces routed the Taliban and al Qaeda, then the Bush team launched its conservative crusade in Iraq. Putin increasingly feared that the longer the Americans stayed, the greater the chance that they would supplant Russia as the region's dominant foreign power. While he was president and later prime minister, after he passed the presidential torch to his protégé, Dmitry Medvedev, Putin pressured those Central Asian countries that had granted the United States base rights to rescind them. That pressure partly worked.

America's war against the Taliban and al Qaeda suffered setbacks in November 2005 when Uzbekistan president Islam Karimov announced that he would expel the United States from the Karshi-Khanabad Air Base, and Kyrgyzstan president Kurmanbek Bakiyev insisted in February 2009 that the United States had three months to evacuate the Manas Air Base at the international airport near Bishkek, the capital. While the Bush administration's ham-fisted demands failed to intimidate Karimov into reversing his government's decision, the Obama White House's more nuanced diplomacy was able to talk and pay Bakiyev into extending America's lease at Manas.

The price the Obama administration had to pay was steep. Bakiyev's eviction notice came with the excuse that the monthly $17 million rent that Washington paid was too miserly. But when the White House declared its willingness to negotiate a higher fee, the Kyrgyz government turned down the offer. One of the excuses for doing so was the Bush administration's rejection of a Kyrgyz request to raise the fee in 2006. Another was a 2006 incident when an American guard shot and killed a Kyrgyz truck driver, apparently fearing he was a suicide bomber.

These were merely excuses. Moscow's pressure was the real reason for the threatened closure. The situation reached a climax during a January 2009 summit in Moscow in which Medvedev and Bakiyev signed an agreement whereby Russia would give Kyrgyzstan a $2 billion loan and $150 million grant, apparently accompanied with the unwritten understanding that the Americans would be sent packing.

Since opening in late 2001, Manas has been a crucial link in the supply network that feeds the American and NATO effort in Afghanistan. As many as five hundred tons of cargo and fifteen thousand personnel pass through Manas each month. The 376th Air Expeditionary Wing based there provides air refueling to aircraft operating throughout the region. The base's importance for the transit of troops and supplies would be even more crucial with the Obama White House's policy of boosting the number of American troops in Afghanistan.[33]

The White House continued to request negotiations for a new base agreement. They reminded the Bakiyev government that the United States had contributed $850 million to Kyrgyzstan since it achieved independence with the breakup of the Soviet empire in 1991. In addition, Washington had supported the 2005 revolution that toppled the corrupt dictatorship of Askar Akayev.

Eventually the parties struck a deal. On June 24, 2009, President Bakiyev agreed to extend Washington's lease in return for a $60 million monthly rent, $36 million to expand the airport, and tens of millions of dollars more to combat the drug trade.

Obama scored an important deal with Medvedev during their Moscow summit on July 8, 2009. Henceforth the United States would be allowed either to fly American troops and supplies bound for Afghanistan over Russian air space or drive them in convoys across the country. That Russian corridor could make up for the increasingly dangerous land routes across Pakistan from the port of Karachi to Afghanistan.

The complex bilateral and at times multilateral diplomacy between the United States and Iran, the five Central Asian states, and Russia pales next to Afghanistan's neighbor to the south and east, Pakistan. General Eikenberry, the current ambassador and former ground commander in Afghanistan, explained that "Pakistan will remain the single greatest source of Afghan instability so long as the border sanctuaries remain. Until this sanctuary problem is fully addressed, the gains from sending additional forces may be fleeting."[34]

12

The War in Pakistan

Pakistan . . . is the most dangerous country in the world today,
where every nightmare of the twentieth century—terrorism,
nuclear proliferation, the danger of nuclear war, dictatorship,
poverty, drugs—come together in one place.
    —Bruce Riedel, CIA officer

The Stakes

The outcome of the war against al Qaeda and the Taliban in Afghanistan has morphed with the struggle against them in Pakistan. Al Qaeda and the Taliban are embedded ever deeper and spreading ever more widely among the over forty million Pashtuns who inhabit the vast, remote, and mostly mountainous region that straddles the fifteen-hundred-mile border between Afghanistan and Pakistan, a region increasingly known as Pashtunistan, Talibanistan, or AfPak.[1]

    The United States appears to be losing that war. The Taliban and an array of other Islamist groups are steadily eating away the already tattered political, economic, and social foundations of both Afghanistan and Pakistan. The heads of that hydra seem to multiply daily. The outcome of the war against Islamism in Afghanistan is important enough, but in Pakistan it is absolutely vital for American and global security. Bruce Riedel, a former CIA officer and now a White House adviser, describes Pakistan as "the most dangerous country in the world today, where every nightmare of the twentieth century—terrorism, nuclear proliferation, the danger of nuclear war, dictatorship, poverty, drugs—comes together in one place."[2]

Islamist terrorism in Pakistan is steadily worsening. The Taliban is only the most prominent of an array of Islamist groups struggling to overthrow Pakistan's government and replace it with rule dictated by a strict interpretation of the Koran and sharia. To that end they have launched bomb and assassination attacks in regions, cities, and towns across Pakistan. The number and severity of those attacks are soaring. In 2001 there were two recorded attacks with no casualties; in 2008 there were 1,820 attacks in which 2,155 civilians, 654 security force members, and 3,906 terrorists died. The most notorious attack to date was the murder of former president and then presidential candidate Benazir Bhutto on December 27, 2007.[3]

Very little holds back Pakistan from total collapse. Pakistan, along with Afghanistan, annually ranks among the top ten countries most prone to failure out of 177 countries.[4] Pakistan has been tottering on the edge ever since Muhammad Ali Jinnah, the brilliant leader of the Muslim League, wrenched it free from India in 1947. But Jinnah died the next year, and the government has since seesawed between military dictatorships and notoriously illiberal democracies. No matter who ruled, the result was massive corruption, exploitation, and repression that extracted and often expatriated much of what little wealth the economy produced. The rich got richer, and the poor got poorer, more numerous, and more desperate. More Pakistanis turned to the one virtuous institution in their midst—the mosque. More mullahs are promising heavenly paradise for those who wage holy war against all infidels, foreign and domestic. Hundreds of madrassas are indoctrinating more young minds in radical Islam. As if all that were not alarming enough, Pakistan tested a nuclear bomb in May 1998 and today may have more than one hundred.

Like Afghanistan, Pakistan is a crazy quilt of different peoples, with 180 million spread among a score of different ethnic groups, sixty languages or dialects, hundreds of tribes, and thousands of clans. Islam is the only force that unifies virtually all Pakistanis. That bond, however, is fraying between its mainstream and increasingly popular militant versions, and between the 70 percent who are Sunni and the 30 percent who are Shiite. The 4 percent of the population who are Hindus, Christians, Sikhs, and other religions suffer worse discrimination and at times outright persecution from Muslim militants. The country's administrative divisions partly reflect that diversity. There are four provinces (Punjab, Sindh, Baluchistan, and North West) and four territories (Islamabad, Federally Administered Tribal Areas, Azad Jammu-Kashmir, and Gilgit-Baltistan). The Tribal Areas alone are composed of seven agencies and six frontier regions, with each a law onto itself, as the federal presence is either symbolic or nonexistent.

Although terrorist groups permeate every province and territory, nowhere are they more entrenched than in the mountainous Tribal Areas, nestled between the North West Province and Afghanistan. The Taliban and al Qaeda escaped there after the American invasion in late 2001, and that remains their epicenter as they spread steadily across more regions of Afghanistan and Pakistan.

As a failing, nuclear-armed state beset by growing poverty, violence, despair, terrorism, and Islamic extremism, Pakistan is indeed the most potentially dangerous country on earth. Although the government remains primarily pro-Western, the population is increasingly anti-Western, anti-American, and zealously Islamist. Factions within both the army and intelligence agency are doing all they can to aid the Taliban, al Qaeda, and other Islamist groups with money, arms, and recruits from the hundreds of madrassas and scores of charities.

The Islamist revolution in Pakistan is steadily strengthening. Should that revolution succeed in toppling the government and taking power, it would control all those nuclear weapons and materials. That would almost certainly trigger an American operation to secure that potential holocaust.

That scenario is disturbing enough. Yet there is another that would be even more catastrophic—nuclear war between Pakistan and India. The result would be tens of millions of dead and dying; political, economic, and social collapse; and a religious war of extermination between Muslims and Hindus. That is a very real possibility. Pakistan and India have gone to the brink of war twice since both countries tested nuclear weapons in 1998.

Friend or Foe?

Ironically, Pakistan's government is largely responsible for its own worsening Islamist insurgency by sponsoring an array of groups, of which the Taliban are the most prominent. Riedel explains that "the jihadist Frankenstein monster that was created by the Pakistani Army and the Pakistani intelligence service is now increasingly turning on its creators."[5]

What fuels Pakistan's seemingly self-destructive policy? The central dilemma for the United States in Pakistan is the Janus-faced nature of the leaders and institutions in Islamabad and beyond. As in many other Muslim states, most notably Saudi Arabia, those in power are torn between two conflicting interests. They would like to modernize and integrate their countries within the global system. Yet the resulting increase in inequalities, corruption, and poverty would provoke more people to heed the call of radical Islam as the solution to all problems. And that can threaten the continued rule of those in power. Added to that is the sincere faith of most of the elite in Islam, a religion in which mosque and state theologically must be inseparable. The result is that people and institutions are trapped in a tug-of-war between modernism and Islamism.

This schizophrenia certainly afflicts Pakistan's army, the only institution that holds the country together and is failing even at that. The army is loyal only to itself and to the concept of Pakistan. Since 1947 generals have overthrown elected governments four times when they felt the political leadership was too corrupt and inept. Indeed soldiers have ruled the country more years than have civilians. Although officially the president is the commander-in-chief, this is effective only when a general holds power. Otherwise the army's loyalty is to its commander. Tragically, soldiers have proven to be just as inept, corrupt, and brutal as civilians when they occupy the presidential palace. These problems are compounded in the field where the army has proven incapable of conducting effective counterinsurgency campaigns.

As if the army's dismal leadership, composition, and effectiveness were not troubling enough for Pakistan's future, there is the ISI. Unlike most intelligence services, the ISI is permeated by ideologues, in this case Islamists, rather than worldly realists. Islamist zeal among the leaders and ranks swelled steadily as the ISI led the jihad against the Soviets in Afghanistan from 1979 to 1989, and then against the communist government of Muhammad Najibullah from then until 1992, when the mujahideen took over. That triumph was short-lived. The mujahideen, which the ISI had nurtured with weapons, money, training, and mullahs, proved to be as damaging as Najibullah's government. The ISI increasingly supported the Taliban or "student" movement led by Mohammad Omar, who not only expressed but fulfilled a version of Islamic puritanism. Pakistan backed the

Taliban's rise to power in Afghanistan and has not-so-secretly aided it since the Americans routed it into Pakistan in December 2001. Omar and his entourage are "hiding" in Quetta, Pakistan. Although Islamabad most likely knows where he is, it has rejected all American requests either to expel or eliminate him.

The Taliban is hardly the only Islamist movement backed by Islamabad, only the most prominent. Peter Bergen explained the blowback engendered by the Pakistanis, who "funneled millions of dollars to anti-Western Afghan factions, which in turn trained militants who later exported jihad and terrorism around the world—including to the United States."[6]

The ISI continues to play both sides of the political and ideological chasm. For years, American military and intelligence officials in Afghanistan and elsewhere have complained that the ISI, especially its S Wing, was aiding the Taliban, al Qaeda, and other militant Islamist groups with money, training, arms, and recruits. It is an open secret that the S Wing supports not just the Taliban but also Hekmatyar's and Haqqani's Islamist movements. In 2007 allegations arose that the ISI had actually put a $1,900-a-head reward for the murder of American and allied troops in Afghanistan. Although ISI chief Ahmed Shuja Pasha claimed that he has purged his organization of Islamists, the White House and Langley remain skeptical of that claim.[7]

As if the Janus-faced nature of the army and intelligence agency is not disturbing enough, there is Abdul Qadeer Khan, once best known as the father of Pakistan's nuclear industry but more recently for an even more dubious distinction. After getting a PhD in nuclear physics from a Belgium university in 1972, he took a high-level position in the Netherlands' nuclear energy industry and proceeded to steal blueprints and bring them back to Islamabad in 1976. The government put him in charge of Pakistan's nuclear energy and weapons programs. Under his leadership, Pakistan successfully detonated nuclear bombs in 1998. Khan's ambitions did not end there. He sold nuclear designs and equipment to Iran, Libya, and North Korea. The proliferation could have been worse. He notably did not sell anything to Iraq and rebuffed several al Qaeda requests to buy nuclear materials.[8]

The United States did not become fully aware of Khan's peddling of nuclear secrets and materials until 2003. The White House pressured President Musharraf to act against Khan. On January 25, 2004, Pakistan's government revealed just what Khan had done and indicted him. This action provoked mass Pakistani protests against the government for its persecution of the national hero. The following day Musharraf pardoned Khan but ordered his indefinite house arrest. But the damage had already been done.

Attempts to spread Pakistan's nuclear technology to anti-Western forces did not end with Khan's nefarious activities. The Ummah Tameer-e-Nau (UTN) is yet another Pakistani institution that sponsors the Taliban, al Qaeda, and other Islamist groups.[9] The UTN is ostensibly a private relief organization that was founded by Sultan Bashiruddan Mahmood, a former director of Pakistan's Atomic Energy Commission, to conduct humanitarian and development projects in Afghanistan. The organization's true purpose is far less noble. Mahmood is an Islamist extremist whose 1987 book, *Doomsday and Life after Death: The Ultimate Faith of the Universe as Seen by the Holy Quran*, argues that a nuclear Armageddon will end the world and bring the final judgment day to Allah. The UTN is filled with scientists who are eager to share their expertise to help al Qaeda and the Taliban get and launch WMD against the infidels. That effort has been aided by Islamist elements in the army and ISI, including its former director General Hamid Gul, who actually met with bin Laden and Zawahiri just weeks before September 11.

After briefing the NSC on this danger, CIA chief Tenet flew to Islamabad to confront Musharraf with that intelligence and get him to shut down UTN. At first Musharraf denied the UTN's malfeasance but eventually had to admit that the evidence was true and promised to end UTN's ties with al Qaeda and the Taliban. To date, that relationship appears to be as tight, if less overt, than ever.

As if the array of terrorist groups festering Pakistan is not formidable enough, there is the homegrown version of the Taliban, known as Tehrik-e-Taliban, that was founded in 2007. That group's leader, Baitullah Mehsud, proved to be as skilled and ruthless an insurgent leader as his Afghan counterpart, Mohammad Omar, until he was killed in August 2009. Yet Mehsud was no dictator; he shared leadership with Hakimullah Mehsud, Hafiz Gul Bahadur, and Maulavi Nazir. And the three of them in turn swore allegiance to Omar, as well as to bin Laden. Hakimullah Mehsud took over Tehrik-e Taliban after Baitullah Mehsud's death

and apparently is just as effective a leader. He and his coterie have tried to carry
the war to the United States, most notably with attacks on the American consulate
in Peshawar in April 2010 and the aborted Times Square bombing in May 2010.
Mehsud is ably assisted by Wali ur Rehman and Qari Hussain, the respective
heads of the military and suicide bomber strategies.[10]

As irony would have it, Islamabad has fought against Pakistan's Taliban version even as it aids the Afghan version. The reason is simple. Afghanistan's Taliban
is devoted to destroying its enemy, the Kabul regime, while the Pakistani version
is devoted to destroying what is considers the apostate regime in Islamabad.

The potentially deadliest groups spawned by Islamabad are Lashkar-e-Taiba
and Jaish-e-Mohammed, both revolutionary movements dedicated to forcing
India to give up Kashmir. On December 13, 2001, five Jaish-e-Mohammed militants attacked India's parliament in New Delhi and murdered five people before
being gunned down. New Delhi was well aware of the links between that group
and Islamabad. During the crisis, both India and Pakistan rushed troops to the
frontier. Fortunately, Secretary of State Colin Powell was able to defuse the crisis
with shuttle diplomacy that got Islamabad and New Delhi to make face-saving
gestures, with Musharraf promising to sever all ties with Lashkar-e-Taiba. That
crisis could easily have escalated into first a conventional and then a nuclear war.

War once again loomed with India following the Mumbai terrorist attack that
began on November 26, 2008, leaving 163 dead, including 136 civilians, 18 security force members, and 9 terrorists. Lashkar-e-Taiba was behind the attack. New
Delhi accused Islamabad of complicity because of its past ties with the group.
Islamabad vigorously denied any current relationship. The Indians and Pakistani
government rattled sabers by swelling their armies on the frontier and conducting
air maneuvers in the skies above. Mercifully, both sides eventually stood down.[11]

The next terrorist attack and crisis is inevitable. The only questions are when,
where, and how Islamabad and New Delhi will react.

American Policy

American policy toward Pakistan is as old as the founding of both that nation-state
and the Cold War in 1947. Pakistan became a key American ally in Washington's
containment policy for Southwest Asia. That relationship peaked during the de-

cade the Soviets spent trying to conquer Afghanistan after their December 1979 invasion. Washington and Islamabad, along with Riyadh, worked together to finance, equip, train, and dispatch the mujahideen who battled and eventually defeated the Soviets and their collaborators.

That close relationship largely evaporated during the 1990s. Islamabad helped bring the Taliban to power and al Qaeda back to Afghanistan in 1996. The Clinton White House voiced its concern but could do no more. Then the Pakistanis followed India in testing nuclear weapons in May 1998. By law the American president was required to cut off military aid and dual-use exports to both countries. In October 1999 Musharraf's coup against the elected government of Nawaz Sharif did replace a corrupt populist fond of spouting anti-Western rhetoric with a less corrupt, generally pro-Western leader. But the nuclear issue kept Washington and Islamabad estranged.

Then came September 11, and suddenly Pakistan was essential once again to American security as a front-line state to enemies in Afghanistan. To cement their relationship, the Bush administration gave Pakistan over $11 billion in mostly military aid from 2002 to 2009. Many question whether that money was well spent. Most of the military aid consisted of weapons systems and equipment that might have bolstered Pakistan's power to fight a conventional war against, say, India, but relatively little went into counterinsurgency efforts. As if that were not wasteful enough, the Government Accountability Office (GAO) found widespread irregularities in how the money was spent. Finally, the Bush team did not use that massive aid as a lever to extract a sustained military campaign by Islamabad against the Taliban and al Qaeda.[12]

As usual there are ironies. During the 1980s, the United States helped underwrite an insurgency against the Soviets in Afghanistan from sanctuaries in neighboring Pakistan. Today the United States faces an insurgency in Afghanistan fueled by recruits, weapons, and ideological zeal emanating largely from neighboring Pakistan. And the White House can do very little to prevent it. Will the United States follow Russia in a humiliating defeat and retreat from the region?

Pakistan's Fight against Terrorism

At times Pakistan has not only cooperated but has inflicted some notable coups against al Qaeda. Islamabad's assistance was essential in the capture of such terrorist kingpins as Ramzi Yousef after the first World Trade Center bombing in 1993, and Abu Zubaydah and Khalid Sheikh Mohammed after September 11. The biggest operation occurred in March 2002 when the CIA and Pakistani security forces launched simultaneous raids on thirteen al Qaeda safe houses, during which they captured two dozen suspects, including Zubaydah. In addition, since September 11, Islamabad has captured over 630 Al Qaeda operatives, at the cost of over 1,600 Pakistani soldiers dead and 3,700 wounded.[13]

Yet Islamabad undercut these efforts by appeasing the Taliban and other rebel Islamist groups in the North West Frontier Province. In return for cease-fires, the government withdrew forces from some areas and released prisoners. The most notorious deal came in September 2006 when Islamabad recognized the Islamic Emirate of Waziristan, an association of tribal chiefs allied with the Taliban and al Qaeda. The result of that appeasement policy has been a domino effect in which the tolerated Taliban mini-states infiltrate, undermine, and eventually take over adjacent regions.

Of course, the most glaring example of Pakistani collaboration was the ability of bin Laden and his entourage to live for years in Abbottabad, just thirty-five miles from Islamabad and a few miles from the nation's military academy. Obviously, key Pakistani officials protected bin Laden. The only question for Washington is how high in Pakistan's government that protection was extended.

Practical reasons may be more important than theological reasons in explaining that appeasement policy. With half a million troops, the Pakistani army may appear to be a formidable force. Experts, however, rate the army as, at best, second-rate, with few units trained for counterinsurgency tactics. Most of the army is deployed along the frontier with India, and much of that is concentrated in the Kashmir region. The Taliban and al Qaeda defeated the army's campaigns into the territories they controlled in 2003, 2004, and 2008.

It took a crisis in Islamabad itself to convince Musharraf to try to fight back against Islamist terrorists wherever they lurked, including the North West Frontier Province. The most powerful Islamist stronghold in Islamabad was the Red Mosque and adjacent Jamia Hafsa madrassa. Since its founding in 1965, the mosque and madrassa have been Islamist hotbeds that have attracted countless pilgrims and trained thousands of militants. Among the regular worshippers were scores of Islamists from within Pakistan's government, including the ISI, whose headquarters shares the same neighborhood.

The government faced a dilemma. It would only provoke more anti-government rhetoric from the mullahs if it tried to suppress their calls for an Islamist revolution. But doing nothing would allow the mullahs to inspire more followers. Musharraf ordered his security forces to search the complex in July 2005 after the terrorist attacks in London but backed off when female students wielding batons blocked the way. Then a crisis erupted on July 3, 2007, when militants from the complex attacked an army post in the neighborhood. This time Musharraf ordered the army to surround the complex while diplomats tried to negotiate with the militants. For the next week over a thousand people came out of the complex, but the militants refused to hand over any among them tied to terrorist attacks. Musharraf broke the stalemate on July 10 by ordering an assault. The army killed eighty-four militants and captured fifty, while ten soldiers and fourteen civilians died in the fighting.

That attack triggered the latest round of fighting in the tribal territories, which became known as the Third Waziristan War. The Taliban ended a truce that was entering its tenth month and launched attacks across both the tribal territories and the rest of Pakistan. Once again Islamabad sent in the army, which was defeated, and signed another truce that ceded yet more land and people to the Taliban.

The Taliban has steadily spread its reign of terror across Pashtunistan and beyond. Their first major incursion into the Punjab was the Swat Valley, inhabited by over 1.3 million people and only a hundred miles north of Islamabad. Although the army had over fifteen thousand troops of four brigades in Swat, by early 2009 as many as four thousand Taliban fighters controlled over two-thirds of the valley. The army had largely ceded control of the valley to the rebels by holing up in its bases except for brief operations. The Taliban took full advantage of the army's meekness. They destroyed truck supply convoys, ambushed patrols, and even shelled the bases. They captured and beheaded any leaders and many supporters of the Islamabad government, including judges, lawyers, police officers, teachers, engineers, businessmen, and politicians from the secular Awami National Party, the most popular political party in the region. They destroyed businesses that sold forbidden products, beat women who did not wear the burqa, and by January 2009 had burned 169 girls' schools. Several hundred thousand people fled from the valley.[14]

Ironically, the Taliban may have made a major push in the Swat Valley in part to escape the deadly Hellfire missile strikes by Predator and Reaper drones against their leadership near the Afghanistan frontier. They at once sought to capture a safer haven and put more pressure on Islamabad to get the Americans to stop their attacks.[15]

That strategy was an overwhelming success. Instead of launching a massive force to drive out the Taliban, Islamabad asked for a truce. The Taliban agreed to a cease-fire for an "indefinite period" in return for Islamabad's promise to make sharia the foundation for justice in the region. The army could stay but could not stir from its bases. That freed the Taliban to operate at will, proselytizing and terrorizing not just in Swat but further south in the district of Bruner, just sixty miles from the capital. Meanwhile, Islamabad became even more strident in criticizing American bombing raids in the North West Frontier Territory. In all, Pakistan, and by extension the United States, had suffered a serious defeat.[16]

Why did the government cave to the rebels? The troops posted in the Swat Valley were second-rate units of a second-rate army whose training and orientation was geared to fighting a conventional war against another second-rate army, that of India. Whenever the Pakistan army tries to conduct counterinsurgency operations, it ends up feeding rather than smothering the insurgents. Its search, destroy, and withdraw tactics kill few rebels and lots of innocent civilians. Many of the survivors who mourn their lost loved ones and destroyed homes end up joining the insurgency. This is what happened in the Swat Valley whenever the army stirred from its lairs.

The Obama administration exerted enormous pressure on Islamabad to destroy rather than appease the Taliban in the Swat Valley. That pressure finally paid off when Islamabad launched a massive counterattack of thirty thousand troops in August 2009. Heavy bombardments and the blanketing of cities and other strategic points with troops managed to drive off or underground most of the Taliban. This in turn provided the security with which most of the two million refugees could return to what remained of their homes. Never before had Pakistan committed as many troops nor won as clear-cut a victory.

Whether this represents a genuine turning point in Pakistan's policies or an anomaly remains to be seen. Despite all that has happened since 2001, Islamabad treated the frontier region with Afghanistan as a secondary front until 2009. Since then the Pakistanis have made a genuine effort to defeating the worsening insurgency. Two inseparable reasons lay behind this dramatic shift in policy. One was the transformation in American policy from that of George W. Bush to Barack Obama. The Obama administration is as committed to defeating al Qaeda and the Taliban in Afghanistan and Pakistan as the Bush administration was indifferent to and neglectful of those enemies. And because of the Bush administration's policies, the Taliban, al Qaeda, and other Islamist groups insidiously mushroomed throughout the country in numbers and deadliness to the point where they threatened to topple Pakistan's government.

The amount of troops that Islamabad has committed to defeating the array of insurgencies tripled from 50,000 in 2001 to 150,000 in 2010. Unlike in previous years, these troops are not mostly hunkered down in their bases, rarely stirring to seek out and engage the insurgents. In 2009 Islamabad launched 209 operations with one or more brigades of 3,000 each, two times as many as in 2007 and 2008 combined. These operations were costly; the Pakistanis lost around 800 troops killed in action in 2009, compared to around 520 NATO troops killed in Afghanistan.[17]

Supplementing the regular army in the North West Frontier Province is a Frontier Corps of ninety thousand troops, up from sixty thousand in 2008 and largely recruited from the region's tribes. That number is not as impressive as it may seem. Most of these troops are poorly trained, equipped, paid, and led. As if these deficiencies were not grave enough, the Taliban and al Qaeda have infiltrated and spread dissension among the Frontier Corps' ranks, uncovered its plans, and impeded operations. Many troops have refused to fight their fellow tribesmen.

Gen. Tariq Khan, who was given command of the Frontier Corps in 2008, has implemented some reforms. He raised the number of troops by ten thousand, began upgrading their weapons and equipment with $40 million of Pentagon aid, allowed thirty American and British experts to train an elite group of four hundred troops in special operations for three months, and launched operations inspired by CIA intelligence and advice.

Although these efforts appeared to be bearing fruit, ultimately they may prove poisonous. By March 2009, after a half-year campaign, the Frontier Corps recaptured the Bajaur district at the northern tip of the tribal areas. General Khan boasted that his troops had killed or captured over fifteen hundred militants. These victories are most likely Pyrrhic. The strategy was little more than one of scorched earth in which heavy bombardments and massive assaults destroyed cities, towns, and countless civilians, and drove over two hundred thousand survivors into refugee camps. Rather than destroy the rebels, the army simply dispersed them while destroying the lives and property of countless fence-sitters caught in the crossfire. The predictable result was the hydra dilemma, where many of the survivors swelled the Taliban ranks.[18]

Thus does the insurgency spread beyond the North West Frontier Province to all regions and more cities and refugee camps across Pakistan. Each Islamist group imposes its own strict version of Islam on whatever population it rules. The Taliban is the largest, and its ranks swell daily with recruits motivated by some mix of belief, pay, and fear. As the Taliban infiltrate an area, the rich and much of the middle class flee, leaving mostly the poor behind. The Taliban reward the rural poor with land and the urban poor with businesses confiscated from those who fled. But the Taliban back these positive inducements by beatings and even executions of anyone who resists the Taliban program.

In early 2010 Islamabad appeared to finally awaken to the reality that the Taliban monster was turning against its creator. The ISI had long turned a blind eye to the known whereabouts of the Taliban's leaders. But in quick succession, the ISI and CIA captured Mullah Abdul Ghani Baradar, the military and financial chief, and Mullah Abdul Kabir, a member of the ruling council. In the short term those were massive blows against Taliban operations, security, prestige, and morale.

Whatever successes Islamabad scored against the Taliban may have literally washed away with the massive flooding of the Indus River valley in August 2010, during which millions of people lost their homes and livelihoods. The Taliban and other Islamist groups were swift to respond by dispensing money, food, and other aid, along with fiery sermons denouncing the government's typically inept and corrupt failure to help. Rebuilding the regions devastated by the floods will take years and billions of dollars. The entire infrastructure of roads, irrigation canals, schools, electricity, health clinics, warehouses, bridges, and dams was swept away across swaths of the country. Islamist movements are blossoming amidst the ruins.

American Operations

Meanwhile America's not-so-secret war in northwestern Pakistan persists. As with many governments, there is often a gap in Islamabad between official and unofficial policies. Officially, the United States is forbidden from violating Pakistan's sovereignty by bombing or raiding al Qaeda and Taliban strongholds in the North West Frontier region, let conducting alone the clear, hold, and build operations that might secure an area. One of these public rejections came in January 2008 after top-ranking American intelligence officials met with Musharraf to brief him on the North West Frontier region situation and ask permission to extend covert operations there. Yet Islamabad does nothing to stop these attacks. Indeed American Predators and Reapers are based in and operate from three secret bases in Pakistan.

The selective American air strikes and commando raids in the region have killed or routed the immediate targets. The air strikes have been especially effective. After taking office, Obama ordered more Hellfire missiles launched from Predator or Reaper drones at al Qaeda and Taliban compounds and training camps to kill scores of operatives and a number of leaders; among the dead were nine of the top twenty al Qaeda and Taliban leaders, including Abu Jihad al-Masri and Osama al-Kini, who were believed to have helped plan the 1998 embassy bombings, and Mustafa Abu al-Yazid, al Qaeda's financial chief. The most significant strike killed the leader of Pakistan's Taliban, Baitullah Mehsud, on August 5, 2009. His death provoked a struggle among factions to fill that leadership vacuum. That disarray helped Pakistan's efforts to retake the Swat Valley.[19]

But the Americans suffered their own terrible blow. Humam Khalil Abu Mulal al-Balawi was a Jordanian doctor and prominent Islamist on the Internet. Jordan's General Intelligence Department recruited and then passed him to the CIA as an asset to infiltrate the Taliban and ideally al Qaeda. On December 30, 2009, Balawi entered the Forward Operating Base Chapman near Khost. He was so trusted that he was let into the compound without being searched. Tragically, Balawi turned out to have been a double agent. When his bomb detonated, it killed the CIA base chief and four other CIA officers, along with two American contractors and a Jordanian intelligence officer, and wounded six others. A week later a video was released in which Balawi appears beside Hakimullah Mehsud, the Taliban chief, who explains that the suicide bombing was retaliation for the killing of his predecessor.

This was the second-worst loss of officers in the agency's history, second only to Hezbollah's suicide bombing attack at the American embassy in Beirut in 1983, which killed eight officers. It also surpassed the loss of four CIA officers in Afghanistan since the invasion in October 2001. Although the CIA retaliated by stepping up the number of Hellfire missile attacks by Predator and Reaper drones against the Taliban and al Qaeda, nothing could soften the devastating blow to the agency's prestige and Afghan operations.[20]

The ability of the drones to gather intelligence and eliminate enemy leaders is crucial to fighting the war. But behind those heartening decapitations of Islamist chiefs lurks the familiar hydra dilemma. The strikes also killed over seven hundred people living near the terrorist compounds. Embittered local people, whose property had been destroyed or loved ones killed, swelled the Taliban's ranks. Islamabad's response is to repeatedly and publicly criticize the United States for those strikes while lauding its own campaigns against those same enemies. According to the official word, somehow America's mostly surgical strikes enhance, while its own ham-fisted poundings diminish, these enemies. In reality, both feed the hydra, although Pakistan's blunderbusses inflict more harm.[21]

Can that vicious cycle be broken? Nothing Washington has done so far appears to have helped much. Buying Islamabad's cooperation is the core of American policy toward Pakistan. The $11 billion that the Bush administration gave Islamabad after September 11, and the $30 billion of international loans that it helped reschedule, did little to bolster the government's counterterrorist efforts, let alone develop Pakistan's economy. Yet there is no question that Pakistan desperately needs all the money it can get. These grants and loans may be all that prevents a failing state from total collapse. So President Obama has continued this aid policy. In April 2009 he asked Congress for $7.5 billion in aid to Islamabad over the next five years. Most of that aid is targeted to bolstering Pakistan's counterinsurgency capacity. Critics question whether the result will merely throw good money after bad.[22]

As in Afghanistan and Iraq, a key White House policy is to train Pakistani security forces in counterterrorist methods. So far these efforts have been modest. During the summer of 2008, a secret task force began training a four-hundred-man unit of Pakistan's Frontier Corps in counterinsurgency warfare. After seven months that unit was deployed in the region. The unit is outside of the army command and reports directly to the president. Initial reports indicate that the unit is performing its mission well enough. Yet that unit is merely a drop in the proverbial bucket of what it vitally needed. In 2010 Americans began ten-week training sessions for up to two thousand recruits at a base in northwestern Pakistan.[23]

The police are a neglected crucial counterterrorist force. The Taliban and other Islamist groups target police for assassination. Increasing numbers of those still alive strip off their uniforms and flee. The police are not just outgunned but outbid by the Taliban. The average policeman makes $200 a month, compared to $440 for a Taliban militant. A policeman's family generally receives nothing if he is killed on duty. The family of a slain Taliban fighter can pocket $20,000.[24]

Economic aid is crucial to Pakistan's survival but tends to be squandered, with very little reaching those who most need it. As during the war against the Soviets, Islamabad refused to let Americans actually distribute the aid. The claim was that for Americans to do so would somehow provoke feelings against both Washington and Islamabad. In reality, the government wanted to take both the credit and a sizable cut of the proceeds. Recently, the Taliban and other Islamist groups mostly use charity groups to infiltrate, proselytize, and recruit among the over two million people crowded in refugee camps. Whenever the government outlaws a charity, the group renames itself and resumes its efforts.[25]

America's dependence on Pakistan for its war against al Qaeda and the Taliban was underlined by attacks on the thousand-mile supply line leading from the port of Karachi on the Indian Ocean north to Kabul. In December 2008 the Taliban destroyed over three hundred trucks at a supply base outside of Peshawar. Then in February 2009 insurgents blew up a bridge in the Khyber Pass just fifteen miles northwest of Peshawar, halting traffic for weeks until the area could be secured and the bridge repaired.[26]

The attacks on truck convoys originating from Karachi and the closure of bases in Uzbekistan and Kyrgyzstan forced the Obama White House to scramble to find and develop new supply routes. Some supplies would actually be trucked in all the way from the port of Riga, Latvia, on the Baltic Sea; traverse Russia; and enter Afghanistan via Uzbekistan or Tajikistan. Other supplies would begin at the port of Poti, Georgia, on the Black Sea and reach Afghanistan via Azerbaijan and Iran. But those two new routes can only handle about five hundred containers a month compared to the two to three thousand containers that journey each month from Karachi. Meanwhile, the number of cargo flights landing at Bagram Air Base outside Kabul would increase by 50 percent. President Karimov agreed to allow nonlethal supplies to be flown into the Navoi Air Base in Uzbekistan and shipped across the nearby frontier. The key is the diversification of supply lines so that a disruption on one or more of the routes does not cripple the American war effort.[27]

One promising development is that Islamabad today, under President Asif Ali Zardari and army commander Gen. Ashfaq Parvez Kayani, appears slightly more willing to cooperate and fight than when Musharraf controlled Pakistan. Zardari, the husband of slain former president Benazir Bhutto, is pro-Western, having spent much of his life in the United States and Europe. Kayani's ties with the Pentagon are close, having trained at the army's infantry school at Fort Benning and the command school at Fort Leavenworth. Yet the government remains deeply divided. Prime Minister Yousaf Raza Gillani, Foreign Minister Shah Mahmood Qureshi, and ISI chief Ahmed Shuja Pasha are more Janus-faced as they try to placate both the Americans and the Islamists.

The latest shift in the seesaw between civilian and army rule is precarious. Zardari became president on September 9, 2008, after Musharraf was forced to resign, mostly because he had alienated too many of Pakistan's elite through corruption and blatant violations of the constitution. But Zardari is widely perceived as much weaker and even more corrupt than his predecessor.

To date, the worst animosities between Washington and Islamabad were provoked by an event that ideally should have been the relationship's greatest triumph.

The Death of Osama bin Laden

Abbottabad is a small city just thirty-five miles north of Islamabad. It is the site for Pakistan's military academy. And for five years it was the refuge for Osama bin Laden and a small circle of his two youngest wives, children, and a few followers who lived together in a three-story building surrounded by a twelve-foot wall.

How did bin Laden pass his time at his Abbottabad compound? He led an austere, quasi-monastic lifestyle within its walls. For security he spent little time in the yard and had no Internet or telephone links with the outside world. He apparently eased some of the tedium by surfing satellite television and occasionally sending messages to his followers via elaborate chains of trusted agents. For videotaped messages he dyed his white beard and hair black.[28]

The CIA finally tracked him down by wielding an array of cutting-edge and more traditional espionage techniques. Even then they could only be 80 percent certain that it was him. The Pentagon gave Obama even worse odds for the success of a mission to kill him—at best only a fifty-fifty chance for Special Forces to evade Pakistan's military, overwhelm him and his bodyguards, and then escape with the body. A failed mission would be a great propaganda coup both for America's enemies and the Republican Party. Operationally the easy alternative was to obliterate everyone and everything inside with a barrage of cruise missiles. That would certainly kill bin Laden if he were there, but the strategy had its own severe drawbacks. If the United States did not have definitive DNA evidence of bin Laden's demise, his followers could claim that he lived on and that the Americans had killed innocent people instead. If the building was destroyed, Langley would never get its hands on the treasure trove of critical information on al Qaeda inside it.

For Obama one choice was clearly superior. He asked the Pentagon to send in Special Forces to kill and carry away bin Laden. When he was briefed on the plan, he added crucial details like adding more men and helicopters and issuing orders for the SEALs to shoot their way out if the Pakistani military or police opened fire. With Islamists permeating Pakistan's government, Obama wisely decided not to inform President Zardari until the operation was over.

On the night of May 2, 2011, twenty-four members of SEAL Team Six, some of America's finest Special Operations troops, descended on the compound in two Black Hawk helicopters equipped with advanced technologies that minimized their radar signature and noise, while other SEALs in two Chinook helicopters as backups landed along the route. One of the Black Hawks crashed in the yard, but the men emerged safely, and with those men from the other Black Hawk, each fulfilled his carefully rehearsed mission. In the yard, bin Laden's courier opened fire and was killed, along with the courier's nearby wife. The SEALs broke into the building and methodically worked their way through it, room by room and floor by floor. They killed his son in the stairwell. They encountered bin Laden on the top floor. One SEAL shot his fifth wife in the leg when she tried to shield her husband. Another SEAL shot bin Laden in the eye and heart. Specialists conducted tests to determine whether the corpse was actually bin Laden's and then put him in a body bag and carried it to one of the helicopters. While some SEALs tied up the dozen surviving women and children, others searched the rooms and scooped up into bags computers, thumb drives, documents, books, and anything else that might contain vital intelligence. The SEAL team then squeezed into the operational Black Hawk and, escorted by the Chinooks, flew low toward the Khyber Pass and the secure base just across the frontier in Afghanistan, where their raid had begun. There, bin Laden's body was transferred to a plane that flew him to an aircraft carrier in the Indian Ocean. After a Muslim cleric performed a brief funeral ceremony, the weighted body was dumped into the ocean's depths. In all, the raid to kill and render bin Laden was a brilliant success.[29]

After Obama announced that U.S. Special Forces had killed, retrieved, and buried bin Laden at sea, Pakistan's leaders and people erupted in a rage fueled both from anger at America's violation of their country's sovereignty and, for many, shame that their own government either was ignorant of the terrorist chief's presence or had actually tolerated it. Islamabad officially responded not with congratulations but with shrill denunciations of the raid, and ordered the United States to cut back its number of CIA officers and other personnel in the country.

This in turn provoked outrage among many Americans who criticized Islamabad for either incompetence or outright treachery. The Obama administration quietly asked some very tough questions of the Pakistani regime's leaders about who may have collaborated with bin Laden to grant him refuge in Abbottabad. Publicly, they tried to dampen some of this animosity by announcing that a preliminary search of the intelligence seized at the compound did not yield any direct link between al Qaeda and the higher echelons of Pakistan's government, leaving unsaid what lower level links they had uncovered. The White House then tested Islamabad's trustworthiness by sharing intelligence of a huge Taliban munitions depot and asking the Pakistanis to seize it. The depot was empty when the army finally showed up. Obviously, high-ranking Pakistani officials tipped off the militants, who were able to truck the weapons caches to safety. Eventually the White House expressed its exasperation with Islamabad's treachery by eliminating $500 million from that year's $1.3 billion military aid package to Pakistan. But such gestures cannot begin to change the regime's duplicitous nature.

Back to the Future

What more can the United States do to try to turn around the war in Pakistan? Bruce Riedel, the Obama White House's counterterrorist chief, recommends a number of ways to gain greater cooperation from Islamabad against the Islamists in the North West Frontier and Tribal Areas. The United States could help negotiate treaties between Pakistan and India to settle the Kashmir conflict and between Pakistan and Afghanistan over a common frontier based on the Durand Line, which was drawn in 1893 but never implemented. These efforts would inspire faith in Washington's goodwill and create a duty to repay that favor. The United States could also refocus its military aid program to emphasize counterinsurgency training, weapons, and equipment. Economic aid should be increased and carefully managed to ensure that it actually helps develop the key sectors of Pakistan's economy.[30]

Yet, ultimately, these policies can do little to alleviate a bleak future facing Pakistan. By 2020 there may well be over 220 million people mostly existing in poverty, violence, and desperation. The political seesaw between inept, corrupt, and brutal military and civilian rule will alienate more of those people. Islamism's appeal as the salvation from all these horrendous worldly problems will spread steadily. The nightmare scenario for American security would be an Islamist revolution led by the Taliban and al Qaeda that takes over Pakistan and gains control over that country's nuclear weapons and materials.

How then could the United States respond? The worst policy option for the White House would be a conservative conquer-and-convert crusade. With over

200 million people mired in worsening poverty, anti-Westernism, and Islamism, Pakistan would surpass Iraq and Afghanistan as a black hole devouring hundreds of thousands of troops and trillions of dollars for a conquest and conversion strategy against an Islamist regime. History has revealed that there are just some wars that the United States is not powerful enough to win, and a war in Pakistan would be among them.

America's only viable choice would be a smash, grab, and run operation to secure and remove Pakistan's nuclear weapons and materials. Ideally that operation could be completed within a few weeks in which all of the elements unfolded at once. The Pakistani air force would be destroyed on the ground. The Islamist government would be decapitated. Special Forces would capture all known nuclear sites. The Indian army could rattle the saber along the frontier to distract most of the Pakistani army. Any Pakistani army forces trying to retake the nuclear sites would be pulverized by bombs and missiles. The CIA would assist pro-Western elements within Pakistan's military to retake the government.

Obviously such an operation would be highly risky. The Pakistani government has widely dispersed and hidden its nuclear facilities, weapons, and materials. There is no guarantee that the CIA knows where all of them are or that the American military could seize them if they did. Even if all of the elements worked as planned, the result would be to kick a hornet's nest of rage and violence in Pakistan and elsewhere across the Muslim world. Terrorist attacks would detonate across India and beyond. But that rage and violence can and must be endured and ultimately contained. There is simply no alternative.

13

Consequences

Are we capturing, killing or deterring and dissuading more terrorists every day than the madrassas and the radical clerics are recruiting, training, and deploying against us?
—Donald Rumsfeld

I truly am not that concerned with him.
—George W. Bush on Osama bin Laden

The Promise

Images of September 11 are forever seared into America's consciousness—the jet airliners exploding into the 110-story Twin Towers; the fireballs engulfing half a dozen floors; the clouds of acrid black smoke billowing away; the thousands of terrified but lucky people streaming out to safety onto the plaza below; the firemen charging into the buildings in a courageous and ultimately doomed attempt to save those still inside; the people trapped above escaping the hellish inferno by hurling themselves into the thousand feet of space before the cement ground; the South Tower and then the North Tower pancaking into ten-story piles of shattered steel, glass, and concrete; and for weeks thereafter the pillars of thick dust and smoke swirling like ghosts from the smoldering ruins below.

In all, the terrorists murdered nearly three thousand people at the World Trade Center, at the Pentagon, and on the hijacked airliner in Pennsylvania. Those attacks blew a hundred billion dollar hole in the economy. The psychic costs for the survivors and all who remember can never be determined.

Most Americans experienced mingled feelings of justice, elation, and relief when, on May 2, 2010, President Obama announced that Special Forces had killed and carried away Osama bin Laden, and that his corpse was now resting at the bottom of the Arabian Sea. That spectacular coup capped a decade of operations that killed or captured scores of al Qaeda's leaders and thousands of its agents around the world.

Yet, despite all that, who could feel anything more than partial closure? Most Americans continue to recall the atrocities of September 11 with helpless horror and rage. Who does not fear that such an attack or one even worse could happen again? Just how much have the counterterrorist campaigns of the United States and its allies around the world eroded the power of al Qaeda and other Islamist groups to commit similar horrendous crimes against humanity in the future?

The Fate of Al Qaeda and Islamism

In the decade after September 11, the American-led global counterterrorist strategy clearly depleted both the operatives and infrastructure of al Qaeda. The United States routed the terrorist organization and its host, the Taliban, from Afghanistan, while American and allied officials have caught and at times killed thousands of operatives elsewhere around the world. That campaign has involved, as John McLaughlin, the CIA's former deputy director, explained, "the relentless grinding away at . . . essential components of the terrorist networks—the couriers, the facilitators, the fundraisers, the safe house keepers, the technicians."[1]

This pressure has forced al Qaeda to reinvent itself. Before 9/11, al Qaeda was much more hierarchical and had strong ties with the network of groups that committed terrorism in its name. Al Qaeda today is much more significant as a movement than an organization, more inspirational than operational, and its links with its affiliates are more virtual than physical. Al Qaeda symbolically spearheads a global Islamist insurgency that, as David Kilcullen describes it, is composed of "dozens of local movements, grievances, and issues" that "have been aggregated (through regional and global players) into a global jihad against the West. These regional and global prey upon, link and exploit local actors and issues that are pre-existing. What makes the jihad so dangerous is its global nature." If so, then the logical strategy for defeating it would be one of "disaggregation" that will "dismantle or break up the links that allow the jihad to function as a global entity."[2]

Al Qaeda reached a nadir in 2007 before staging a brief comeback for several years. That year's NIE concluded that while al Qaeda's ability to attack the United States or its foreign assets had diminished, it remained a threat as it steadily rebuilt, while its affiliates were spreading elsewhere. Charles Allen, the DHS's intelligence chief, explained that al Qaeda has "regained its equilibrium. It has a safe haven in [Pakistan's] Federally Administered Tribal Areas; its top leadership is generally intact; it has able new lieutenants; it has new recruits to train; and it is training operatives who were born in the West or who have lived in the West."[3]

For several years after 2007, al Qaeda and its ally, the Taliban, steadily expanded their power over Afghanistan and Pakistan, and conducted terrorist attacks in the capitals of Kabul and Islamabad and in the other major cities. The Taliban even wielded the power to reach out of that region to terrorize the relatives of Pakistan and Afghan immigrants in New York and elsewhere in the United States, or kidnap for ransom immigrants who returned for visits. There were also two aborted terrorist attacks, one by a would-be bomber on a Christmas Day 2009 flight to Detroit and the other a May 2010 attempted car bombing in New York City's Times Square.[4]

The resurgence of al Qaeda and the Taliban was the direct result of the Bush team's disinterest, neglect, and incompetence. Although Obama implemented a surge in Afghanistan, that may have been too little to transform the country. Afghanistan today is essentially a failed state and is unlikely to ever become viable, no matter how many more troops, relief workers, and tens of billions of dollars are deployed there. President Hamid Karzai presides over the city-state of Kabul in fragile alliances with most other warlords across the country. Pakistan, meanwhile, is a failing state, locked in its own vicious cycle of poverty, corruption, violence, and radicalism. Here too all the tens of billions of the dollars that Washington has ladled out since September 11 have not slowed, let alone reversed, that cycle.

The good news is that the Americans and their allies have all but obliterated the original al Qaeda as an organization. The bad news it is that al Qaeda remains virulent as a movement of related organizations. Over forty groups declared their affiliation with al Qaeda from 2005 through 2007 alone. Al Qaeda's ties with two groups, Pakistan's Lashkar-e-Taiba and Sri Lanka's Tamil Tigers, may be seen in operational similarities in the attacks on Mumbai, India, in November 2008 and Lahore, Pakistan, in February 2009. Al Qaeda and its affiliates also share ways to hide or move people, money, arms, and information. Abu Zubaydah, one of al Qaeda's inner circle, was run to ground in a Lashkar-e-Taiba safe house.[5]

The international efforts to block al Qaeda's sources of money and freeze financial assets squirreled away in banks, front companies, charities, and other businesses and institutions have succeeded to a point. The loss of that money and records makes donors ever more hesitant to contribute. To finance operations al Qaeda increasingly relies on the face to face hawala system of passwords that debit an account in one place and fork over money elsewhere. That small-scale system is inefficient and impedes al Qaeda operations.

Al Qaeda has had to diversify its sources of money. An increasingly important source of cash is reaped from the heroin trade in Afghanistan, where al Qaeda skims money from transit and protection fees. Islamic charities are another vital source of revenue. Groups like the International Islamic Relief Organization, al-Haramain Foundation, and Muslim World League have been linked to Islamist groups, including al Qaeda. Also, it was estimated that as much as one-quarter of the four thousand non-governmental organizations working in Iraq were actually paying protection money to the insurgents. Al Qaeda and its affiliates increasingly rely on smuggling cash as well as gold, diamonds, and heroin. With its unregulated markets, Dubai has become the financial headquarters for al Qaeda and other Islamist groups. In late 2001 and 2002 couriers were spiriting around $2 million to $3 million a day on flights from Islamabad to Dubai, where the money was usually exchanged for gold.[6] And then there is strong-arm crime, which was especially blatant in Iraq. Al Qaeda was able to raise from $70 million to $200 million a year through protection rackets, kidnappings for ransom, and oil smuggling. Al Qaeda was hardly alone in raising cash through crime. To varying degrees, most other insurgent groups wield those tactics.[7]

Like its ability to raise and move money, al Qaeda's communications have been complicated rather than eliminated by the counterterrorist efforts of the United States and its allies. Electronic surveillance forces terrorist groups to limit their cell phone calls and conspire together in whispers. Al Qaeda can still communicate fairly freely, however, over the Internet, with coded messages embedded in the pixels of the most innocent of images.

Today no government openly admits any links, let alone alliance, with al Qaeda. Nonetheless, some governments do surreptitiously aid the group. Officially the governments of Iran, Syria, and Yemen claim that al Qaeda is an ideological enemy, yet they deliberately turn a blind eye to al Qaeda operatives and operations in their territories. Although Saudi Arabia and Pakistan are officially allied with the United States in the war against al Qaeda, elements in both governments share intelligence, money, arms, and refuge with the terrorists.

After September 11 Osama bin Laden became a mass cult figure comparable to Che Guevara as an international icon for enemies of Western civilization and the United States. This popularity was attributable not just to his message and powerful quiet charisma, but to possibly true stories of him repeatedly slipping through the fingers of American and other allies. The escape of bin Laden and several hundred other al Qaeda fighters from Tora Bora in late December 2001 is well known. Recent stories credit him with sneaking back across into Afghanistan several times to organize resistance against the Americans and their allies. The most dramatic tale involves an alleged escape in 2004 when he and his followers were able to break through British forces that had encircled them. Certainly no one, including those Pakistanis aware of his home in Abbottabad, dared to act on that $50 million price on bin Laden's head, up from $5 million in 1999. Bin Laden's legend gave al Qaeda a tremendous source of power to raise funds and recruits. Indeed Milt Bearden, a CIA officer, argued as far back as 1998 that "the following of Osama bin Laden that has been created by the romantic mythology has become more dangerous than the man himself," and his legions of devoted followers are "more often inspired by him than controlled by him."[8] How much the successful American raid to kill and rid the world of bin Laden has diminished his cult-like status remains to be seen.

Through a series of ideologically driven blunders that they committed after taking power on January 20, 2001, the Bush administration unwittingly fed the power of bin Laden and al Qaeda. Indeed it can be argued that different counterterrorist policies might not only have destroyed al Qaeda but might well have prevented the September 11 attacks.

The first blunder was to ignore the warnings of the outgoing Clinton administration experts, and thereafter Richard Clarke and George Tenet, that al Qaeda
posed the worst threat to America; the CIA's Presidential Daily Brief (PDB) of
August 6, 2001, more than a month before the actual attacks, could not have been
more clear—it was titled "Bin Laden determined to strike in U.S." Yet the president and his fellow conservatives ignored all those warnings because they did not
fit with their ideological mind-set and political agenda.

Then, after September 11, the Bush team lost crucial time in a tug-of-war between the realists and conservatives over whether to retaliate against Afghanistan
or Iraq. The realists finally prevailed but only after giving in to the demand that
Saddam Hussein's regime would be targeted for destruction after defeating al
Qaeda and the Taliban.

The third blunder was not circling and destroying al Qaeda when it made
what might have been its last stand in Afghanistan at its Tora Bora mountain
fortress complex. Rather than airdrop thousands of Special Forces to seal off
the mountain passes leading to a safe haven in neighboring Pakistan, the Bush
team farmed the job out to local tribal militia. Al Qaeda paid them to look the
other way at a rate of $5,000 for each fighter; bin Laden was among the hundreds
who slipped over the frontier to safety in Pakistan. According to a 2009 Senate
Foreign Relations Committee report, the consequences of the Bush administration allowing bin Laden, his henchmen, and hundreds of al Qaeda fighters to escape have been disastrous for American national security. The result was for "bin
Laden to emerge as a potent symbolic figure, who continues to attract a steady
flow of money and inspire fanatics worldwide" while laying "the foundation for
today's protracted Afghan insurgency and inflaming the internal strife now en-
dangering Pakistan."[9]

The fourth blunder was not blanketing Afghanistan with enough troops and
relief organizations to clear, hold, and rebuild the entire country. Instead, the
Bush team diverted crucial military, intelligence, and development assets from
Afghanistan to its conservative crusade in Iraq. As a result, al Qaeda and the
Taliban steadily infiltrated Afghanistan and took over numerous regions.

The fifth blunder was the conservative crusade in Iraq itself, which drained
American blood, treasure, and honor, and fed the hatreds that nourish al Qaeda

and other Islamist terrorist groups. By the time the Bush administration left office, the United States had directly squandered over four thousand lives and $850 billion in Iraq, while surveys revealed a huge blow to American prestige and honor for violations of international law, morality, and the Constitution. Meanwhile, the war against Iraq acted like a giant Islamist recruiting poster. A National Intelligence Report issued in July 2007 notably cited "the rejuvenating effect the Iraq War has had on al Qaeda."[10]

The al Qaeda movement, including scores of affiliated groups, remains committed to its jihad against the United States, Western civilization, and the so-called apostate governments of Muslim populations. Those groups recruit, train, finance, and commit terror largely on their own. The bombings that targeted westerners in Bali on October 12, 2002; Madrid on March 11, 2004; Taba, Egypt, on October 7, 2004; London on July 7 and 21, 2005; and Sharm el-Sheikh, Egypt, on July 23, 2005, were committed by local groups with either no or limited links with al Qaeda operatives in Pakistan.[11]

At times those attacks can have a decisive political effect. The Madrid bombing was the most notable. Prime Minister José María Aznar and his conservative People's Party, which had supported the Iraq War and even contributed a small contingent of Spanish troops, lost the general election on March 14, four days after the bombing, to the Socialist Worker's Party and a coalition of smaller leftist parties led by José Luis Rodríguez Zapatero. Among the new government's first acts was to announce that it would withdraw Spanish troops from Iraq.

The greatest threat would be if al Qaeda or another Islamist group could obtain a WMD and detonate it in the United States or in one of its allied nations. While counterterrorist efforts have sharply reduced the likelihood, that nightmare scenario will never disappear. Indeed a study by the Commission on the Prevention of Weapons of Mass Destruction Proliferation and Terrorism concluded in December 2008 that such an attack was likely in the next five years.[12] Of course, al Qaeda has already used WMD against the United States, on September 11, 2001.

While no terrorist group has the capacity to make nuclear weapons, they do have the potential to create a radiological bomb. A perennial threat lies in the smuggling of enriched uranium and plutonium from nuclear plants into the hands of terrorists. There are hundreds of large- and small-scale nuclear reactors around the world. Any of them can potentially be turned into a radiological bomb if a terrorist group were able to induce a meltdown in its nuclear core.

Al Qaeda and the Islamist network have created a kind of transnational virtual state, fighting an all too real global war against its enemies. That virtual state has no concrete territory, economy, or other resources besides what it can exploit haphazardly as opportunities fleetingly arise then disappear as real states employ countermeasures. The only tangible elements of power are the committed terrorists; the people who shelter, fund, arm, and train them; and the leaders who organize, plan, propagandize, and deploy those assets.[13]

That virtual state, however, has some weaknesses. David Kilcullen explains that "the Islamists ultimately cannot offer the material benefits of statehood—protection, stability, and economic prosperity—and thus cannot compete with nation-states for the long-term allegiance of uncommitted populations."[14] Should an Islamist group capture a state, like the Taliban did in Afghanistan from 1996 to 2001, it faces the challenges of actually fulfilling its promises and having fixed sites of power that can be systematically destroyed by American missiles and bombs.

There are other potential weaknesses in al Qaeda's transformation from a hierarchy into a network. Perhaps the most crucial is that "al Qaeda's core now has to rely on the affiliates to train operatives and carry out attacks, while the affiliates need al Qaeda's brand name to gain credibility and attention."[15] As for the mushrooming of all those children of al Qaeda, few of them have the capacity to operate beyond the country or region where they originate.

Yet another weakness is the lack of universal support among Islamists for al Qaeda and its strategies. One prominent radical, Montasser al-Zayyat, spoke for many when he argued that "Islamists across the globe were adversely affected by the September 11 attacks on the United States. Even Islamic movements that did not target the United States are paying the price of this folly." He lamented the loss of the Taliban Islamist regime in Afghanistan. Sheikh Salman bin Fahd al-Awdah, a leading Saudi cleric, wrote an open letter to bin Laden, asking: "How much blood has been spent? How many innocent people, children, elderly, and women have been killed, dispersed, or evicted in the name of al Qaeda?[16]

NCTC director Michael Leiter asserts that "al Qaeda is—in the end—its own worst enemy."[17] The al Qaeda affiliate in Iraq under Zarqawi self-destructed by its indiscriminate murders of thousands of Iraqis regardless of their faith. Increasing numbers of the Sunnis who were at first inspired by al Qaeda's presence turned their guns against its operatives and drove them underground or out of Iraq. What happened in Iraq can happen elsewhere if al Qaeda commits similar atrocities.

Nonetheless, any gains against al Qaeda and its affiliates may be fleeting. Islamism and failed states are inseparable. A demographic time bomb is ticking away across the Arab and the Muslim world. The populations of those countries are growing faster than their economies, which means that more people are mired deeper into poverty. About half of the population is under twenty years old, and these young people are growing into economies that not only fail to provide them with jobs but also with basic needs like adequate schools, health care, housing, electricity, sewage, water, and recreation. These countries are locked into vicious economic and political cycles in which more poor people struggle to survive while the governments are more corrupt, brutal, and inept. Without jobs, young men cannot marry or acquire any other status in society. The result is a greater desperation to escape a dead-end existence.

To a greater portion of the billion and a half Muslims on earth, especially the hundreds of millions leading the bleakest of lives, the zealous rhetoric of bin Laden and other Islamist leaders is vastly gripping. The only hope for increasing numbers of Muslims is that radical version of their faith. Islamism explains the reasons for their poverty and despair as the result of Western imperialism that planted Israel in their midst and imposed corrupt apostate government atop them. If only true Muslims could rise up and drive out the Western imperialists, destroy Israel, and overthrow the corrupt apostate governments, then a new caliphate ruling through sharia will resolve all problems and bring peace and prosperity to all of the faithful.

The 9/11 Commission succinctly captured that reality: "Because the Muslim world has fallen behind the West politically, economically, and militarily for the past three centuries, and because few tolerant or secular Muslim democracies provide alternative models for the future, Bin Laden's message finds receptive ears. . . . The resentment of America and the West is deep, even among leaders of relatively successful Muslim states."[18]

Ultimately the futures of the al Qaeda and related Islamist movements depend on the policies of the United States and its allies. The containment, deterrence, and reduction of the Islamist terrorist threat rather than its eradication is the more realistic goal. The United States and its allies have adapted their counterterrorist strategies as the threat posed by al Qaeda and its affiliates has mutated. The result, as Leiter put it, is that "we are safer. But we are not safe."[19]

Al Qaeda and its spawn will continue to pose a threat to the United States for the foreseeable future. Undoubtedly more terrorist attacks lay ahead. People will die and property will be destroyed. It is quite possible, however, that fears of another attack as devastating as September 11 are misplaced. The enhanced security measures in the United States and around the world make an attack that destructive unlikely, if not impossible.

These successes have come at an enormous and steadily growing cost. The price tag for the wars against al Qaeda, the Taliban, other possible terrorist threats, and Iraq in the decade after September 11, 2011, was $3.3 trillion dollars, or $6.6 million for every one dollar that al Qaeda spent on that attack. Al Qaeda itself inflicted $55 billion in physical damage and $123 billion in economic damage on the United States. Washington then spent $589 billion on homeland security and $1.646 trillion on the two wars, including $803 billion in Iraq and $402 billion in Afghanistan. Those costs, of course, will persist for the indefinite future. Winding down those wars will impose $277 billion on taxpayers and veterans benefits and health care another $589 billion. Then there are America's human costs to date of 4,500 dead in Iraq, 1,800 dead in Afghanistan, and tens of thousands of men and women crippled physically and emotionally.[20]

Did America overreact to the September 11 attacks? If so, then al Qaeda won. Terrorists cannot destroy their enemy, but they can stampede their enemy into destroying itself. The threat that Islamist terrorism poses to the United States must be put in perspective. In 2009 there were two attacks and one aborted attack by Islamists in the United States. Fourteen Americans were murdered, thirteen by a lone gunman at Fort Hood, Texas, and one by a lone gunman at an army recruiting office in Little Rock, Arkansas. Far more would have died had a terrorist succeeded in detonating a bomb on an airliner bound for the United States on Christmas Day. Those fourteen murders by Islamists were all tragedies. Yet they are insignificant compared to the murders inflicted by Americans against each other—14,000 in 2009.[21] And, to date, those were the last Islamist inspired terrorist attacks in the United States.

Terrorists win to the extent that they terrorize governments and populations, and goad them into acting self-destructively. All of the Bush administration's hyperbole about a "global war on terror" and the unconstitutional measures it took to that end strengthened rather weakened America's enemies. In reality, the al Qaeda movement and all other terrorist groups pose absolutely no threat to the existence of the United States itself. Only Americans can destroy their nation and only then by destroying the ideals and institutions upon which it is based. Terrorists can play a hand in pushing Americans into that act, but ultimately it would be zealous, extreme American leaders and a hateful, fearful public that would pull the trigger.

NOTES

Introduction

1. Joby Warrick, "Little Blue Pills Among the Ways the CIA Wins Friends in Afghanistan," *Washington Post*, December 26, 2008.
2. While most people have vivid images of terrorism, experts offer differ over just how to define and apply the term. For some goods summaries of those differences, see: Walter Reich, ed., *The Origins of Terrorism: Psychologies, Theologies, States of Mind* (Washington, DC: Woodrow Wilson Center, 1998); Bruce Hoffman, "The Confluence of International and Domestic Trends in Terrorism," *Terrorism and Political Violence* 9, no. 1 (1997): 1–15; Edward Mickolus, and Todd Sandler, and Peter Fleming, *International Terrorism: Attributes of Terrorist Events* (Dunn Loring, VA: Vinyard Software, 2004); and Todd Sandler and Walter Enders, "An Economic Perspective on Transnational Terrorism," *European Journal of Political Economy* 20, no. 2 (2004): 301–16.
3. "Uniting Against Terrorism: Recommendations for a Global Counter-Terrorism Strategy," United Nations, April 27, 2006, http://www.un.org/uniting againstterrorism/sg-terrorism-2may06.pdf.
4. Anonymous, *Imperial Hubris: Why the West Is Losing the War on Terror* (Washington, DC: Brassey's, 2004), xxi.

Chapter 1. September 11, 2001

1. "Dead and Missing," *New York Times*, April 10, 2002; Eric Liptor, "Sept. 11 Death Toll Declines as 2 People Are Found Alive," *New York Times*, November 3, 2002; Dan Barry, "A New Account of September 11 Loss, with 40 Fewer Souls to Mourn," *New York Times*, October 29, 2003.
2. For the best overview of the Bush administration's policymaking following September 11, see Bob Woodward, *Bush at War* (New York: Simon & Schuster, 2002), and Richard Clarke, *Against All Enemies: Inside America's War on Terror* (New York: Free Press, 2004).

3. "Bush's Remarks to the Nation on the Terrorist Attacks," *New York Times*, September 12, 2001.

Chapter 2. Know Your Enemy: Al Qaeda versus Its Enemies

1. Sun Tzu, *The Art of War*, trans. Ralph D. Sawyer (New York: Barnes and Noble Book, 1994), 179.

2. For some of the leading works on Osama bin Laden and al Qaeda, see Steve Reeve, *The New Jackals: Ramzi Youssef, Osama bin Laden, and the Future of Terrorism* (Boston: Northeastern University Press, 1999); Youssef Bodansky, *Bin Laden: The Man Who Declared War on America* (New York: Prima, 2001); Peter Bergen, *The Holy War, Inc.: Inside the Secret World of Osama bin Laden* (New York: Free Press, 2002); Rohan Gunaratna, *Inside Al Qaeda: Global Network of Terror* (New York: Penguin, 2003); Jane Corbin, *Al Qaeda: In Search of the Terror Network that Threatens the World* (New York: Nation Books, 2003); Stephen Coll, *Ghost Wars: The Secret History of the CIA, Afghanistan, and Bin Laden, from the Soviet Invasion to September 10, 2001* (New York: Penguin, 2004); Marc Sageman, *Understanding Terror Networks* (Philadelphia: University of Pennsylvania Press, 2004); Jason Burke, *Al Qaeda: Casting a Shadow of Terror* (New York: I. B. Tauris, 2004); National Commission on Terrorist Attacks upon the United States, *The 9/11 Commission Report, Final Report of the National Commission on Terrorist Attacks on the United States* (New York: Norton, 2004); Bruce Lawrence, ed., *Messages to the World: The Statements of Osama bin Laden* (New York: Verso, 2005); Richard Whelan, *Al Qaedaism: The Threat to Islam, The Threat to the World* (London: Ashfield Press, 2005); Paul Williams, *The Al Qaeda Connection: International Terrorism, Organized Crime, and the Coming Apocalypse* (New York: Prometheus Books, 2005); Michael Scheuer, *Through Our Enemies' Eyes: Osama bin Laden, Radical Islam, and the Future of America, 2nd ed.* (Washington, DC: Potomac Books, 2006); Peter Bergen, *The Osama bin Laden I Know* (New York: Free Press, 2006); Lawrence Wright, *The Looming Tower: Al-Qaeda and the Road to 9/11* (New York: Knopf, 2006); Abdal Ari Atwan, *The Secret History of Al Qaeda* (Berkeley: University of California, 2006); Jason Burke, *Al Qaeda: The True Story of Radical Islam* (New York: Penguin, 2007); and Bruce Riedel, *The Search for Al Qaeda: Its Leadership, Ideology, and Future* (Washington, DC: Brookings Institute, 2008).

3. Elizabeth Bumiller, "Prepare for Casualties, Bush Says, While Asking Support of Nation," *New York Times*, September 21, 2001.

4. Daniel Byman, "Scoring the War on Terrorism," *The National Interest* (Summer 2003): 80.

5. "Transcript of bin Laden's October Interview," CNN.com, February 5, 2002, http://articles.cnn.com/2002-02-05/world/binladen.transcript_1_ incitement-fatwas-al-qaeda-organization?_s=PM:asiapcf. For an excellent list and analysis of al Qaeda's attempts to gain WMDs, see Alistair Miller

and Jason Ipe, "Cutting the Deadly Nexus: Preventing the Spread of Weapons of Mass Destruction to Terrorists," in David Cortright and George A. Lopez, eds., *Uniting Against Terror: Cooperative Nonmilitary Responses to the Global Terrorist Threat* (Cambridge, MA: MIT Press, 2007), 123–55.

6. Douglas Streusand, "What Does Jihad Mean?" *Middle East Quarterly* 4, no. 3 (September 1997). See also Bernard Lewis, *The Crisis of Islam: Holy War and Unholy War* (New York: Random House, 2004).

7. For some of the leading works on Islamism, see John Esposito, *Unholy War: Terror in the Name of Islam* (New York: Oxford University Press, 2002); Bernard Lewis, *The Crisis of Islam: Holy War and Unholy Terror* (London: Weidenfeld & Nicholson, 2003); Olivier Roy, *Globalized Islam: The Search for a New Ummah* (New York: Columbia University Press, 2004); Marc Sageman, *Understanding Terror Networks* (Philadelphia: University of Pennsylvania Press, 2004); Gilles Keppel, *Jihad: The Trail of Political Islam* (London: I. B. Tauris, 2004); Faisal Devji, *Landscapes of the Jihad: Militancy, Morality, Modernity* (Ithaca, NY: Cornell University Press, 2005); Gerges Fawaz, *The Far Enemy: Why Jihad Went Global* (New York: Cambridge University Press, 2005); Gerges Fawaz, *Journey of the Jihadist: Inside Muslim Militancy* (New York: Harcourt, 2006); Mary Habeck, *Knowing the Enemy: Jihadist Ideology and the War on Terror* (New Haven, CT: Yale University Press, 2006); Charles Allen, *God's Terrorists: The Wahhabi Cult and the Hidden Roots of Modern Jihad* (London: Abacus, 2006).

8. Scheuer, *Through Our Enemies' Eyes*, 62.

9. "The Century's First War Speech by Osama bin Laden," Al Jazeera Television, November 3, 2001.

10. See the outstanding analysis by David Kilcullen, "Countering Global Insurgency," *Small Wars Journal* (November 30, 2004): 16.

11. Kilcullen, "Countering Global Insurgency," 13–14, 27.

12. Scheuer, *Through Our Enemies' Eyes*, 88–96.

13. Robert D. Kaplan, *Soldiers of God: With the Mujahidin in Afghanistan* (Boston: Houghton Mifflin, 1990); Kurt Lohbeck, *Holy War, Unholy Victory: Eyewitness to the CIA's Secret War in Afghanistan* (Washington, DC: Regnery, 1993); Mark Galeotti, *Afghanistan: The Soviet Union's Last War* (New York: Houghton Mifflin, 2001); George Crile, *Charlie Wilson's War: The Extraordinary Story of the Largest Covert Operation in History* (New York: Atlantic Monthly Press, 2003).

14. James Risen and Judith Miller, "Pakistani Intelligence Had Ties to Al Qaeda, U.S. Officials Say," *New York Times*, October 29, 2001.

15. Bergen, *Holy War*, 56.

16. Ahmed Rashid, *The Taliban, Militant Islam, Oil, and Fundamentalism in Central Asia* (New Haven, CT: Yale University Press, 2000); Larry Goodson, *Afghanistan's Endless War* (Seattle: University of Washington Press, 2001); Barnett R. Rubin, *The Fragmentation of Afghanistan* (New Haven, CT: Yale University Press, 2002).

17. *9/11 Commission Report*, 182–83.
18. *9/11 Commission Report*, 169; Kathryn L. Gardner, "Terrorism Defanged: The Financial Action Task Force and International Efforts to Capture Terrorist Finances," in David Cortright and George A. Lopez, eds., *Uniting Against Terror: Cooperative Nonmilitary Responses to the Global Terrorist Threat* (Cambridge, MA: MIT Press, 2007), 160.
19. *9/11 Commission Report*, 169–73.
20. John Roth, Douglas Greenburg, and Serena Wille, *Monograph on Terrorist Financing* (Washington, DC: 9/11 Commission, 2004), 93; Jamal al-Fadl, Testimony in *United States v. Usama bin Laden et al.*, February 2001.
21. Scheuer, *Through Our Enemies' Eyes*, 21.
22. Bruce Hoffman, *Inside Terrorism* (New York: Columbia University Press, 2006).
23. Scheuer, *Through Our Enemies' Eyes*, xxiii.
24. *9/11 Commission Report*, 67.
25. Some believe that figure is exaggerated and that al Qaeda actually numbered hundreds rather than thousands at its peak. For conflicting views, see Gunaratna, *Inside Al Qaeda*, 8, 95, and Bergen, *Holy War*, 35; for Khalid Sheikh Mohammed's estimate, see *9/11 Commission Report*, 232.
26. Scheuer, *Through Our Enemies' Eyes*, 72; George Tenet, *At the Center of the Storm: My Years at the CIA* (New York: Harper, 2007), 259–80.

Chapter 3. Know Your War: Terrorism versus Counterterrorism

1. Carl von Clausewitz, *On War* (Princeton, NJ: Princeton University Press, 1976), 88.
2. Ronald Reagan, quoted in Walter Laqueur, *The New Terrorism: Fanaticism and the Arms of Mass Destruction* (New York: Oxford University Press, 1999), 6.
3. Bruce Hoffman, *Inside Terrorism* (New York: Columbia University Press, 2006); Gary Sick, "The Political Underpinnings of Terrorism," in Charles W. Kegley, ed., *International Terrorism: Characteristics, Causes, Controls* (New York: St. Martin's, 1990), 51.
4. David Apter and Tony Sach, *Revolutionary Discourse in Mao's Republic* (Cambridge, MA: Harvard University Press, 1994).
5. Bruce Hoffman, "Defining Terrorism," in Russell D. Howard and Reid L. Sawyer, eds., *Terrorism and Counterterrorism: Understanding the New Security Environment* (Guilford, CT: McGraw-Hill/Dushkin, 2003), 22.
6. Jonathan White, *Terrorism: An Introduction* (Belmont, CA: Wadsworth, 2002), 63–77.
7. Brian Jenkins, "International Terrorism: A New Mode of Conflict," in David Carlton and Carlo Schaerf, eds., *International Terrorism and World Security* (London: Croon Helms, 1975).
8. Robert Pape, *Dying to Win: The Strategic Logic of Suicide Terrorism* (New York: Random House, 2005), 4; Mia Bloom, *Dying to Kill: The Allure of*

Suicide Terror (New York: Columbia University Press, 2005); Ami Pedahzur, *Suicide Terrorists* (Malden, MA: Polity Press, 2005); Ami Pedahzur, ed., *The Root Causes of Suicide Terrorism: The Globalization of Martyrdom* (New York: Routledge, 2005); Diego Gambetta, ed., *Making Sense of Suicide Missions* (New York: Oxford University Press, 2005); Mohammad Hafez, *Manufacturing Human Bombs: The Making of Palestinian Bombers* (Washington, DC: United States Institute of Peace, 2005).

9. Ted Gurr, *Why Men Rebel* (Princeton, NJ: Princeton University Press, 1970); Konrad Kellen, *On Terrorists and Terrorism* (Santa Monica, CA: Rand Corporation, 1982); Jerrold Post, "Terrorist Psycho-Logic: Terrorist Behavior as a Product of Psychological Forces," in Walter Reich, ed., *The Origins of Terrorism: Psychologies, Ideologies, Theologies, States of Mind* (New York: Cambridge University Press, 1990); Richard Pearlstein, *The Mind of the Political Terrorist* (Wilmington, DE: SR Books, 1991); Maxwell Taylor and Ethel Quayle, *Terrorist Lives* (Washington, DC: Brassey's, 1994); Rex Hudson, *The Sociology and Psychology of Terrorism: Who Becomes a Terrorist and Why* (Washington, DC: The Division, 1999); Andrew Silke, "Cheshire Cat Logic: The Recurring Theme of Terrorist Abnormality in Psychological Research," *Psychology, Crime, and Law* 4 (1998): 51–69; John Horgan, "The Search for The Terrorist Personality," in Andrew Silke, ed., *Terrorists, Victims, and Society: Psychological Perspectives on Terrorism and Its Consequences* (Chicester, UK: John Wiley, 2003); Tore Bjorgo, ed., *The Root Causes of Terrorism* (Oslo: Norwegian Institute of International Affairs, 2003); Jerrold Post, *Leaders and Followers in a Dangerous World: The Psychology of Political Behavior* (New York: Cornell University Press, 2004); Fathali Moghaddam and Anthony Marsella, eds., *Understanding Terrorism: Psychosocial Roots, Consequences, and Interventions* (Washington, DC: American Psychological Association, 2004); John Horgan, *The Psychology of Terrorism* (London: Taylor & Francis, 2005).

10. Alan B. Krueger and Jitka Maleckova, "Education, Poverty, and Terrorism: Is There a Casual Connection?" *Journal of Economic Perspectives* 17, no. 4 (Fall 2003): 138.

11. Clinton Watts, "Beyond Iraq and Afghanistan: What Foreign Fighter Data Reveals About the Future of Terrorism," *Small Arms Journal*, April 17, 2008.

12. For some recent prominent studies, see Paul Wilkinson, *Terrorism Versus Democracy: The Liberal State Response* (London: Frank Cass, 2001); Alexander T. J. Lennon, ed., *The Battle for Hearts and Minds: Using Soft Power to Undermine Terrorist Networks* (Cambridge, MA: MIT Press, 2003); Richard A. Clarke et al., *Defeating the Jihadists: A Blueprint for Action* (Washington, DC: Century Foundation Press, 2004); David Benjamin and Steven Simon, *The Next Attack: The Failure of the War on Terror and a Strategy for Getting It Right* (New York: Times Books, 2005); and David Cortright and George A. Lopez, eds., *Uniting Against Terror: Cooperative Nonmilitary Responses to the Global Terrorist Threat* (Cambridge, MA: MIT Press, 2007).

13. National Strategy for Combating Terrorism, White House, February 2003, https://www.cia.gov/news-information/cia-the-war-on-terrorism/Counter_ Terrorism_Strategy.pdf, 29.
14. David Cortright and George A. Lopez, "Strategies and Policy Challenges for Winning the Fight Against Terrorism," in David Cortright and George A. Lopez, eds., *Uniting Against Terrorism: Cooperative Nonmilitary Responses to the Global Terrorist Threat* (Cambridge, MA: MIT Press, 2007), 238.
15. Sun Tzu, *The Art of War*, 179.
16. Lawrence Freedman, "The Coming War on Terrorism," in Lawrence Freedman, ed., *Superterrorism: Policy Responses* (Oxford: Blackwell, 2002), 44–45.
17. For an excellent discussion of this and related questions, see Seumas Miller, *Terrorism and Counterterrorism: Ethics and Liberal Democracy* (New York: Blackwell, 2009).
18. Quoted in John Tillson et al., *Learning to Adapt to Asymmetrical Threats* (Alexandria, VA: Institute for Defense Analysis, 2005), 7.
19. Michael Braun, "Drug Trafficking and Middle Eastern Terrorist Groups: A Growing Nexus?" Washington Institute for Near East Policy, July 18, 2008, http://www.washingtoninstitute.org/templateC05.php?CID=2914.
20. International Monetary Fund, Statistics Department, "International Transactions in Remittances: Guide for Compilers and Users," September 2008, http://www.imf.org/external/pubs/ft/bop/2008/08-09b.pdf.
21. "Bush Delivers West Point Commencement Address," May 27, 2006, http:// transcripts.cnn.com/TRANSCRIPTS/0605/27/se.01.html.
22. Robert A. Miller and Irving Lachow, "Strategic Fragility: Infrastructure Protection and National Security in the Information Age," *Defense Horizons* 59 (January 2008): 5.
23. Andrew Bacevich, "The Petraeus Doctrine," *Atlantic Monthly*, October 2008. For classic works on counterinsurgency, see Robert Thompson, *Defeating Communist Insurgence: The Lessons of Malaya and Vietnam* (London: Hailer, 1966); Michael McClintock, *Instructions of Statecraft: U.S. Guerrilla Warfare, Counterinsurgency, and Counterterrorism, 1940–1990* (New York: Pantheon Books, 1992); John A. Nagl, *Learning to Eat Soup with a Knife: Counterinsurgency Lessons from Malaya and Vietnam* (Chicago: University of Chicago Press, 2005); Dan Baum, "Battle Lessons: What the Generals Don't Know," *New Yorker*, January 17, 2005; Kilcullen, "Countering Global Insurgency," 597–617; David J. Kilcullen, "Twenty-Eight Articles: Fundamentals of Company-level Counterinsurgency," *Military Review* 86, no. 3 (May–June 2006): 103–8; Eliot Cohen, Conrad Crane, Jan Horvath, and John Nagl, "Principles, Imperatives, and Paradoxes of Counterinsurgency," *Military Review* 86, no. 2 (March–April 2006): 49–53; David Galula, *Counterinsurgency Warfare: Theory and Practice* (Westport, CT: Praeger, 2006); Steven Metz, *Learning from Iraq: Counterinsurgency in American Strategy* (Carlisle, PA: Strategic Studies Institute, 2007); Sarah Sewall, "Modernizing U.S. Counterinsurgency Practice: Rethinking Risk

and Developing a National Strategy," *Military Review* (September–October 2006): 103–20; David H. Petraeus and James F. Amos, *The U.S. Army and Marine Corps Counterinsurgency Field Manuel* (Chicago: University of Chicago Press, 2007).

24. Russell F. Weigley, *The American Way of War: A History of United States Military Policy and Strategy* (Bloomington: University of Indiana Press, 1977).

25. Harry G. Summers, *On Strategy: A Critical Analysis of the Vietnam War* (New York: Presidio, 1995).

26. Petraeus and Amos, *Counterinsurgency Manual*.

27. Ibid., xxv.

28. Jessica Stern, "How America Created a Terrorist Haven," *New York Times*, August 20, 2003.

29. Petraeus and Amos, *Counterinsurgency Manual*, lii.

30. Ibid., 47–51.

31. "Defeating Terrorist Groups," Rand Corporation, September 19, 2008, http://www.rand.org/content/dam/rand/pubs/testimonies/2008/RAND_CT314.pdf.

32. Arthur Keller, "In Afghanistan, Less Can Be More," *New York Times*, March 10, 2009.

33. Celestine Bohlen, "'Graveyard of Empires' with a Lesson for U.S.," *International Herald Tribune*, March 4, 2009.

34. Helene Cooper, "Dreams of Splitting the Taliban," *New York Times*, March 8, 2009.

35. Seymour Martin Lipset, *Political Man: The Social Bases of Politics* (London: Heinemann, 1983), 64.

36. Sun Tzu, *Art of War*, 210.

37. Dell Dailey, "An 'All Elements of Power' Strategy for Combating Terrorism," December 12, 2007, http://merln.ndu.edu/archivepdf/terrorism/state/97165.pdf.

38. Larry Diamond, "What Went Wrong In Iraq," *Foreign Affairs* 83, no. 5 (September–October 2004): 37.

39. Peter Baker and Colum Lynch, "At UN, Bush Links War on Terrorism to Anti-Poverty Efforts," *Washington Post*, September 15, 2005.

40. Ali Mohammandi, ed., *Islam Encountering Globalization* (London: Routledge, 2002), 190; R. Brahramitash, *Myths and Realities of the Impact of Political Islam on Women: Female Employment in Indonesia and Iran* (London: Routledge, 2004); Pia Karlsson, and Amir Mansory, "Islamic and Modern Education in Afghanistan: Conflictual or Complementary?" Development Studies Research Conference, Lund University, 2003, http://ddp-ext.worldbank.org/EdStats/AFGstu08.pdf.

41. Sun Tzu, *Art of War*, 232.

42. Director's Statement to the Senate Select Committee on Intelligence, Central Intelligence Agency, February 5, 2008, https://www.cia.gov/news-information/speeches-testimony/speeches-testimony-archive-2008/february08-statement-to-ssci.html.

43. Roberta Wohlstetter, *Pearl Harbor: Warning and Decision* (Stanford, CA: Stanford University Press, 1962).

44. Daniel Byman, "Six Years Later: Innovative Approaches to Defeating Al Qaeda," Brookings Institute, February 14, 2008, http://www.brookings.edu /testimony/2008/0214_al_qaeda_byman.aspx.

45. Sun Tzu, *Art of War*, 168.

46. Michelle K. Van Cleave, "Counterintelligence and National Strategy," National Defense University, April 2007, http://www.dtic.mil/cgi-bin/Get TRDoc?AD=ADA471485, 18.

47. Ibid., 30, 15, 4.

48. Ibid., 5–11.

49. Christopher Felix, *A Short Course in the Secret War* (Lanham, MD: Madison Books, 2001), 121.

50. *9/11 Commission Report*, 374–75; Office for the Coordinator of Counterterrorism, "Country Reports on Terrorism 2007," U.S. Department of State, April 2008, http://www.state.gov/documents/organization/105904.pdf.

51. Paul Pillar, *Terrorism and U.S. Foreign Policy* (Washington, DC: Brookings Institution Press, 2001), 218.

Chapter 4. Clinton and Bush versus al Qaeda before September 11

1. Coll, *Ghost Wars*, 155, 255.

2. *9/11 Commission Report*, 109.

3. Clarke, *Against All Enemies*, 144.

4. Ibid., 97; Coll, *Ghost Wars*, 318.

5. Benjamin and Simon, *Age of Sacred Terror*, 315.

6. Coll, *Ghost Wars*, 362.

7. Benjamin and Simon, *Age of Sacred Terror*, 322.

8. *9/11 Commission Report*, 117–18; Bodansky, *Bin Laden*, 283–90. For a justification of the missile attack against the al Shifa plant, see Benjamin and Simon, *Age of Sacred Terror*, 353–63.

9. James Risen and Judith Miller, "Pakistani Intelligence had Ties to Al Qaeda, U.S. Officials Say," *New York Times*, October 28, 2001.

10. Benjamin and Simon, *Age of Sacred Terror*, 294–96.

11. Ibid., 318.

12. Ibid., 298–307.

13. *9/11 Commission Report*, 130–32; Coll, *Ghost Wars*, 421–23.

14. Benjamin and Simon, *Age of Sacred Terror*, 317.

15. Coll, *Ghost Wars*, 447.

16. *9/11 Commission Report*, 187–88.

17. Tenet, *At the Center of the Storm*, 125.

18. Jim Pavitt, "DDO Addresses Duke University Law School Conference," Central Intelligence Agency, April 11, 2002, https://www.cia.gov/news -information/speeches-testimony/2002/pavitt_04262002.html.

19. Tenet, *At the Center of the Storm*, 130.

20. For the best accounts of the Bush team's policy debate in the weeks after 9/11, see Bob Woodward, *Plan of Attack* (New York: Simon and Schuster, 2003); Clarke, *Against All Enemies*; Ron Suskind, *The Price of Loyalty: George W. Bush, the White House, and the Education of Paul O'Neill* (New York: Simon & Schuster, 2004). See also "Glimmers of Warning: Who Knew What, and What Happened?," *New York Times*, May 17, 2002; Barton Gellman, "Before September 11, Little in Bush's Anti-Terror Steps Set Him Apart," *New York Times*, May 18, 2002.

21. Benjamin and Simon, *Age of Sacred Terror*, 328; Clarke, *Against All Enemies*, 229.

22. *9/11 Commission Report*, 254; Pavitt, "DDO Addresses Duke University Law School Conference"; Philip Shenon, "September 11 Panel Wasn't Told of Meeting, Members Say," *New York Times*, October 2, 2006; Philip Shenon and Mark Mazzetti, "Records Confirm that C.I.A. Chief Warned Rice on Al Qaeda," *New York Times*, October 3, 2001.

23. Tenet, *At the Center of the Storm*, 144.

24. David Sanger, "Bush Was Warned Bin Laden Wanted to Hijack Planes," *New York Times*, May 17, 2002; Judith Miller, "Sheik's Son and Bin Laden Spoke of Plots, Officials Say," *New York Times*, May 18, 2002.

25. Condoleezza Rice testimony before the 9/11 Commission, March 8, 2004, http://www.9-11commission.gov/archive/hearing9/9-11Commission_Hearing_2004-04-08.htm.

26. Benjamin and Simon, *Age of Sacred Terror*, 336–39, 344.

27. George Tenet, "DCI's Worldwide Threat Briefing," February 7, 2001, https://www.cia.gov/news-information/speeches-testimony/2001/UNCLASWWT_02072001.html.

28. Bob Woodward, *State of Denial* (New York: Simon & Schuster, 2006), 50.

29. Tenet, *At the Center of the Storm*, 151–54; Clarke, *Against All Enemies*, chapter 1; Woodward, *State of Denial*, 49–52.

30. *9/11 Commission Report*, 212.

31. David Sanger and Elisabeth Bumiller, "Answer to Critics," *New York Times*, May 17, 2002; Alison Mitchell, "Cheney Rejects Broader Access to Terror Brief," *New York Times*, May 20, 2002.

32. Eric Lichtblau and Josh Meyer, "Terrorist Ties Cited in Memo," *Los Angeles Times*, May 23, 2002; *9/11 Commission Report*, 272–76; Tenet, *At the Center of the Storm*, 192–200.

33. Tenet, *At the Center of the Storm*, 192–204.

34. Philip Sheldon, "Lawmakers Say Misstatements Cloud F.B.I. Chief's Credibility," *New York Times*, May 25, 2002.

35. Woodward, *State of Denial*, 79–80.

36. James Mann, *The Rise of the Vulcans* (New York: Penguin, 2004).

37. "Excerpts from 1992 Draft 'Defense Planning Guidance,'" http://www.pbs.org/wgbh/pages/frontline/shows/iraq/etc/wolf.html.

38. Charles Krauthammer, "The Bush Doctrine: ABM, Kyoto, and the New American Unilateralism," *Weekly Standard*, June 4, 2001.

39. For the best insights into the psychology of neoconservatives, see Eric Hoffer, *The True Believer: Thoughts on the Nature of Mass Movements* (New York: Harper Perennial Modern Classic, 2002); Mann, *Rise of the Vulcans*; and George Packer, *The Assassin's Gate: America in Iraq* (New York: Farrar, Straus, and Giroux, 2005), 8–38, 39–65. As for the psyche of George W. Bush, all the biographies give insights, but two excellent books are devoted to the subject: Justin A. Frank, *Bush on the Couch: Inside the Mind of the President* (New York: Harper, 2007), and Dan P. McAdam, *George W. Bush and the Redemptive Dream: A Psychological Portrait* (New York: Oxford University Press, 2010).

40. Ron Suskind, "Without a Doubt," *New York Times*, October 17, 2004.

Chapter 5. The Post-9/11 Neoconservative War on Terror and Tyranny

1. For insiders' accounts of the policy debates in the weeks following 9/11, see Clarke, *Against All Enemies*; Suskind, *The Price of Loyalty*; and Tenet, *At the Center of the Storm*. See also David Sanger, "Bush Was Warned Bin Laden Wanted to Hijack Planes," *New York Times*, May 17, 2002; and Judith Miller, "Sheik's Son and bin Laden Spoke of Plots, Officials Say," *New York Times*, May 18, 2002.

2. Clarke, *Against All Enemies*, 30; Bill Keller, "The World According to Powell," *New York Times Magazine*, November 25, 2001; Rohan Gunaratna, "Iraq and Al Qaeda: No Evidence of an Alliance," *International Herald Tribune*, February 19, 2003.

3. Todd Purham, "Leaders Face Challenges Far Different from those of Last Conflict," *New York Times*, September 15, 2001.

4. Woodward, *Bush at War*, 243.

5. "The National Security Strategy," September 2002, http://merln.ndu.edu/whitepapers/USnss2002.pdf, 5, 29.

6. William Pfaff, "The American Mission?" *New York Review of Books* 51, no. 6 (April 8, 2004): 23; Jeffrey Record, *Bounding the Global War on Terrorism* (Carlisle, PA: Strategic Studies Institute, 2004), v, 1.

7. "The National Security Strategy," 1, 15.

8. Condoleezza Rice, "Promoting the National Interest," *Foreign Affairs* (January/February 2000): 61.

9. Quote from Michael Dobbs, "North Korea Tests Bush's Policy of Preemption," *Washington Post*, January 6, 2003.

10. George W. Bush, "There Is No Justice Without Freedom," *Washington Post*, January 21, 2005.

11. "Bush: 'We Will Do What Is Necessary,'" *Washington Post*, September 8, 2003.

12. Condoleezza Rice, "Transforming the Middle East," *Washington Post*, August 7, 2003; Charles Krauthammer, "Three Cheers for the Bush Doctrine," *Time*, March 7, 2005.

13. Lee Hamilton, foreword, in David Cortright and George A. Lopez, eds., *United Against Terror: Cooperative Nonmilitary Responses to the Global Terrorist Threat* (Cambridge, MA: MIT Press, 2007), vii.

Chapter 6. The War in Afghanistan: Round One

1. Elisabeth Bumiller, "Bush and Blair Trade Praise at White House Love Fest," *New York Times*, November 8, 2001.
2. John Burns, "Pakistan Fights U.S. Move Linked to Anti-Taliban Drive," *New York Times*, September 25, 2001.
3. Patrick Tyler, "Powell, in Pakistan, Focuses on Shape of Post-Taliban Regime," *New York Times*, October 16, 2001.
4. Michael Wines, "To Free the Way for the U.S. or Not? Either Way, a Fateful Choice for Russia," *New York Times*, September 25, 2001.
5. Elaine Sciolino and Neil Lewis, "Iran and U.S. Dance 'Ballet' About War in Afghanistan," *New York Times*, October 16, 2001.
6. Nazila Fathi, "Iran Softens Tone against the United States," *New York Times*, September 21, 2001; Sciolino and Lewis, "Iran and U.S. Dance 'Ballet' about War in Afghanistan"; Elaine Sciolino and Nazila Fathi, "British Minister Meets with Top Iranians Over Afghanistan," *New York Times*, September 26, 2001.
7. John Kifner, "56 Islamic Nations Avoid Condemning U.S. Attacks, but Warn on Civilian Casualties," *New York Times*, October 11, 2001; John Kifner, "Arab League Condemns bin Laden and His War," *New York Times*, November 4, 2001.
8. John Burns, "Adding Demands, Afghans Leaders Show Little Willingness to Give Up Bin Laden," *New York Times*, September 19, 2001; Elisabeth Bumiller, "Bare Talks, Saying Hosts Will Share the Terrorists' Fate," *New York Times*, September 20, 2001.
9. John Burns, "Afghans Coaxing bin Laden but U.S. Rejects Clerics' Bid," *New York Times*, September 21, 2001; John Burns, "Clerics Answer 'No, No, No!,'" *New York Times*, September 22, 2001.
10. "The United States Military Presence," *New York Times*, September 21, 2001.
11. "Deployments Around the Region," *New York Times*, December 9, 2001.
12. "Offers of Help from Other Countries," *New York Times*, November 8, 2001; Eric Schmitt, "Many Eager to Help, but Few Are Chosen," *New York Times*, November 30, 2001.
13. "Offers of Help from Other Countries," *New York Times*; Schmitt, "Many Eager to Help, but Few Are Chosen."
14. Coll, *Ghost Wars*, 84–88.
15. Jim Pavitt, "DDO Addresses Duke University Law School Conference."
16. Tenet, *At the Center of the Storm*, 120.
17. Coll, *Ghost Wars*, 11–12, 151, 190.
18. Coll, *Ghost Wars*, 460.

19. James Carney and John F. Dickerson, "Inside the War Room," *Time*, December 31, 2001; David Rohde, "Rift Grows Among Anti-Taliban Leadership," *New York Times*, November 11, 2001.

20. Barry Bearak, "Slain Taliban Foe is Buried. So They Say," *New York Times*, October 29, 2001; Tenet, *At the Center of the Storm*, 218.

21. Gary Bernstein, *Jawbreaker: The Attacks on Bin Laden and Al Qaeda; A Personnel Account by the CIA's Key Field Commander* (New York: Crown, 2005).

22. Woodward, *Bush at War*, 184; Gary Schroen, *First In: An Insider's Account of How the CIA Spearheaded the War on Terror in Afghanistan* (New York: Random House, 2005).

23. "Bush's Remarks on War," *New York Times*, October 8, 2001.

24. John Burns, "Bin Laden Taunts U.S. and Praises Hijackers," *New York Times*, October 8, 2001.

25. Elisabeth Bumiller, "President's Remarks on the War on Terrorism," *New York Times*, October 12, 2001.

26. Woodward, *Bush at War*, 220.

27. Ibid.

28. Elisabeth Bumiller, "U.S. Will Buy Asian Wheat to Give Afghans," *New York Times*, November 1, 2001.

29. Tenet, *At the Center of the Storm*, 210.

30. "Excerpts from the President's Remarks on the War on Terrorism," *New York Times*, October 12, 2001.

31. John Burns, "Taliban Chief Urges Troops: Defy 'Infidel,'" *New York Times*, October 18, 2001.

32. Tenet, *At the Center of the Storm*, 219–21.

33. Ibid., 215–17.

34. Woodward, *Bush at War*, 314.

35. Fouad Ajami, "What the Muslim World is Watching," *New York Times Magazine*, November 18, 2001; Col. John Jogerst, "What's So Special about Special Operations?: Lessons from the War in Afghanistan," *Aerospace Power Journal* (Summer 2002).

36. Woodward, *Bush at War*, 194.

37. Ibid., 220.

38. Ibid.

39. Steve Erlanger, "Britain Presses U.S. for 'Nation-Building' in Afghanistan," *New York Times*, October 12, 2001.

40. "Excerpts from the President's Remarks on the War on Terrorism," *New York Times*.

41. Elizabeth Becker, "U.S. Questions Its Share of Reconstruction Costs," *New York Times*, October 13, 2001.

42. Patrick Tyler, "Britain Ready to Lead Force for the U.N. After the War," *New York Times*, December 12, 2001.

43. "Powell Hints at Role for Taliban Moderates in Coalition," *New York Times*, October 17, 2001.

44. Steven Erlanger "Delegates Meet in First Step toward Post-Taliban Rule," *New York Times*, November 27, 2001.

45. Alan Sipress, "U.S. Prepares to Release $221 million to Afghans," *International Herald Tribune*, January 16, 2002.

46. James Dao, "Lawmakers Urge Bush to Expand Afghan Force Beyond Kabul," *New York Times*, June 27, 2002.

47. Michael Gordon, "U.S. Backs Increase in Peacekeepers for Afghanistan," *New York Times*, August 30, 2002.

48. Hamid Mir, "How Osama Has Survived for Six Years," September 11, 2007, http://www.rediff.com/news/2007/sep/11hamid.htm.

Chapter 7. The War on Terror at Home

1. Ron Suskind, *The One Percent Doctrine: Deep Inside America's Pursuit of Its Enemies Since 9/11* (New York: Simon & Schuster, 2006), 62. See also Stephen Flynn, *America the Vulnerable: How Our Government Is Failing to Protect Us from Terrorism* (New York: HarperCollins, 2004); Michael Ignatieff, *The Lesser Evil: Political Ethics in an Age of Terror* (Princeton, NJ: Princeton University Press, 2004); Matthew Brzezinski, *Fortress America: On the Front Lines of Homeland Security, An Inside Look* (New York: Bantam, 2004); Samuel Dash, *The Intruders: Unreasonable Searches and Seizures from King John to John Ashcroft* (New Brunswick, NJ: Rutgers University Press, 2004); John Firman, *The Maze of Power: Security and Migration after 9/11* (New York: New Press, 2004); Howard Ball, *The USA Patriot Act: A Reference Handbook* (Santa Barbara, CA: ABC-CLIO, 2004); Robert Byrd, *Losing America: Confronting a Reckless and Arrogant Presidency* (New York: W. W. Norton, 2005); John Dean, *Worse Than Watergate: The Secret Presidency of George W. Bush* (New York: Warner, 2005); Sasha Abramasky, *Conned: How Millions of Americans Went to Prison, Lost the Vote, and Helped Send George W. Bush to the White House* (New York: New Press, 2006); Clark Kent Ervin, *Open Target: Where America Is Vulnerable to Attack* (New York: Palgrave Macmillan, 2006); Frances Fox Piven, *The War on Terror: The Domestic Cost of Bush's Militarism* (New York: New Press, 2006); Charles Tifer, *Veering Right: How the Bush Administration Subverts the Law for Conservative Causes* (Berkeley: University of California Press, 2006); and Eric Posner and Adrian Vernuel, *Terror in the Balance* (New York: Oxford University Press, 2007).

2. Philip Shenon, "A Man with Connections: Tom Ridge," *New York Times*, November 26, 2002.

3. "The Plan: 'We Have Concluded That Our Government Must Be Reorganized,'" *New York Times*, June 7, 2002.

4. Charles Allen, "Terrorism in the Twenty-First Century: Implications for Homeland Security," in Matthew Levitt and Michael Jacobson, eds., *Terrorist*

Threat and U.S. Response, The Washington Institute for Near East Policy, September 2008, http://www.washingtoninstitute.org/pubPDFs/PolicyFocus 86.pdf, 30.

5. Pavitt, "DDO Addresses Duke University Law School Conference."

6. Mark Mazzetti, "Report Faults Spy Chief for Inaction on Turf Wars," *New York Times*, April 2, 2009.

7. Benjamin and Simon, *Age of Sacred Terror*, 299–300.

8. *9/11 Commission Report*, 76.

9. U.S. Senate Select Committee on Intelligence, "Joint Inquiry Into Intelligence Community Activities Before and After the Terrorist Attacks of September 11, 2001," December 2002, http://intelligence.senate.gov/pdfs /1071086v2.pdf, 363–68.

10. Philip Sheldon, "Lawmakers Say Misstatements Cloud FBI Chief's Credibility," *New York Times*, June 1, 2002.

11. Michelle K. Van Cleave, "Counterintelligence and National Strategy," National Defense University, April 2007, http://www.dtic.mil/cgi-bin/Get TRDoc?AD=ADA471485, 23.

12. Ibid.

13. Juan Zarate, "Winning the War on Terror: Marking Success and Confronting Challenges," in Levitt and Jacobson, *Terrorist Threats and U.S. Response*, 35.

14. Barton Gellman, "Secret Unit Expands Rumsfeld's Domain," *Washington Post*, January 23, 2005.

15. Dan Eggen, "FBI Agents Still Lacking Arabic Skills," *Washington Post*, October 11, 2006.

16. *9/11 Commission Report*, 92.

17. Frank Rich, "The Road from K Street to Yusufiya," *New York Times*, June 25, 2006.

18. Eric Lipton, "Former Anti-Terror Officials Find Industry Pays Better," *New York Times*, June 18, 2006.

19. Ibid.

20. Eric Lipton, "Big Cities Will Get More in Antiterrorism Grants," *New York Times*, December 20, 2004; Eric Lipton, "Come One, Come All, Join the Terror Target List," *New York Times*, July 12, 2006; Raymond Hernandez, "New York Officials Complain of Unfair Share of Homeland Security Money," *New York Times*, March 30, 2003.

21. Lipton, "Come One, Come All, Join the Terror Target List."

22. Raymond Hernandez, "Panel Defeats Effort to Give Billions More to New York," *New York Times*, November 15, 2001; Robert Peer, "Senate Rejects Increase in Aid for New York," *New York Times*, December 8, 2001.

23. Mark Grossman, *Political Corruption in America: An Encyclopedia of Scandals, Power, and Greed* (New York: Grey House, 2008); Elizabeth Drew, *The Corruption of American Politics: What Went Wrong and Why* (New York: Overlook Books, 2000); Matthew Continetti, *The K Street Gang: The Rise and Fall of the Republican Machine* (New York: Doubleday, 2006).

24. Eric Lipton, "U.S. Airline Security Is Said to Be 5 Years Behind Schedule," *New York Times*, February 21, 2007.

25. Patrick Radden Keefe, "Don't Privatize Our Spies," *New York Times*, June 25, 2007.

26. Ibid.

27. Michael Ignatieff, "Lesser Evils," *New York Times Sunday Magazine*, May 2, 2003.

28. "Ability to Reason Vital in Fighting Terrorism, Secretary-General Tells Conference," United Nations, September 22, 2003, http://www.un.org /News/Press/docs/2003/sgsm8885.doc.htm.

29. Tamar Lewin, "For Many of Those Held in a Legal Limbo," *New York Times*, November 1, 2001; "A Nation Challenged: Civil Rights and Security," *New York Times*, November 25, 2001; William Glabereson, "Closed Immigration Hearings Criticized as Prejudicial," *New York Times*, December 7, 2001.

30. *Al-Marri v. Wright*, 06-7427 (2nd Circuit, 2007), 76–77.

31. Susan Sacks, "U.S. Defends the Withholding of Jailed Immigrants' Names," *New York Times*, May 21, 2002; Adam Liptak, "A Court Backs Open Hearings on Deportation," *New York Times*, August 27, 2002.

32. Jodi Wilgoren, "Michigan 'Invites' Men from Mideast to be Interviewed," *New York Times*, November 27, 2001; Barbara Crosette, "Diplomats Protest Lack of Information," *New York Times*, December 20, 2001.

33. Both quotes from Seumas Miller, *Terrorism and Counterterrorism: Ethics and Liberal Democracy* (New York: Blackwell Publishing, 2007).

34. Lowell Bergman et al., "Spy Agency Data After September 11 led FBI to Dead Ends," *New York Times*, January 17, 2006; "Spies, Lies, and Wiretaps," *New York Times*, January 26, 2006; Eric Lichtblau and James Risen, "U.S. Wiretapping of Limited Value, Officials Report," *New York Times*, July 11, 2009.

35. Adam Liptak and Eric Lichtblau, "U.S. Judge Finds Wiretap Actions Violate the Law," *New York Times*, July 10, 2009.

36. Eric Lichtblau, "Former Prosecutors in U.S. Say Departure was Pressured," *International Herald Tribune*, March 6, 2007; Paul Krugman, "Department of Injustice," *New York Times*, March 9, 2007.

37. Adam Nagourney, "New Poll Finds Mixed Support for Wiretaps," *New York Times*, January 27, 2006.

38. OpentheGovernment.org; William Broad, "U.S. Cuts Assess to Technical Documents," *International Herald Tribune*, February 18, 2002.

39. "The Costly Right to Know," *International Herald Tribune*, February 3, 2005; Scott Shane, "Bipartisan Support Emerges for Federal Whistle-Blowers," *New York Times*, February 17, 2006.

40. William Broad, "Researchers Say Science Is Hurt by Secrecy Policy Set Up by the White House," *New York Times*, October 19, 2003.

41. Amy Harmon, "U.S. Scientific Journals Make a Pact to Censor," *International*

Herald Tribune, February 17, 2003; William Broad, "U.S. Cuts Access to Technical Documents," *International Herald Tribune*, February 18, 2003.

42. Fox Butterfield, "Justice Department Bars Use of Gun Checks in Terror Inquiry," *New York Times*, December 6, 2001.

43. Eric Lichtblau, "Terror Suspects Buying Firearms, U.S. Report Finds," *New York Times*, March 5, 2005.

44. Eric Lichtblau, "On Terrorist Watch List, But Allowed to Buy Guns," *New York Times*, June 20, 2009.

45. U.S. Department of Homeland Security, "National Infrastructure Protection Plan," 2006, http://www.dhs.gov/xlibrary/assets/NIPP_Plan_noApps .pdf, 103.

46. Congressional Research Service, "Vulnerability of Concentrated Critical Infrastructure: Background and Policy Options," December 21, 2005, http:// www.dtic.mil/cgi-bin/GetTRDoc?AD=ADA450527, 4.

47. Robert Pear, "U.S. Pressuring Foreign Airlines over Manifests," *International Herald Tribune*, December 19, 2001; Eric Lipton, "New Scrutiny for Air Cargo Screening," *International Herald Tribune*, February 8, 2007.

48. Hans Binnedijk et al., "The Virtual Border: Countering Seaborne Container Terrorism," *Defense Horizons*, no. 16 (August 2002); Eric Lipton, "Big U.S. Ports Left at Risk," *New York Times*, February 21, 2005; Clark Ervin, "Strangers at the Door," *New York Times*, February 23, 2006.

49. Matthew Wald, "White House Hasn't Sought Money to Guard Atomic Plants, Energy Official Says," *New York Times*, April 22, 2002; Matthew Wald, "White House Cut 93 percent of Funds Sought to Secure Sources of Radiation," *New York Times*, March 12, 2002.

50. "Unnecessary Security," *New York Times*, February 22, 2005.

51. Danny Hakim, "State Sues E.P.A. for Files on Household Pollutants," *New York Times*, February 15, 2006; "Chemical Insecurity," *New York Times*, February 22, 2005.

52. Sanger and Bumiller, "Answer to Critics." "Excerpts from Senator Clinton's Speech," *New York Times*, May 18, 2002.

53. "Excerpts from the Attorney General's Testimony before Senate Judiciary Committee, *New York Times*, December 7, 2001.

54. William Nester, *Haunted Victory: The American Crusade to Destroy Saddam and Impose Democracy in Iraq* (Washington, DC: Potomac Books, 2012).

55. Don Van Natta, "Democrats Raise Questions Over Remarks on Warnings," *New York Times*, May 16, Elisabeth Bumiller, "New Tone, Old Goal," *New York Times*, June 6, 2002.

56. David Rosenbaum, "Bush Bucks Tradition on Investigation," *New York Times*, May 25, 2002.

57. David Firestone, "Two Senators Say White House Is Thwarting 9/11 Inquiry," *News York Times*, October 12, 2002.

58. Ibid.

59. *9/11 Commission Report*, xv–xvi.

60. David Kay Griffin, *The 9/11 Commission Report: Omissions and Distortions* (New York: Interlink Publishing, 2005).

61. *9/11 Commission Report*, xvi.

62. Tenet, *At the Center of the Storm*, 257.

63. Eric Litchblau, "Study Finds Sharp Drop in the Number of Terrorism Cases Prosecuted, *New York Times*, September 4, 2006.

Chapter 8. The Global War on Terror

1. "Transcript of President Bush's Address," CNN, September 21, 2001, http://articles.cnn.com/2001-09-20/us/gen.bush.transcript_1_joint-session-national-anthem-citizens?_s=PM:US; "The Vice President appears on Meet the Press with Tim Russert," The White House, September 16, 2001, http://911research.wtc7.net/cache/disinfo/alibis/whitehouse_cheney.html; Suskind, *The One Percent Doctrine*, 62.

2. "Testimony of J. Cofer Black Before the National Commission on Terrorist Attacks upon the United States," Federation of American Scientists, April 13, 2004," http://www.fas.org/irp/congress/2004_hr/black_statement.pdf; Shaun Waterman, "CIA 'Too Cautious' in Killing Terrorists, Critics Say," United Press International, February 28, 2005.

3. Patrick Hayden et al., eds., *America's War on Terror* (London: Ashgate, 2003); Michael Ledeen, *The War Against the Terrorist Master: Why It Happened, Where We Are Now, How We'll Win* (New York: St. Martin's, 2003); Ronald Kessler, *The CIA at War: Inside the Secret War Against Terror* (New York: St. Martin's, 2004); Philip Smucker, *Al Qaeda's Great Escape: The Military and the Media on Terror's Trail* (Washington, DC: Potomac Books, 2004); Paul Rogers, *A War on Terror: Afghanistan and After* (London: Pluto, 2004); George Friedman, *America's Secret War: Inside the Hidden Worldwide Struggle Between the United States and Its Enemies* (New York: Broadway Books, 2005); James Hoge and Gideon Rose, eds., *Understanding the War on Terror* (Washington, DC: Foreign Affairs, 2005); Suskind, *The One Percent Doctrine*; Eric Schmitt and Thom Shanker, *Counter Strike: The Untold Story of America's Secret Campaign against Al Qaeda* (New York: Times Books, 2012).

4. Serge Schemann, "United Nations to Get a U.S. Anti-Terror Guide," *New York Times*, December 19, 2001.

5. Edward Luck, "Tackling Terrorism," in David Malone, ed., *The United Nations Security Council: From the Cold War to the Twenty-First Century* (Boulder, CO: Lynne Rienner, 2004), 85–100.

6. "Joint Testimony Daniel Glaser, Deputy Assistant Secretary for Terrorist Financing and Financial Crimes," U.S. Treasury Department, April 18, 2007, http://www.treasury.gov/press-center/press-releases/Pages/hp361.aspx.

7. "Hearing of the House Permanent Select Committee on Intelligence: Annual Worldwide Threat Assessment," Office of the Director of National

Intelligence, February 7, 2008, http://www.dni.gov/testimonies/20080207_
transcript.pdf; "Letter from al-Zawahiri to al-Zarqawi," Globalsecurity.
org, http://www.globalsecurity.org/security/library/report/2005/zawahiri
-zarqawi-letter_9jul2005.htm; Evan Kohlmann, "Al-Qaida Leader in Afghanistan Begs for Cash Donations," Counterterrorism Blog, May 25, 2007,
http://counterterrorismblog.org/2007/05/alqaida_leader_in_afghanistan
.php.

8. Eric Rosand and Alistair Millar, "Strengthening International Law and
Global Implementation," in David Cortright and George A. Lopez, eds.,
*Uniting Against Terror: Cooperative Nonmilitary Responses to the Global
Terrorist Threat* (Cambridge, MA: MIT Press, 2007), 61.

9. David T. Armitage, *The European Union: Measuring Counterterrorism Cooperation* (Washington, DC: Institute for National Strategic Studies, 2007), 3.

10. Edwin Bakker, "Jihadi Terrorists in Europe: Their Characteristics and the
Circumstances in Which They Joined the Jihad; An Exploratory Study,"
Netherlands Institute of International Relations, January 2007, http://www
.clingendael.nl/publications/2006/20061200_cscp_csp_bakker.pdf.

11. For an excellent exploration of international law and moral dilemmas of war
and terrorism, see Miller, *Terrorism and Counterterrorism.*

12. T. R. Reid, "U.S. Criticized Over Prisoners," *International Herald Tribune*,
January 18, 2002; Katharine Seelye and Steven Erlanger, "Under Criticism
U.S. Suspends Prisoner Flow to Base in Cuba," *International Herald Tri-
bune*, January 24, 2002; Lee Dembart, "For Afghans in Cuba, Untested Legal
Limbo," *International Herald Tribune*, January 25, 2002; David Sanger, "An
Aversion to Applying Old Treaties in a New Era," *International Herald Tri-
bune*, January 29, 2002; David Sanger, "Bush Decision on Detainees Fails
to Satisfy Red Cross," *International Herald Tribune*, February 23, 2002.

13. William Safire, "Kangaroo Courts," *New York Times*, November 27, 2001.

14. Thom Shanker, "A Chorus of Dissent Led Bush to Reversal on Prisoners,"
International Herald Tribune, February 23, 2002.

15. Adam Liptak, "The Court Enters the War, Loudly," *New York Times*, July 2,
2006; Mark Mazzetti and Kate Zernike, "White House Says Terror Detainees Hold Basic Rights," *New York Times*, July 12, 2006.

16. Scott Shane, "Site for Terror Trial Isn't Its Only Obstacle," *New York Times*,
January 31, 2010.

17. "USA: Guantanamo and Beyond: The Continuing Pursuit of Unchecked Executive Power," Amnesty International, May 13, 2005, http://www.amnesty
.org/en/library/asset/AMR51/063/2005/en/0e3f8b95-d4fe-11dd-8a23
-d58a49c0d652/amr510632005en.pdf, 11.

18. "USA: Below the Radar: Secret Flights to Torture and 'Disappearance,'"
Amnesty International, April 4, 2006, http://www.amnesty.org/en/library/
asset/AMR51/051/2006/en/b543c574-fa09-11dd-b1b0-c961f7df9c35/amr
510512006en.pdf, 31.

19. Condoleezza Rice, "Remarks Upon Her Departure for Europe," U.S. Department of State, December 5, 2005, http://merln.ndu.edu/archivepdf/terrorism/state/57602.pdf.

20. Tim Golden, "After Terror, A Secret Rewriting of Military Law," *New York Times*, October 24, 2004; Joel Brinkley, "U.S. Interrogators Are Saving European Lives, Rice Says," *New York Times*, December 8, 2005; Neil Lewis, "U.S. Spells Out New Definition Curbing Torture," *New York Times*, January 1, 2006.

21. Tim Golden, "Administration Officials Split Over Stalled Military Tribunals," *New York Times*, October 25, 2004; Kate Zernike, "Military Lawyers Urge Protections for Detainees," *New York Times*, July 14, 2006.

22. For the best overview of the interrogation/torture issue, see Ali Soufan, *The Black Banners: The Inside Story of 9/11 and the War against Al Qaeda* (New York: W. W. Norton, 2011). See also Ali Soufan, "My Tortured Decision," *New York Times*, April 23, 2009; Scott Shane, "C.I.A. to Close Secret Overseas Prisons for Terrorism Suspects," *New York Times*, April 10, 2009; Scott Shane, "Divisions Arose on Rough Techniques for Qaeda Figure," *New York Times*, April 18, 2009; Scott Shane, "Waterboarding Used 266 Times on Two Suspects," *New York Times*, April 20, 2009.

23. For classic books on the psychology of why "good" people do "bad" things, see Theodore Adorno et al., *The Authoritarian Personality* (New York: Harper, 1950); William Golding, *Lord of the Flies* (London: Faber & Faber, 1954); Stanley Milgram, *Obedience to Authority: An Experimental View* (New York: Harper & Row, 1974); James Waller, *Becoming Evil: How Ordinary People Commit Genocide and Mass Killing* (New York: Oxford University Press, 2002); and Philip Zimbardo, *The Lucifer Effect: Understanding How Good People Turn Evil* (New York: Random House, 2007).

24. "Few Punished in Abuse Cases," *New York Times*, April 27, 2006; "Deaths in Custody," *New York Times*, March 16, 2005; "Abusive Gin's Not Pursued, Survey Finds," *New York Times*, February 23, 2006; David Johnson and Mark Mazzetti, "Legal and Political Hurdles Stand in the Way of Prosecuting Interrogation Abuses," *New York Times*, August 20, 2009.

25. Steven Kleinman and Matthew Alexander, "Try a Little Kindness," *New York Times*, March 11, 2009; Matthew Alexander, *How to Break a Terrorist: The U.S. Interrogators Who Used Brains, Not Brawn, to Take Down the Deadliest Man in Iraq* (New York: Free Press, 2008).

26. Jen Banbury, "Rummy's Scapegoat," Salon, November 10, 2005, http://www.salon.com/2005/11/10/karpinski/; Zimbardo, *The Lucifer Effect*; Seymour Hersh, *Chain of Command: The Road from 9/11 to Abu Ghraib* (New York: HarperCollins, 2004).

27. "Limbaugh on Torture of Iraqis: U.S. Guards Were 'Having a Good Time,' 'blow[ing] some steam off," Media Matters, May 5, 2004, http://mediamatters.org/research/200405050003.

28. For an in-depth discussion, see Daniel Byman, "Hearing before the Senate Foreign Relations Committee on 'Extraordinary Renditions, Extraterritorial Detention, and Treatment of Detainees: Restoring Our Moral Credibility and Strengthening Our Diplomatic Standing,'" July 26, 2007, http://www.foreign.senate.gov/imo/media/doc/BymanTestimony070726.pdf.

29. George Tenet, "Written Statement for the Record of the Director of Central Intelligence Before the Joint Inquiry Committee," Federation of American Scientists, October 17, 2002, http://www.fas.org/irp/congress/2002_hr/101702tenet.html; Dana Priest, "CIA's Assurances on Transferred Suspects Doubted," *Washington Post*, March 17, 2005; Douglas Jehl and David Johnson, "Rule Change Lets CIA Freely Send Suspects Abroad," *New York Times*, March 6, 2005.

30. George Tenet, "DCI Statement: The Worldwide Threat in 2000," Central Intelligence Agency, February 2, 2000, https://www.cia.gov/news-information/speeches-testimony/2000/dci_speech_020200.html.

31. Condoleezza Rice, "Remarks Upon Her Departure for Europe."

32. Dana Priest, "Italy Knew about Plan to Grab Suspect," *Washington Post*, June 20, 2005.

33. Steve Hendricks, *A Kidnapping in Milan: The CIA on Trial* (New York: W. W. Norton, 2010).

34. Arthur M. Schlesinger, *The Imperial Presidency* (New York: Mariner Books, 2004); Mann, *Rise of the Vulcans*.

35. Eric Schmitt, "Two Prisons, Similar Issues for President," *New York Times*, January 27, 2009.

36. Katherine Zoepf, "Deprogramming Jihadists," *New York Times*, November 9, 2008.

37. Robert Worth, "Saudis Issue List of 85 Terrorism Suspects," *New York Times*, February 4, 2009.

38. Elisabeth Bumiller, "1 in 7 Detainees Rejoined Jihad Pentagon Finds," *New York Times*, May 21, 2009; Robert Worth, "Freed by U.S., Saudi Becomes a Qaeda Chief," New York Times, January 23, 2009.

39. Scott Shane, "CIA to Close Secret Overseas Prisons for Terrorist Suspects," *New York Times*, April 10, 2009.

40. President Barack Obama, "Reassurance on the Economy, Addressing Afghanistan," *New York Times*, March 8, 2009.

41. Kilcullen, "Countering Global Insurgency," 43.

42. Cofer Black, preface, in "Patterns of Global Terrorism," Department of State, 2003, http://www.state.gov/documents/organization/31912.pdf; Jonathan Stevenson, ed., "Perspectives," *Strategic Survey 2003/4* 104, no. 1 (May 2004): 6.

43. "Fifth Report of the Analytic Support and Sanctions Monitoring Team Appointed Pursuant to Resolutions 1526 (2004) and 1617 (2005) Concerning Al Qaeda and the Taliban and Associated Individuals and Entities," United

Nations Security Council, September 20, 2006, http://www.nefafoundation
.org/file/FeaturedDocs/UN_1267Report.pdf.

44. "Patterns of Global Terrorism."

Chapter 9. The War for American Hearts and Minds

1. Sarah E. Igo, *The Averaged American: Surveys, Citizens, and the Making of a Mass Public* (Cambridge, MA: Harvard University Press, 2008); Pew Research Center for the People and the Press (http://pewresearch.org/about/.)

2. Eric Alterman, *What Liberal Media?: The Truth About Bias and the News* (New York: Basic Books, 2004); Craig Crawford, *Attack the Messenger: How Politicians Turn You Against the Media* (New York: Rowman & Littlefield, 2005); Mary Mapes, *Truth and Duty: The Press, the President, and the Privilege of Power* (New York: St. Martin's, 2006); Eric Boehlert, *Lapdogs: How the Press Rolled Over for Bush* (New York: Free Press, 2006); Frank Rich, *The Greatest Story Never Told: The Decline and Fall of the Truth from 9/11 to Katrina* (New York: Penguin, 2006).

3. Fred Greenstein, "The Leadership Style of George W. Bush," in Fred Greenstein, ed., *The George W. Bush Presidency: An Early Analysis* (Baltimore: Johns Hopkins University Press, 2003), 7.

4. Jim Rutenberg and Bill Carter, "Network Coverage a Target of Fire from Conservatives," *New York Times*, November 7, 2001.

5. Jim Rutenberg and Bill Carter, "Fox Portrays a War of Good and Evil, and Many Applaud," *New York Times*, December 3, 2001.

6. Alessandra Stanley, "Battling the Skepticism of a Global TV Audience," *New York Times*, November 1, 2001.

7. Bill Carter and Felicity Barringer, "Networks Agree to U.S. Request to Edit Future Bin Laden Tapes," *New York Times*, October 11, 2001.

8. Jayson Blair, "Some Comic Strips Take an Unpopular Look at US," *New York Times*, October 22, 2001.

9. Rick Lyman, "Hollywood Discusses Role in War Effort," *New York Times*, November 12, 2001; Jim Rutenberg, "Hollywood Enlists Muhammad Ali to Explain War," *New York Times*, December 23, 2001; Jean-Michel Valautin, *Hollywood, the Pentagon, and Washington: The Movies and National Security from World War II to the Present* (New York: St. Martin's, 2005).

10. Bill Carter and Felicity Barringer, "Networks Agree to Edit Future Bin Laden Tapes," *New York Times*, October 11, 2001.

11. Scott Shane, "Behind Bush's Fury, a Vow Made in 2001," *New York Times*, June 29, 2006.

12. Byron Calame, "Eavesdropping and the Election: An Answer to the Question of Timing," *New York Times*, August 13, 2006.

13. David Barstow and Robin Stein, "Under Bush, A New Age of Prepackaged News," *New York Times*, March 13, 2005; David Barstow, "Report Faults Video Reports Shown as News," *New York Times*, April 6, 2006; Frank Rich, "When Real News Debunks Fake News," *New York Times*, February 19, 2005.

14. Todd Purdam and Alison Mitchell, "Bush, Angered by Leaks, Duels with Congress," *New York Times*, October 10, 2001; Todd Purdum, "Bush Lifts Some Restrictions on Classified Information," *New York Times*, October 11, 2001.

15. Dana Millbank, "For Bush, Facts Are Malleable," *Washington Post*, March 18, 2003.

16. For an excellent overview of the case, see Max Frankel, "The Washington Back Channel," *New York Times Magazine*, March 25, 2007, along with Adam Liptak, "In Leak Cases, New Pressure on Journalists," *New York Times*, April 30, 2006.

17. "Mixed Views on Civil Liberties," *New York Times*, December 12, 2001.

Chapter 10. The War for International Hearts and Minds

1. For two very diverse accounts, see Peter Tomsen, *The Wars of Afghanistan: Messianic Terrorism, Tribal Conflicts, and the Failures of Great Powers* (New York: Public Affairs, 2011); and Sean Parnell, *Outlaw Platoon: Heroes, Renegades, Infidels, and the Brotherhood of War in Afghanistan* (New York: William Morrow, 2012).

2. Thom Shanker, "Pentagon Closes Office Accused of Issuing Propaganda Under Bush," *New York Times*, April 16, 2009.

3. Fouad Ajami, "What the Muslim World Is Watching," *New York Times Magazine*, November 18, 2001.

4. Eric Schmitt, "Rumsfeld to Appeal to Arab Public on Mideast TV Network," *New York Times*, October 17, 2001.

5. Thomas Friedman, "Fighting bin Ladenism," *New York Times*, November 6, 2001.

6. Ibid.

7. Judith Miller and Elisabeth Bumiller, "Bin Laden on Tape Boasts of Trade Center Attack; U.S. Says It Proves His Guilt," *New York Times*, December 14, 2001.

8. Clarke, *Against All Enemies*, 264.

9. Samuel P. Huntington, *The Clash of Civilizations and the Remaking of World Orders* (New York: Simon & Schuster, 1996), 217.

10. Levitt and Jacobson, *Terrorist Threat and U.S. Response*, 56; Juan Zarate, "Winning the War on Terror: Marking Success and Confronting Challenges," in Levitt and Jacobson, *Terrorist Threat and U.S. Response*, 40.

11. Helene Cooper and David Sanger, "Obama's Positive Message to Iran Is an Opening Bid in a Diplomatic Drive," *New York Times*, March 21, 2009.

12. Hillary Clinton, Nomination Hearing to be Secretary of State, January 13, 2009, http://www.state.gov/secretary/rm/2009a/01/115196.htm; Peter Baker, "A Quieter Approach to Spreading Democracy Abroad," *New York Times*, February 22, 2009.

13. David Brooks, "Continuity We Can Believe In," *New York Times*, December 2, 2008.

14. Jeff Zeleny, "Obama to Change Contract Awarding," *New York Times*, March 5, 2009.
15. *9/11 Commission Report*, 376.
16. Ibid., 363.

Chapter 11. The War in Afghanistan: Round Two

1. Craig Whitlock, "National Security Team Delivers Grim Appraisal of Afghanistan War," *Washington Post*, February 9, 2009.
2. Thom Shanker, "U.S. Plans Afghan Effort to Thwart Road Bombs," *New York Times*, February 26, 2009.
3. Eric Schmitt, "Afghan Arms Are at Risk, Report Says," *New York Times*, February 12, 2009.
4. Dexter Filkins, "Afghan Leader Finds Himself Hero No More," *New York Times*, February 8, 2009.
5. Richard D. Oppel and Carlotta Gall, "Opposition Leaders Accuse Afghan President of Abusing His Power to Stay in Office," *New York Times*, March 4, 2009; Richard D. Oppel and Sangar Rahimi, "Afghan Leader Refuses to Step Down Before Election in August," *New York Times*, March 8, 2009.
6. Mark Landler and Helene Cooper, "Afghan Ballot Uncertainty Creates Dilemma for U.S.," *New York Times*, September 18, 2009.
7. Dexter Filkins, Mark Mazzetti, and James Risen, "Brother of Afghan Leader Said to Be Paid by CIA," *New York Times*, October 28, 2009.
8. Eric Schmitt, "U.S. Envoy's Cables Show Concerns on Afghan War Plans," *New York Times*, January 26, 2010.
9. Dexter Filkins, "With U.S. Aid, Warlord Builds Afghan Empire," *New York Times*, June 6, 2010; Dexter Filkins, "U.S. Money Financing Afghan Warlords for Convoy Protection, Report Says," *New York Times*, June 22, 2010.
10. Rod Nordland, Alissa Rubin, and Mathew Rosenberg, "Gulf Widens Between U.S. and an Increasingly Hostile Karzai," *New York Times*, March 18, 2012.
11. For an excellent overviews see Vanda Felbab-Brown, "Afghanistan: When Counternarcotics Undermines Counterterrorism," *Washington Quarterly*, Autumn 2005, 55–72; Ali A. Jalali, Robert B. Oakley, and Zoe Hunter, "Combating Opium in Afghanistan," *Strategic Forum*, no. 224 (November 2006).
12. Hamid Karzai, statement on counter narcotics, International Counter Narcotics Conference, August 22, 2006, http://www.unodc.org/pdf/afg/afg_intl_counter_narcotics_conf_2004.pdf.
13. James Risen, "U.S. Identifies Mineral Riches in Afghanistan," *New York Times*, June 14, 2010.
14. Emmanuel Duparcq, "US Mission in Afghanistan is Tougher than Iraq," January 14, 2009, France 24 International News. Channel NewsAsia, channel newsasia.com.
15. Helene Cooper and Thom Shanker, "Obama Afghan Plan Focuses on Pakistan Aid and Appeal to Militants," *New York Times*, March 13, 2009.

16. Jane Perlez, "Pakistan Is Said to Pursue Role In Afghan Talks with U.S.," *New York Times*, February 10, 2010.

17. Helene Cooper, "Putting Stamp on Afghan War, Obama Will Send 17,000 Troops," *New York Times*, February 17, 2009.

18. Thom Shanker, "With Afghan People in Mind, a New Commander Rethinks How to Measure Success," *New York Times*, June 20, 2009.

19. Thom Shanker and John Cushman, "Reviews Raise Doubt on Training of Afghan Forces, *New York Times*, November 6, 2009.

20. Alissa Rubin, "Taliban Overhaul Image in Bid to Win Allies," *New York Times*, January 21, 2010.

21. Richard Oppell, "Corruption Undercuts U.S. Hopes for Improving Afghan Police," *New York Times*, April 9, 2009; Richard Oppel and Elisabeth Bumiller, "Afghanistan's President Says Army Will Need Allies' Help Until 2024 or Longer," *New York Times*, December 9, 2009.

22. Thom Shanker, "Afghan Push Went Beyond Traditional Military Goals," *New York Times*, February 20, 2010.

23. Jason Campbell et al., "The States of Iraq and Afghanistan," March 20, 2000; David Sanger, "In Assessing the Damage in Afghanistan, Fears of an Emboldened Taliban," *New York Times*, March 11, 2012.

24. "State of Conflict: An Update," *New York Times*, July 29, 2011; Elisabeth Bumiller, "U.S. to End Combat Role in Afghanistan as Early as Next Year, Panetta Says," *New York Times*, February 2, 2012: Rod Nordland and Alissa Rubin, "Taliban Captives Dispute U.S. View on State of War," *New York Times*, February 2, 2012.

25. Helene Cooper and Thom Shanker, "Obama Afghan Plan Focuses on Pakistan Aid and Appeal to Militants," *New York Times*, March 13, 2009.

26. President Barack Obama, "Reassurance on the Economy, and Addressing Afghanistan," *New York Times*, March 8, 2009.

27. John F. Burns, "In Bold Move, Karzai Offers Safe Passage to Taliban Leader If He Agrees to Talks," *New York Times*, November 17, 2008; Carlotta Gall, "As U.S. Weighs Taliban Negotiations, Afghans Are Already Talking," *New York Times*, March 11, 2009.

28. Carlotta Gall and Ruhullah Khapalwak, "U.S. Has Met with a Top Aide to the Taliban Leader, Officials Say," *New York Times*, May 27, 2011.

29. Mark Landler, "Obama Got Message Supporting Talks with Taliban, but Maybe Not from Its Leader," *New York Times*, February 4, 2012.

30. Dexter Filkins, "Overture to Taliban Aggravates Ethnic Tensions in Afghanistan," *New York Times*, June 27, 2010.

31. "Rumseld: Iraq Inspections Would Be 'Very Difficult,'" CNN.com, August 13, 2002, http://edition.cnn.com/2002/ALLPOLITICS/08/13/iraq.pentagon/index.html.

32. Dexter Filkins, "Iran Said to Give Top Karzai Aid Cash by Bagful," *New York Times*, October 24, 2010; Dexter Filkins and Alissa Rubin, "Karzai Confirms That Iran Gives 'Bags of Money,'" *New York Times*, October 26,

2011; Helene Cooper, "Treasury Department, Citing Six People as Operatives, Accuses Iran of Aiding Al Qaeda," *New York Times*, July 29, 2011.

33. Elisabeth Bumiller and Ellen Barry, "U.S. Searches for Alternative to Kyrgyz Base," *New York Times*, February 6, 2009.

34. Eric Schmitt, "U.S. Envoy's Cables Show Concerns on Afghan War Plans," *New York Times*, January 26, 2010.

Chapter 12. The War in Pakistan

1. Carlotta Gall, "Taliban's 2 Branches Agree to Put Focus on an Offensive," *New York Times*, March 27, 2009.

2. Riedel, *The Search for Al Qaeda*. See also Tariq Ali, *The Duel: Pakistan on the Flight Path of American Power* (New York: Scribner, 2009).

3. "Major Incidents of Terrorism-Related Violence in Pakistan, 1988–2009; "Casualties of Terrorist Violence in Pakistan," Fault Lines, South Asia Terrorism Portal.

4. Foreign Policy Journal, Critical List of Countries, 2009, 2010, 2011, www.foreignpolicy.com.

5. Eric Schmitt and Jane Perlez, "Strikes Worsen Qaeda Threat, Pakistan Says," *New York Times*, February 25, 2009.

6. Bergen, *Holy War*, 70.

7. "Pakistan Accused of Placing Bounty on NATO Soldiers," *New York Times*, April 5, 2007; Mark Mazzetti and Helene Copper, "CIA Pakistan Campaign Is Working," *New York Times*, February 26, 2009; Mark Mazzetti and Eric Schmitt, "U.S. Says Agents of Pakistan Aid Afghan Taliban," *New York Times*, March 26, 2009; Carlotta Gall, "Report Says Pakistan Intelligence Agency Exerts Great Sway on Afghan Taliban," *New York Times*, June 13, 2010; Mark Mazzetti, Jane Perlez, Eric Shultz, and Andrew Lehren, "Pakistan Spy Unit Aiding Insurgents, Reports Suggests," *New York Times*, July 26, 2010.

8. Tenet, *At the Center of the Storm*, 261.

9. Ibid., 262–68.

10. Jane Perlez and Pir Zubair Shah, "Pakistani Taliban Leader Is Reported Dead," *New York Times*, February 1, 2010; Declan Walsh, "Leadership Rift Emerges in Pakistani Taliban," *New York Times*, March 6, 2012.

11. Tim Weiner, "The Kashmir Connection," *New York Times*, December 7, 2008.

12. David Sanger, "Revamping Aid to Pakistan Is Expected in Bush Report," *New York Times*, December 7, 2008.

13. Eric Schmitt and Jane Perlez, "Strikes Worsen Qaeda Threat, Pakistan Says," *New York Times*, February 25, 2009.

14. Richard Oppel and Pir Zubair Shah, "Radio Spreads Taliban's Terror in Pakistani Region," *New York Times*, January 25, 2009.

15. Jane Perlez, "Pakistan Makes a Taliban Truce, Creating a Haven," *New York Times*, February 17, 2009; Schmitt and Perlez, "Strikes Worsen Qaeda Threat, Pakistan Says."

16. Jane Perlez, "Pakistan Makes a Taliban Truce, Creating a Haven," *New York Times*, February 17, 2009; Jane Perlez, "Taliban Accepts Pakistan Ceasefire," *New York Times*, February 25, 2009.

17. Michael E. O'Hanlon, "Pakistan's War of Choice," *New York Times*, March 24, 2010.

18. Eric Schmitt, "Officer Leads Old Corps in New Role in Pakistan," *New York Times*, March 7, 2009; Jane Perlez and Pir Zubair Shah, "Pakistan Regains Control of Remote Area for Now," *New York Times*, March 9, 2009.

19. Marc Mazzetti and David Sanger, "Obama Widens Missile Strikes Inside Pakistan," *New York Times*, February 21, 2009; Eric Schmitt, "Top Militant Killed by U.S. in Pakistan, Al Qaeda Says," *New York Times*, June 1, 2010.

20. Richard Oppel et al., "Attacker in Afghanistan Was a Double Agent," *New York Times*, January 5, 2010.

21. Schmitt and Perlez, "Strikes Worsen Qaeda Threat, Pakistan Says." David Kilcullen and Andrew Exum, "Death from Above, Outrage Below," *New York Times*, May 17, 2009.

22. Eric Schmitt and Thom Shanker, "U.S. Seeks $3 billion for Pakistani Military," *New York Times*, April 3, 2009.

23. Eric Schmitt and Jane Perlez, "U.S. Unit Secretly in Pakistan Lends Ally Support," *New York Times*, February 23, 2009; Eric Schmitt and Jane Perlez, "Distrust Slows U.S. Training of Pakistanis," *New York Times*, July 12, 2010.

24. Paul Wiseman and Zafar M. Sheikh, "Pakistan Cops Underfunded, Overwhelmed," *USA Today*, May 6, 2009.

25. Jane Perlez and Pir Zubair Shah, "In Refugee Aid, Pakistan's War Has New Front," *New York Times*, July 2, 2009.

26. Salman Masood, "Bridge Attacks Halt NATO Supplies to Afghanistan," *New York Times*, February 4, 2009.

27. Sabrina Tavernise, "Avoiding Pakistan, New Supply Route to Afghanistan Opens," *New York Times*, March 4, 2009; Thom Shanker and Elisabeth Bumiller, "U.S. Seeks New Afghan Supply Routes, Even in Iran," *New York Times*, March 12, 2009.

28. Elisabeth Bumiller, Carlotta Gall, and Salman Masood, "Bin Laden's Secret Life in a Shrunken World," *New York Times*, May 8, 2011.

29. Eric Schmitt, Thom Shanker, and David Sanger, "Bigger Raid Unit Braced for Fight with Pakistanis," *New York Times*, May 10, 2011.

30. Riedel, *The Search for Al Qaeda*.

Chapter 13. Consequences

1. Cofer Black, preface, "Patterns of Global Terrorism"; Department of State, Stevenson, "Perspectives," 6; "Fifth Report of the Analytic Support and Sanctions Monitoring Team"; John McLaughlin, "The Changing Face of Terror—a Post 9/11 Assessment," The Investigative Project on Terrorism, June 6, 2006, http://www.investigativeproject.org/documents/testimony/257.pdf.

2. Kilcullen, "Countering Global Insurgency," 37.

3. Charles Allen in Levitt and Jacobson, "Terrorist Threat and U.S. Response."

4. Kirk Semple, "From Pakistan, Taliban Threats Reach New York," *New York Times*, February 17, 2009.

5. Michael Scheuer, "Al-Qaeda and Algeria's GSPC: Part of a Much Bigger Picture," The Jamestown Foundation, April 6, 2007, http://www.james town.org/programs/gta/single/?tx_ttnews%5Btt_news%5D=4058&tx_ ttnews%5BbackPid%5D=240&no_cache=1; Tim Weiner, "The Kashmir Connection: A Puzzle," *New York Times*, December 7, 2008.

6. Douglas Farah, "Al Qaeda's Gold: Following the Trail to Dubai," *International Herald Tribune*, February 18, 2002.

7. John Burns and Kurt Semple, "U.S. Finds Iraq Insurgency Has Funds to Sustain Itself," *New York Times*, November 26, 2006.

8. Mir, "How Osama Has Survived for Six Years"; Milt Bearden, "Making Osama bin Laden's Day," *New York Times*, August 13, 1998.

9. Scott Shane, "Senate Report Explores Bin Laden's 2001 Escape," *New York Times*, November 29, 2009.

10. Karen De Young and Walter Pincus, "Al-Qaeda's Gains Keep U.S. at Risk, Report Says," *Washington Post*, July 18, 2007.

11. Daniel Benjamin and Steven Simon, *The Next Attack: The Failure of the War on Terrorism and a Strategy for Getting It Right* (New York: Times Books, 2005), 6; Mark Mazzeti and David Rohde, "Terror Officials See Qaeda Chiefs Regaining Power, *New York Times*, February 19, 2007.

12. Eric Schmitt, "Panel Fears Use of Unconventional Weapon," *New York Times*, December 1, 2008.

13. Kilcullen, "Countering Global Insurgency," 28–29.

14. Ibid., 28.

15. Matthew Levitt and Michael Jacobson, "Preface," in Levitt and Jacobson, "Terrorist Threat and U.S. Response," 2.

16. Richard Bonney, *Jihad: From Qur'am to bin Laden* (Basingstoke, UK: Macmillan, 2004), 361; Juan Zarate, "Winning the War on Terror: Marking Success and Confronting Challenges," in Levitt and Jacobson, "Terrorist Threat and U.S. Response," 38.

17. Michael Leiter, "Looming Challenges in the War on Terror," in Levitt and Jacobson, "Terrorist Threat and U.S. Response," 57.

18. *9/11 Commission Report*, 362.

19. Leiter, "Looming Challenges in the War on Terror, 58.

20. Amanda Cox, "A 9/11 Tally: $3.3 Trillion," *New York Times*, September 11, 2011; David Sanger, "The Price of Lost Chances," *New York Times*, September 11, 2011.

21. Scott Shane, "A Year of Terror Plots, Through a 2nd Prism," *New York Times*, January 13, 2010.

INDEX

ABOUT THE AUTHOR

Dr. William Nester is a professor in the Department of Government and Politics at St. John's University in New York. He is the author of thirty previous books on different aspects of international relations.